AMC'S BEST DAY HIKES IN THE

CATSKILLS & HUDSON VALLEY

FOUR-SEASON GUIDE TO 60 OF THE BEST TRAILS
FROM THE HUDSON HIGHLANDS TO ALBANY

PETER W. KICK

SECOND EDITION

Appalachian Mountain Club Books
Boston, Massachusetts

AMC is a nonprofit organization and sales of AMC Books fund our mission of protecting the Northeast outdoors. If you appreciate our efforts and would like to make a donation to AMC, contact us at Appalachian Mountain Club, 5 Joy Street, Boston, MA 02108.

www.outdoors.org/publications/books/

Distributed by The Globe Pequot Press, Guilford, Connecticut.

Front cover photograph © Michael Nelson
Back cover photographs (l-r) © Michael Nelson, © Jerry and Marcy Monkman/
    EcoPhotography.com
All interior photographs © Peter Kick and Lori Lee Dickson
Maps by Ken Dumas © Appalachian Mountain Club
Cover design by Gia Giasullo/Studio eg
Interior design by Eric Edstam

Library of Congress Cataloging-in-Publication Data
Kick, Peter, 1951-
  AMC's best day hikes in the Catskills and Hudson Valley : four-season
guide to 60 of the best trails from the Hudson highlands to Albany /
Peter W. Kick. -- 2nd ed.
    p. cm.
Includes bibliographical references and index.
ISBN 978-1-934028-45-2 (alk. paper)
  1. Hiking--New York (State)--Catskill Mountains--Guidebooks. 2.
Hiking--Hudson River Valley (N.Y. and N.J.)--Guidebooks. 3. Trails--New
York (State)--Catskill Mountains--Guidebooks. 4. Trails--Hudson River
Valley (N.Y. and N.J.)--Guidebooks. 5. Catskill Mountains
(N.Y.)--Guidebooks. 6. Hudson River Valley (N.Y. and N.J.)--Guidebooks.
I. Appalachian Mountain Club. II. Title. III. Title: Best day hikes in
the Catskills and Hudson Valley.
GV199.42.N652C3736 2011
917.47'3804--dc22
                                2010049699

Interior pages contain 30% post-consumer recycled fiber.
Cover contains 10% post-consumer recycled fiber.
Printed in the United States of America,
using vegetable-based inks.

Mixed Sources
Product group from well-managed forests, controlled sources and recycled wood or fiber
www.fsc.org   Cert no. SCS-COC-002464
©1996 Forest Stewardship Council
FSC

10 9 8 7 6 5 4 3 2 1   11 12 13 14 15 16 17

For Lori Lee Dickson

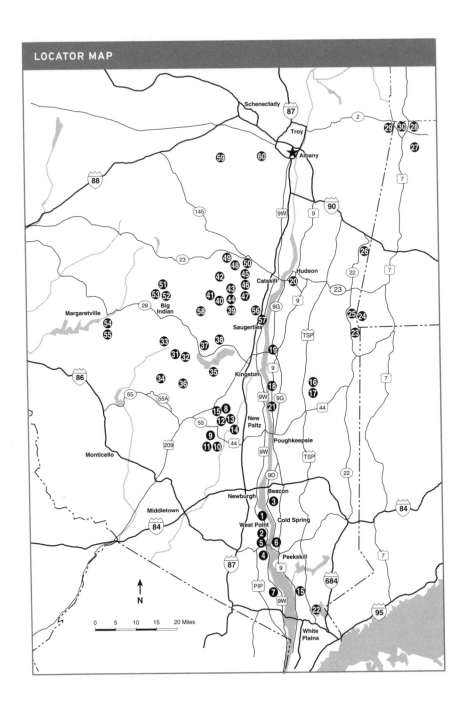

CONTENTS

AT-A-GLANCE TRIP PLANNER

#	Trip	Page	Location	Difficulty	Distance and Elevation Gain
THE HUDSON HIGHLANDS					
1	Storm King	3	Cornwall-on-Hudson, NY	Moderate	6 mi, 400 ft
2	Popolopen Gorge and the Torne	8	Fort Montgomery, NY	Moderate	4.5 mi, 1,250 ft
3	Breakneck Ridge to South Beacon Mountain	13	Beacon, NY	Strenuous	9.0 mi, 1,400 ft
4	Bear Mountain	18	Bear Mountain, NY	Strenuous	4.0 mi, 1,000 ft
5	Hessian Lake and Fort Montgomery State Historic Site	23	Fort Montgomery, NY	Easy	3.25 mi, 350 ft
6	Anthony's Nose	28	Cortlandt and Bear Mountain, NY	Moderate	4.0 mi, 700 ft
7	The Hook	32	Nyack, NY	Moderate	5.3 mi, 1,200 ft

Estimated Time	Fee	Good for Kids	Dogs Allowed	Public Transit	X-C Skiing	Snow-shoeing	Trip Highlights
3.0 hrs			✔				Signature Highlands hike with scenic views of the Hudson River
3.5 hrs			✔	✔		✔✔	360-degree views of the Hudson Valley
6.0 hrs			✔	✔			Quiet forests, views from open ridges, exposed scenic trail
3.5 hrs	$		✔	✔			360-degree views
2.0 hrs	$	✔	✔	✔			Park, zoo, Revolutionary War site
4.0 hrs	$		✔	✔			Memorable views of the Hudson River and Bear Mountain Bridge
3.5 hrs	$		✔	✔			Scenic walk and climb of section of the northern Palisades

Estimated Time	Fee	Good for Kids	Dogs Allowed	Public Transit	X-C Skiing	Snow-shoeing	Trip Highlights
2.5 hrs	$						Vertical cliffs, excellent views
6.5 hrs	$		🐕		⛷	⛄⛄	Swimming in Lake Awosting, valley views from Castle Point
5.5 hrs	$		🐕			⛄⛄	Glacial cobble fields, pine-pitch balds, sheer cliffs
2.5 hrs	$		🐕		⛷	⛄⛄	Beautiful lake, far-reaching views
2.0 hrs	$	👪	🐕		⛷	⛄⛄	Easy hike, rock climbing
4.0 hrs	$						Exciting boulder scramble, easy walk back
3.5 hrs	$				⛷	⛄⛄	Carriage road to gazebos and cliffs with Catskills views
3.0 hrs		👪	🐕	🚌	⛷	⛄⛄	Flat walk through deep woods ideal for children, bicycles
2.0 hrs		👪	🐕				Views of Southern Taconic Plateau and Catskills
2.0 hrs		👪			⛷	⛄⛄	Pond, wetlands, golden eagles; great for families
3.0 hrs		👪	🐕		⛷	⛄⛄	Shoreline hike along Hudson River; great for families
1.5 hrs		👪	🐕		⛷	⛄⛄	Open fields, rustic gazebos, unforgettable views

Estimated Time	Fee	Good for Kids	Dogs Allowed	Public Transit	X-C Skiing	Snow-shoeing	Trip Highlights
3.0 hrs	$	✓			✓	✓	Picturesque castle, ponds, gardens, woods
2.5 hrs		✓	✓	✓	✓	✓	FDR museum, library, and home
2.0 hrs		✓			✓	✓	Bogs and wetlands; ideal for children and bird-watchers
4.0 hrs			✓			✓	Valley and mountain views
6.0 hrs			✓			✓	Gradual climb with generous views, free camping
3.0 hrs			✓			✓	Stream crossing, Bash Bish Falls
2.5 hrs		✓	✓		✓	✓	Blueberry knoll, free camping
7.0 hrs			✓				Greylock massif, Bascom Lodge, sugar-maple forest
2.5 hrs		✓	✓				Popular Williamstown hike; quartzite limestone summit
3.5 hrs		✓	✓				Scenic ridge hike to deep, icebound crevice
2.0 hrs		✓	✓		✓	✓	Quiet hike through old settlement area, cross-country ski trail
5.5 hrs	$		✓			✓	Scenic day-long hike up Catskills' highest peak

Estimated Time	Fee	Good for Kids	Dogs Allowed	Public Transit	X-C Skiing	Snow-shoeing	Trip Highlights
7.0 hrs	$		🐕				Rustic area; a favorite of many Catskill hikers
2.5 hrs			🐕			⛄⛄	Scenic cliffs of glacial cirque, meteorite impact zone
5.0 hrs		🚶	🐕				Quiet boreal summits with southwesterly views
2.0 hrs		🚶			🎿	⛄⛄	Intimate views of the Catskills; wheelchair accessible
5.5 hrs		🚶	🐕			⛄⛄	Blueberry heath, intimate views of high peaks
4.0 hrs		🚶	🐕			⛄⛄	Quarry, lean-tos, summit fire tower
3.0–4.0 hrs		🚶	🐕		🎿	⛄⛄	Hotel ruins, fire tower, Eagle Cliff
4.5 hrs			🐕			⛄⛄	Interior forest hike to boreal summit, exciting views
5.0 hrs		🚶	🐕			⛄⛄	Double-peaked mountain with superior views
6.0 hrs			🐕				Stony Clove Notch, isolated views
6.0 hrs			🐕		🎿	⛄⛄	Kaaterskill Wild Forest area, spectacular views
4.5 hrs			🐕			⛄⛄	Quiet ledge overlooking Kaaterskill Clove
3.5 hrs			🐕			⛄⛄	Hemlock and pitch-pine woods, scenic overlook
4.5 hrs	$	🚶	🐕			⛄⛄	Escarpment Trail's cliffs; popular outing
4.0 hrs			🐕			⛄⛄	North-South Lake Public Campground

THE HELDERBERGS

Estimated Time	Fee	Good for Kids	Dogs Allowed	Public Transit	X-C Skiing	Snow-shoeing	Trip Highlights
1.5 hrs			🐕				State's highest waterfall; Catskills' most popular short hike
3.0 hrs			🐕			🏷️🏷️	Lockwood Gap, Escarpment Trail
5.0 –7.0 hrs		🧑‍🧒	🐕			🏷️🏷️	Spruce plantations, sweeping views to the north
3.0 hrs		🧑‍🧒	🐕			🏷️🏷️	Isolated lookout above Black Dome Valley
7.0 hrs			🐕			🏷️🏷️	Catskills' second-highest peak, quiet westerly viewpoint
3.5 hrs		🧑‍🧒	🐕			🏷️🏷️	Ski and hiking trail
6.5 hrs			🐕			🏷️🏷️	Demanding hike, scenic area
5.0 hrs			🐕			🏷️🏷️	First-growth forest
4.5 hrs		🧑‍🧒	🐕			🏷️🏷️	Spruce-fir summit, 360-degree views of the Catskills
5.0 hrs			🐕		⛷️	🏷️🏷️	Peaceful lookouts over Kaaterskill Clove and the Hudson Valley
40 min		🧑‍🧒	🐕			🏷️🏷️	River views, picnic area
40 min	$	🧑‍🧒	🐕		⛷️	🏷️🏷️	Camping, boating, hiking; ideal for children
2.0 hrs			🐕			🏷️🏷️	Sweeping views of Schoharie floodplain and Catskills
3.0 hrs	$		🐕				Narrow catwalk trail, world's oldest exposed surface limestone

ACKNOWLEDGMENTS

THE JOB OF A GUIDEBOOK WRITER (especially when the subject is hiking) is often a harsh, solitary, and tedious one. I am still of the mind, of course, that a "bad day hiking is better than a good day at work." During the creation of this book there were many long days of travail and research; however, friends and acquaintances along the trail helped make this an entirely enjoyable and fascinating bipedal experience—from tip to toe.

In view of that, I'd like to recognize those who supported me. Foremost among them is the vibrant Inverna Lockpez of the Catskill Center for Conservation and Development (CCCD). For several successive summers, Inverna selected me as an artist in residence at the Platte Clove Preserve cabin, a woodsy retreat of waterfalls and old-growth forest abutting the Indian Head Wilderness Area, where I worked on this book. Thanks also to the CCCD's former executive director, Tom Alworth, as well as to the CCCD's watershed coordinator, Aaron Bennett. My appreciation also goes to the rest of the CCCD staff, who manage the Catskills' largest environmental watchdog agency.

My indebtedness extends to the many hiking companions who joined me on the trails, among them my good friends Barry Knight and Rita Berman, Dori O'Connell, Nick and Erika Minglis, and the Catskill Center's artist-in-residence Susan Mayr. I thank Bleecker's Creepers Hiking Club. Thanks also go to Lori Lee Dickson, who helped to research this second edition.

I am indebted to the rangers and foresters who've helped me with this and other books, including the Rudges (Pat and Bill), Dennis Martin, Steve Preston, Stephen Scherry, Fred Dearstyne, Pete Evans, and George Profous. Thank you as well to Drew Jones, manager, Hopkins Memorial Forest; Bob Spear, Rough Mountain fire warden, Sterling Forest State Park; Dr. John C. Dwyer, historian; Jim Morton, lifelong Platte Clove resident; and Dr. Mike Kudish, botanist, author of Catskill-related books and dissertations, and professor of forest history.

Gratitude goes to my woods-roving neighbors from the Hutterian Bruderhof's Catskill Community, especially the peripatetic Emmy, Lizzy, Abigail, and Eirlys for their humble and lighthearted company on the trail and their sustained, cordial invitations to visit the community.

I am compelled to recognize, albeit posthumously, my old friend and one-time mentor Barbara McMartin, who died in the fall of 2005 at the age of 73 after a long struggle with cancer. Barbara was one of the Adirondacks' most dedicated preservationists and writers. Together, we co-authored *50 Hikes in the Hudson Valley* (1984), now out of print.

Of course, my endless appreciation goes to all of my readers. It's such a pleasure to find people carrying your book in the woods (especially if they're not lost), or leaving it on the dashboard of their car, parked at a trailhead, where I might see it.

My appreciation also goes to Eric Edstam, who designed this book, and to Ken Dumas, who created all of the featured maps. Several current and former members of the AMC staff managed to push this project along through several hardships. Thanks go to AMC's publisher, Heather Stephenson, to editors Dan Eisner and Kimberly Duncan-Mooney, and to production manager Athena Lakri, whose patience and dedication made this second edition possible.

INTRODUCTION

I thank God I was born on the banks of the Hudson.
                                        —Washington Irving

WELCOME TO THE HUDSON VALLEY AND CATSKILL REGION, birthplace of a nation. The Hudson River begins at the Adirondacks' Lake Tear of the Clouds at 4,300 feet in elevation, making its way 315 miles to New York City's Battery at sea level as it drains an area of more than 13,000 square miles. Except for the Saint Lawrence, it is the only river that provides such deep and cordial invitation into the North American continent—a fact that has had the largest single influence on the growth and development of the United States. Geologically the Hudson River is a fjord, a long, narrow coastal inlet, its steep slopes formed by glacial action. It is one of only two water gaps that penetrate the Appalachian Mountain chain at a point that is below sea level (the other is Maine's Somes Sound). Its deepest point is 216 feet, near West Point; its widest is 3.5 miles, at Haverstraw Bay; and its narrowest is at the Hudson Highlands, where it is constricted into the notorious throat of often rough and windy water dubbed the Devil's Horse Race by early mariners.

The history of the region is a study in change. After the Paleo Indians left the Hudson Valley 12,000 years ago, when the glaciers retreated, the hunter-gatherer people of the Woodland Period arrived, leaving evidence of their existence in the form of oyster middens (mounds), fishing weirs (traps), camps, and villages. By 1,000 BCE they began to cultivate crops, which required permanent villages and seasonal encampments, many positioned at the mouths of Hudson River tributaries. For crop rotation and soil revitalization, these villages were moved every 8 to 12 years. This culture was altered permanently with the arrival of Europeans. Like its rival the English Hudson Bay Company, the Dutch East India Company (which employed Henry Hudson) was primarily interested in fur. American Indians, lured by the false promise of progress and prosperity, entered the business of commercial trapping and trade. This, along with broken treaties (particularly by the Dutch director-general Peter Stuyvesant), led to the destruction of a traditional lifestyle that was also subjected to conflict, disease, and ultimately, displacement.

Realizing that whoever controlled the Hudson River would also control the American frontier and its rich promise for trade, the British took control of New Amsterdam (now New York) from the Dutch by force in 1664. Stuyvesant had become so unpopular that he was unable to raise a militia. The French and the English, using Mohawk and Algonquian mercenaries as their allies, then fought over the region, hoping to establish and maintain trade interests. The French and Indian Wars put an end to French aspirations south of the Great Lakes. The British focused on the Hudson Valley, and were finally defeated by the Americans in the 1777 Saratoga campaign. The empire-building period was about to begin.

By this time, writers and artists had begun to praise the region's scenic character, part of an international Romantic movement that envisaged the world as a place both picturesque and sublime. This enhanced the valley's appeal as a place to live and and also made it the first American tourist destination. For both Americans and Europeans by the early 1820s, the valley was a rural retreat, with a focus on the river and the Catskills in celebration of the aesthetic conventions of the time. Tremendous industrial growth was also taking place, spurred by the nationalistic pride created by the Revolution. During the nineteenth century, the valley would be intensively developed for fishing, logging, agriculture, shipping, and power generation, while also becoming widely settled residentially. Throughout the twentieth century, these conditions would bring about habitat destruction, the depreciation of scenic resources, continual alterations of the natural shoreline of the river, and diminished public access. Major factors in the preservation of open space through this development period were the farms and patroonships, and, in the Catskills, the tenant farming system of the Hardenburgh Patent (a large land grant given by Queen Anne to a small group of investors).

Today, 70 percent of the Hudson's shore is inaccessible because of rail corridors and private property. The river is also home to a 35-foot-deep shipping channel maintained from New York Harbor to the Port of Albany; the Hudson drops only about 5 feet in this span, making it an ideal in-route for heavy shipping and a recreational route connecting the Atlantic to the Great Lakes.

At the same time, improvements in the river's water quality; a heightened, positive public perception of the river; and increasing population have created demands for more public access and more open space. Of the 3.9 million acres in the Hudson River Valley National Heritage Area, only 5 percent (203,000 acres) is protected open space. Fortunately, early in its settlement history, sentiment was strong for the preservation of open space. This led to hard-fought battles by the environmental movement that resulted in the preservation of the Hudson Valley as we see it today.

Below Troy, the Hudson River is a rich and productive tidal estuary inhabited by ospreys, eagles, harbor seals, muskrats, beavers, herons, rails, deer, foxes, turkeys, coyotes, fishers, and even bears. Its diverse habitat is the result of a broad salinity gradient determined by the mixing of the Atlantic's sea water with the river's fresh water. The Hudson is home to 185 species of fish, and is the last estuary on the East Coast to retain self-sustaining spawning stocks of its original native fish species, such as the once commercially important shad and sturgeon and the very popular game fish the striped bass. Under the Federal Clean Water Act, the Environmental Protection Agency designated these resources the Hudson River National Estuarine Research Reserve. It contains 2,400 acres of tidal freshwater fish and wildlife habitat, with an additional 1,500 acres undesignated. All of the reserves in the Hudson River estuary are protected and managed as field laboratories for research and education.

Beyond the river is a seemingly endless assortment of mountains, lakes, ponds, valleys, and geological intrusions that give the Hudson Valley its character and appeal. The valley's historical development is almost as diverse as its habitat. The region is so striking in appearance that early German Palatine settlers from the Palatinate county of the Rhine Valley region called it the American Rhineland. The first European visitors, the members of Henry Hudson's crew (who were looking for China), called it "as fine a place as we have ever seen . . . so pleasant with grass and flowers, and goodly trees." Klara Sauer, the former director of Scenic Hudson, put the river's beauty into another perspective, remarking, "Had this continent been settled west-to-east, the Hudson Valley would be a national park today." It is interesting to reflect on Sauer's comment now that the National Park Service has designated the Hudson Valley a National Heritage Area (1998). Because the Hudson River valley is so large and its resources so diffuse, and because it is so developed, the NPS realized it could not create a national park in the traditional sense, such as a Yellowstone or Yosemite, but it did recognize that the region's cultural and natural attributes were worthy of federal protection, preservation, and interpretation for the benefit of the nation. Congressman Maurice Hinchey drafted the legislation that created the Hudson River Valley National Heritage Area.

The designation is based on the region's Revolutionary War history; its role as a living canvas for the first American school of art (the Hudson River School of landscape painting, whose celebration of nature contributed to the creation of our national parks system); the river's function as the nation's principal artery of commerce; and the fact that the Hudson Valley was the birthplace of the modern environmental movement—the basis of environmental law was formed by a fight that took place here in the Hudson Valley.

This book will lead you to the Hudson's greatest scenic landscapes: the Highlands, the ancient Taconics, the white cliffs of the Shawangunks, and the recesses of the distant Catskills. It reaches west to the Delaware watershed, east to the Taconics, and north to the fortress of the Helderbergs. It penetrates the Southern and Northern Taconics and the Greylock Range. It brings you to the tops of this series of ranges, allowing you the best views of their succession and of the Hudson Valley. From the resistant limestone of the Helderberg Escarpment to the dissected plateau of the Catskills and into the crystalline Hudson Highlands lying beside the younger folded rocks of the Appalachians, you can see the parts of the puzzle that make up the region's geological history, and that have earned the Hudson River its place as one of America's premier scenic and recreational assets.

AUTHOR'S NOTE

Guidebooks directly affect the shape and development of recreational resources. New York State's Department of Environmental Conservation (DEC) welcomes such publications from the private sector, which allow it to cut back substantially on costly in-house guide and map production. During the 25 years or so that I have written outdoor material about specific destinations, I have watched some areas change because of increased public use. The state has responded by designating trails and adding signage in such areas, and by including them on maps and pamphlets. Such "pressure" increases as more books are written and more trails are built, a fact that some people lament.

But I do not feel this pressure has brought harm, especially given that education fosters appreciation for the land and, thus, preservation. (With few exceptions, the region's trails have not exceeded their carrying capacity.) Nor do I offer apologies for divulging the whereabouts of these trails. Revealing what I feel are the most desirable hikes is my promise to my readers.

The natural environment is our single largest human resource, and it's there to be used and enjoyed. It is my sincere wish that this book and its carefully selected inventory of special, scenic places helps you to do that. Just be prepared to rub up against the world a bit. Get wet, get dirty, get hungry, and get sore. But whatever you do, get out there and enjoy the trails!

HOW TO USE THIS BOOK

THERE ARE MANY WAYS TO ENJOY THESE WALKS. Social hikers will find many outdoor groups that offer regularly scheduled hikes and trips. Appalachian Mountain Club (AMC) chapters provide members with hiking schedules. The New York–New Jersey Trail Conference (NY–NJTC) will put you in touch with many other groups. Organizations such as the Catskill 3500 Club, the Sierra Club, the Catskill Mountain Club, and chapters of the Adirondack Mountain Club all offer outing schedules for a variety of hikers. Each organization also provides ways for hikers to return something to the land with programs of trail maintenance, conservation, and education to promote wise use. These organizations help not only to protect our wild lands, but also to acquire more of them.

Those who seek quiet in the wildlands can find ways to do that here. Some of these routes are never heavily used. Others are, and these trails may best be hiked in early spring, late fall, or on weekdays, when solitude can be mixed with expanded vistas in ways that are sure to please any wilderness seeker.

There are relatively few hikes on the east side of the Hudson Valley. Its gentler hills were settled early, and although the farms are shrinking, settlements have grown to fill most of the open land. In contrast, the forests on the west side of the Hudson have been protected as the valley's water source and as part of the New York State Forest Preserve, whose unique state constitutional protection ensures its land will remain "forever wild." Lands within the Blue Line (as it appears on many maps) of the Catskill Park make up the largest group of hikes in this guide.

Almost all the lands traversed by today's trails were once settled and used by soldiers, farmers, miners, loggers, and romantics. Their presence inevitably is reflected in the lore that surrounds the trails. While this guide serves as an invitation to the mountain ranges and valleys of the southern part of the state (as well as a few Hudson Valley watershed hikes in neighboring states), it cannot begin to probe the vast history that enlivens each route.

With 60 hikes to choose from, you may wonder how to decide where to go. The locator map at the front of this book will help you narrow down the trips by location, and the At-a-Glance Trip Planner that follows the Table of Contents will provide more information to guide you toward a decision.

Once you settle on a destination and turn to a trip in this guide, you will find icons that indicate whether the hike is a good place for children, whether dogs are permitted, whether you can go snowshoeing or cross-country skiing there, and whether there are fees.

Information on the basics follows: location, difficulty rating, distance, elevation gain, estimated time, and available maps. The difficulty ratings are based on the author's perception and are estimates of what the average hiker will experience; you may find the hikes to be easier or more difficult than stated. Elevation gain (or vertical rise) is the total change in cumulative elevation for the hike. Hiking time is for walking the trail as described at a leisurely pace. The text often suggests that you allow more time for sightseeing.

Information is included about the relevant U.S. Geological Survey (USGS) maps, as well as about where you can find trail maps. While you will find the trail map in the book helpful, take the recommended maps too. These maps give the larger picture, and you will have more fun on a mountaintop if you can identify the surrounding countryside. A cautionary note on USGS maps: While contours and elevations are by and large reliable, some of the manufactured features, including trails, are out of date. All of the supplementary maps mentioned in the hike headings are more convenient and up-to-date than the USGS quads, and I recommend acquiring them. In particular, I suggest the *Appalachian Mountain Club Catskill Mountains* map that was designed to accompany my book *Catskill Mountain Guide,* published by AMC. That book is sold with a paper-printed map, but a waterproof version of the map can also be purchased separately and could prove helpful for the Catskills-related trips in this book.

The directions explain how to reach the trailhead. Global Positioning System (GPS) coordinates for parking lots are also included. When you enter the coordinates into your vehicle's navigational GPS device, it will provide driving directions. (Set your device to "degrees and decimal minutes" format. Please remember that trailheads can be obscured by foliage. While the author and AMC have made every effort to ensure accuracy, GPS coordinates may direct you very near, but not directly to, the trailhead.) Whether or not you have a GPS device, bring an atlas or a county or state road map with you, such as the *DeLorme Atlas & Gazetteer for New York State* and *DeLorme Atlas & Gazetteer for Massachusetts*. Don't rely on finding small preserve maps and other handouts at kiosks. Often the supplies are exhausted. Try to find the map you need online, where many are available these days.

If you do not know how to read a map, you should learn to do so before hiking all but about a dozen of the simplest trails in this guide. Spend time walking with someone who does know how to read a map, such as the friendly hikers from your local AMC chapter. The same instructions are appropriate for the use of a compass. You may not need either on the easiest of this guide's trails, but walking the easier routes with map and compass will allow you to become comfortable with their use so you can extend your hikes beyond the ones described, or to the more difficult hikes in this book. Get the best compass you can afford. I've had the same Silva Ranger for 30 years, and highly recommend a similar type of orienteering compass with a flip-up sight that will also be useful in identifying far-away peaks or triangulating your position from a set of known peaks.

Some of the trips are accessible by public transportation. For those that are, basic instructions are included in the Directions section. However, remember to call ahead for schedules and to confirm routes. AMC's New York–North Jersey Chapter has helpful information on its website: www.amc-ny.org/trans_ codes. You can also find other resources online, such as the Metro-North website or the Coach USA website.

In the trail description, you will find instructions on where to hike, the trails on which to hike, and where to turn along the trail. You will also learn about the natural and human history along your hike, along with information about flora, fauna, and any landmarks and objects you will encounter.

Each trip ends with a More Information section that provides details about the locations of bathrooms, access times and fees, the property's rules and regulations, and contact information for the place where you will be hiking.

TRIP PLANNING AND SAFETY

THERE IS A WIDE RANGE OF HIKES IN THIS GUIDE, from easy walks to strenuous climbs. The information about distance, estimated time, and elevation gain should help you gauge the difficulty of each hike and prepare properly. Almost all hikes follow clearly marked trails, although this can change. The greatest source of confusion seems to be the constant revisions in trail designation for the more southerly trails, particularly in the Highlands region, where interconnecting routes can be confusing and color changes in the markings have been common.

Preparedness is key to your hiking enjoyment, and you should be well equipped before you start. If you are new to hiking, it is a good idea to join an AMC group and learn from those with experience. The more background you have in the woods, the greater will be your safety and your enjoyment. Even with the best of forecasts, you should know that you will face the unexpected.

Elevations in and around the Hudson Valley are varied, and often steep and rugged. Some of the walks traverse moderately rugged terrain along rocky hills, while others lead to ponds and fields where you'll have of sun exposure and to areas where walking is slow in soft soil or mud. Many parks in the Hudson Valley have complex trail networks based on old cart and carriage roads, a few of which are unmarked. Always allow extra time in case you get lost.

Before heading out for your hike, consider the following:

- Select a hike that everyone in your group is comfortable making. Match the hike to the abilities of the least capable person in the group. If anyone is uncomfortable with the weather or is tired, turn around and complete the hike another day.
- Plan to be back at the trailhead before dark. Before beginning your hike, determine a turnaround time. Don't diverge from it, even if you have not reached your intended destination.
- Check the weather. Whenever possible, wait for a sunny day. But even on sunny days you should be prepared for changes and extremes. It can be at least 20 degrees colder on the mountaintops of the Catskills than in the valley, close to the river. Storms can appear with little warning. Many prefer walking in southern New York State during fall and spring; just remember these are the most volatile times—extremes ranging from heat waves to snowstorms can occur. But the less-populated trails and expanded distant vistas in the leafless season make hiking at such times worthwhile.
- If you are planning a ridge or summit hike, start early so you will be off the exposed area before the afternoon hours when thunderstorms most often strike, especially in summer. The weather in the Hudson Valley is highly variable. Significant storms—including heavy winter snowfalls, spring rainstorms, and tropical storms in late summer and fall—can cause flooding and other hazards.
- Bring a pack with the following items:
  - ✓ Water: Two quarts per person is usually adequate, depending on the weather and the length of the trip. These mountains are dry much of the year. It is becoming increasingly dangerous to trust open water sources because of the spread of the Giardia parasite.
  - ✓ Food: Even if you plan just a 1-hour hike, bring high-energy snacks such as nuts, dried fruit, or snack bars. Pack a lunch for longer trips.
  - ✓ Map and compass: Be sure you know how to use them. A handheld GPS device may also be helpful, but is not always reliable.
  - ✓ Headlamp or flashlight with spare batteries
  - ✓ Extra clothing: rain gear, a wool sweater or a fleece, a hat, and mittens. Experiment with layers of light, waterproof gear. In the mountains, you will want a layer of pile or wool even in summer, so carry a sweater in your day pack.
  - ✓ Sunscreen
  - ✓ First-aid kit, including adhesive bandages, gauze, pain medicine, and moleskin
  - ✓ Pocketknife or multitool

✓ Matches and a lighter
✓ Trash bag
✓ Toilet paper
✓ Whistle
✓ Insect repellent
✓ Sunglasses
✓ Cell phone: Be aware that service is sometimes unreliable in low or remote areas. Use the phone only for emergencies to avoid disturbing the backcountry experience for other hikers.
✓ Binoculars (suggested)
✓ Camera (suggested)

- Wear appropriate footwear and clothing. Wool or synthetic hiking socks will keep your feet dry and help prevent blisters. Comfortable, waterproof hiking boots will provide ankle support and good traction. Avoid wearing cotton clothing, which absorbs sweat and rain. Polypropylene, fleece, and wool all wick moisture away from your body and keep you warmer in wet or cold conditions.

- A sturdy pair of broken-in, over-the-ankle boots is essential. Boots of lightweight Gore-Tex or a similar material are ideal; they will give you good traction and support, and they will be all the footwear you will need, except when you're hiking on the higher mountain trails in early spring or winter. In even the worst winter conditions, I have never needed crampons, even in the Catskills, but a pair of studded ice creepers is a good thing to bring along on winter or spring hikes. You will also be more sure-footed with a pair of trekking poles or a staff, which will take some weight off your knees too.

- If you see downed wood that appears to be purposely covering a trail, it probably means the trail is closed due to overuse or hazardous conditions.

- If a trail is muddy, walk through the mud or on rocks, never on tree roots or plants. Waterproof boots will keep your feet comfortable. Staying in the center of the trail will keep it from eroding into a widening footway.

- Poison ivy is always a threat when you're hiking. To identify the plant, look for clusters of three leaves that shine in the sun but are dull in the shade. If you do come into contact with poison ivy, wash the affected area with soap as soon as possible.

- Wear blaze-orange items during hunting season. In New York, the peak hunting season for big game and birds generally runs from mid-October to the end of December, with high-powered rifles permitted in most counties from mid-November to mid-December. Seasons for small game extend into March. Turkey season is held in fall and spring. Yearly schedules are available at www.nys.dec.gov and in fliers and brochures available at town halls and in other public areas.

- After you complete your hike, check for deer ticks, which carry dangerous diseases, such as Lyme disease. The deer ticks that transmit Lyme disease are now found far north and west of Westchester County, where the problem has reached epidemic proportions. Their range is expanding rapidly north and west, and you should take a few preventive measures: wear long, light-colored pants; wear socks; check yourself for ticks; keep to the trail; avoid high grass; and use repellent.

- Biting insects are present during warm months, particularly in the vicinity of wetlands. They can be a minor or significant nuisance, depending on seasonal and daily conditions. One serious concern is the eastern equine encephalitis virus (commonly referred to as EEE), a rare but potentially fatal disease that can be transmitted to humans by infected mosquitoes. The Hudson Valley's many swamps and wetlands provide ideal mosquito habitats.

- Many Hudson Valley hikers have expressed concern about the recent appearance of the West Nile Virus, a mosquito-borne infection that has been known to cause encephalitis. The chances of infection are small, but are greater in infants, the elderly, and people with weak or damaged immune systems. Symptoms include low-grade fevers and headaches, but more severe infections can result in high fever, headaches and body aches. There is no cure for viral infections—only the symptoms can be treated. Of the 65 mosquito species in New York State, only the most common species, *Culex pipiens,* is associated with the virus. If you're concerned, you can protect yourself with insect repellent, long shirt sleeves and pant legs, and a hat or bug shirt during mornings and evenings, when mosquitoes are most active.

- There are a variety of options for dealing with bugs, ranging from sprays that include the active ingredient diethyl-meta-toluamide (commonly known as DEET) to more skin-friendly products. Head nets, which often can be purchased more cheaply than a can of repellent, are useful during especially buggy conditions.

Remember, hiking should be fun. If you are uncomfortable with the weather or are tired, turn back and make the complete hike another day. Don't create a situation where you risk yourself or your companions. And, try not to walk alone. Be sure someone knows your intended route and expected return time. Always sign in at a trailhead register if one is available. The unexpected can occur. Weather can change, trail markings can become obscured, you can fall, and you can get lost. But you will not be in real danger if you have anticipated the unexpected.

LEAVE NO TRACE

THE APPALACHIAN MOUNTAIN CLUB is a national educational partner of Leave No Trace, a nonprofit organization dedicated to promoting and inspiring responsible outdoor recreation through education, research, and partnerships. The Leave No Trace program seeks to develop wildland ethics—ways in which people think and act in the outdoors to minimize their impact on the areas they visit and to protect our natural resources for future enjoyment. Leave No Trace unites four federal land management agencies—the U.S. Forest Service, the National Park Service, the Bureau of Land Management, and the U.S. Fish and Wildlife Service—with manufacturers, outdoor retailers, user groups, educators, organizations such as AMC, and individuals.

The Leave No Trace ethic is guided by these seven principles:

1. **Plan Ahead and Prepare.** Know the terrain and any regulations applicable to the area you're planning to visit, and be prepared for extreme weather or other emergencies. This will enhance your enjoyment and ensure that you've chosen an appropriate destination. Small groups have less impact on resources and the experiences of other backcountry visitors.
2. **Travel and Camp on Durable Surfaces.** Travel and camp on established trails and campsites, rock, gravel, dry grasses, or snow. Good campsites are found, not made. Camp at least 200 feet from lakes and streams, and focus

activities on areas where vegetation is absent. In pristine areas, disperse use to prevent the creation of campsites and trails.

3. **Dispose of Waste Properly.** Pack it in, pack it out. Inspect your camp for trash or food scraps. Deposit solid human waste in cat holes dug 6 to 8 inches deep, at least 200 feet from water, camps, and trails. Pack out toilet paper and hygiene products. To wash yourself or your dishes, carry water 200 feet from streams or lakes and use small amounts of biodegradable soap. Scatter strained dishwater.

4. **Leave What You Find.** Cultural or historic artifacts, as well as natural objects such as plants and rocks, should be left as found.

5. **Minimize Campfire Impacts.** Cook on a stove. Use established fire rings, fire pans, or mound fires. If you build a campfire, keep it small and use dead sticks found on the ground.

6. **Respect Wildlife.** Observe wildlife from a distance. Feeding animals alters their natural behavior. Protect wildlife from your food by storing rations and trash securely.

7. **Be Considerate of Other Visitors.** Be courteous, respect the quality of other visitors' backcountry experiences, and let nature's sounds prevail.

AMC is a national provider of the Leave No Trace Master Educator course. AMC offers this 5-day course, designed especially for outdoor professionals and land managers, as well as the shorter 2-day Leave No Trace Trainer course, at locations throughout the Northeast.

For Leave No Trace information and materials, contact the Leave No Trace Center for Outdoor Ethics, P.O. Box 997, Boulder, CO 80306. Phone: 800-332-4100 or 302-442-8222; fax: 303-442-8217; web: www.lnt.org. For information on the AMC Leave No Trace Master Educator training course schedule, see www.outdoors.org/education/lnt.

1

THE HUDSON HIGHLANDS

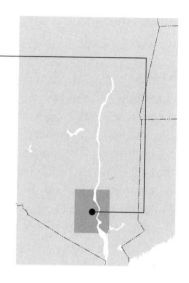

PERHAPS NO OTHER LANDMARK CHARACTERIZES the Hudson Valley like its Highlands, the scenic and rugged group of Appalachian hills that rise between Dunderberg Mountain and the Fishkill Ridge. Here, where the river is deep and narrow and the mountains rise steeply from its shores, is the topography that determined the military, cultural, and environmental history of the region.

Geologically known as the Highlands Province, its rocks are crystalline in structure, originating from Precambrian and early Paleozoic igneous and metamorphic action rather than from the sedimentation that created a great deal of the surrounding region's surface rock. Hikers will see marble, schist, and gneiss embedded, ribboned, and sprinkled throughout the open outcrops and exposed ridges. Surface scars of Pleistocene glacial activity are also visible, and visitors will walk across solidified, granitic magma chambers that were once buried deep in the earth (such as Bear Mountain). Stripped of their overburden of softer geology, the hard, weather-resistant crystalline rocks remain exposed. The upper-elevation ridges are dry and relatively open, with frequent sweeping views. Today's Highlands are geologically equivalent to and scenically comparable to the Blue Ridge Mountains of North Carolina and Virginia.

Beyond its significance as a commercial trade route, the Highlands' topography determined the settlement of the continent in other ways. Military leaders considered it the most important strategic location in the American colonies. It was here in 1778 that the great Hudson River Chain—wrought in the forges of Sterling Forest at Stirling Iron Works and floated on log booms— was stretched across the river to stop the British from advancing northward. Already in control of Canada and the Atlantic coast, the British sought to control the Hudson in order to hinder military transport and travel between the north and south. Several chains would span the river between New York City and Fort Montgomery, but the West Point Chain, built after the defeat of the north-lying forts Montgomery and Clinton, was the most notable in terms of engineering: its 2-foot-long links weighed in excess of 125 pounds each and the entire 1,500-foot span weighed nearly 200 tons. Defended from both sides of the river, the chain was never challenged or penetrated. The treasonous Benedict Arnold attempted to help the British overcome it, but he was captured before he could put his plan into action. The chain changed the course of the war, shortening it substantially. Thirteen of the original links can still be seen at West Point, but the rest were re-smelted for armament at the West Point Foundry in Cold Spring, near the point that the east end of the chain was anchored on Constitution Island. Today, the island is an Audubon nature preserve and popular canoeing destination.

A few decades after Independence, the picturesque and sublime landscapes of the Hudson Valley gave rise to the Hudson River School of landscape painting, which first focused on the Highlands area and northward. Most of the era's painters worked from New York City studios and painted to please European audiences until, in the early 1820s, Thomas Cole burst upon the scene, including among his Catskill scenes several of the Highlands. Inspired by Cole's nearly instant fame and by the existence of a growing audience of prosperous patrons and admirers with widening tastes, other artists began to emulate and train under Cole. Among them were John Frederick Kensett, Sanford R. Gifford, George Inness, Jasper Cropsey, and Frederic Church, who was Cole's star student.

Developing alongside this artistic revolution were the New York literati known as the Knickerbockers, who shared the popularity and Romantic vision of their counterparts in the art world. They included Washington Irving, Nathaniel Parker Willis, William Cullen Bryant, and James Fenimore Cooper (when his Tory sympathies could be overlooked), among others.

These artists and writers, , inspired by the beauty and grandeur of the Highlands, celebrated an America that could stand on its own in the world of arts and letters, a young country with a fierce stamp of individuality. That pride would later be called into play to protect these same resources from ruin.

TRIP 1
STORM KING

Location: Cornwall-on-Hudson, NY
Rating: Moderate
Distance: 6.0 miles
Elevation Gain: 400 feet
Estimated Time: 3 hours
Maps: USGS Cornwall; USGS West Point; NY–NJTC West Hudson Trails

This signature Highlands hike begins with a steep ascent, then eases up. It is among the shorter and easier hikes in the Highlands, with a scenic destination with views up and down the Hudson River.

DIRECTIONS

Getting to the scenic parking area where the yellow-blazed Stillman Trail begins is tricky, since it's located on a "no turns" section of US 9W in the northbound lane. If you are traveling south (from Cornwall), drive past the parking area and make a U-turn at the intersection of US 9W and NY 293/218 at the West Point Reservation, 3.0 miles south. As you are driving south from Cornwall on US 9W, you will see the parking turnout at the top of the pass, 1.5 miles beyond the Angola Road overpass. From the intersection of US 9W and NY 293/218 (the U-turn) you must turn around and drive the 3.0 miles north, back to the parking area. *GPS coordinates:* 41° 25.390′ N, 74° 00.087′ W.

TRAIL DESCRIPTION

Storm King (1,340 feet) is among the most popular hiking destinations in the Hudson Highlands, and is a mountain that has had a decisive influence on the national environmental movement. If there is one symbol of the struggle to preserve scenic open space, this is it. Dramatic views and open rock ledges characterize the trails in Storm King State Park, which is managed by the Palisades Interstate Park Commission. Until recently, some interesting destinations in the park were inaccessible, but proactive trail advocacy by the New York–New Jersey Trail Conference has provided more access, particularly in the southern area bordering the West Point Military Reservation.

This prominent little mountain draws its name from its tendency to bottleneck storms at the head of the Highland Gap. It is among the easiest walks in

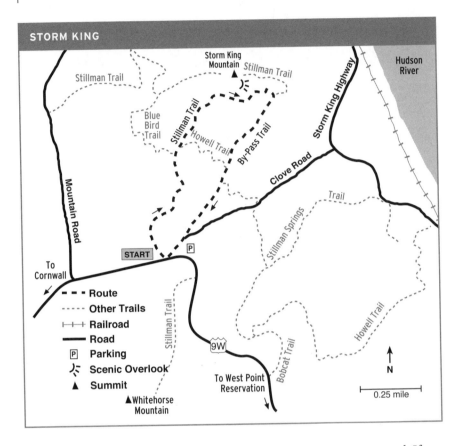

STORM KING

the region, ideal when a moderate, half-day's scenic outing is your goal. If you want to add distance and elevation, there are several choices—the Highlands may not be as lofty as surrounding mountain groups, but the trails are extensive and as steep as many others in the Catskills.

The Stillman Trail is the most popular approach to Storm King with casual day-hikers, largely because the trailhead lies in the upper elevations west of the mountain, making for a fairly easy hike. The Stillman Trail makes up most of that portion of the Highlands Trail running from the Sutherland Pond area of adjacent Black Rock Forest to Cornwall.

Park at the turnout and walk west (to the edge of the turnout) to reach the Stillman trailhead. Marking is inconspicuous from the parking lot but is consistent throughout the hike. Look closely for reddish orange paint blazes that lead uphill. Walk to the extreme west edge of the parking area or you may not find the trail. There is no signage here aside from a plaque describing the return route of the hostages who were taken in Iran in 1979.

The large, round, rocky hill you see directly north of the parking area is your first objective. This is not Storm King, but Butter Hill, or Boterberg.

After you make a fairly steep climb up an open series of shrubby slabs for a few minutes, the terrain levels out at the ruins of the Spy Rock House, the summer cottage of a park commissioner from 1913 to 1930 (there are open views to 1,461-foot Spy Rock to the south-southwest). Next, descend into a shady ravine full of talus that has fractured away from the upper ledges of Butter Hill. The trail rises sharply from here, turning northeast past several interesting south-facing vistas.

About 20 minutes after leaving the parking lot, you will ascend to the small, open, grassy summit of Butter Hill. Take a moment to enjoy some of the sights you will not see from the east ledges of Storm King. To the west, the long, serpentine ridge is the low-lying Schunemunk, over which the Long Path travels for roughly 6.0 miles on its way to the southern Shawangunks. The long trestle to the north of Schunemunk is the Moodna Viaduct, the longest rail trestle east of the Mississippi (built in 1906–1908, it is 3,200 feet long). In the far, low western foreground, with binoculars you can see a few of the large, welded-steel sculptures at the Storm King Arts Center. (See if you can identify bits of Andy Goldsworthy's 2,278-foot-long *Storm King Wall* at the south end.)

As you look through the south and across the Black Rock highlands' Mount Misery (1,268 feet) and the fire tower beyond, your gaze crosses from West Point Reservation lands and the Hudson River to Mount Taurus' lower slopes and the open quarry scar above the village of Cold Spring. The entire Shawangunk Ridge is visible in the west–northwest, all the way to Sky Top Tower in the Mohonk Preserve (5 degrees magnetic). Several major Catskill wilderness areas are also can also be seen (Slide Mountain is at magnetic north). There are three USGS triangulation benchmarks on Butter Hill (1,300 feet).

On a clear day you will most likely encounter several hikers on Butter Hill. Beyond Butter Hill, follow blue (or turquoise) and yellow paint blazes. Continue on the trail through an oak forest, dropping in elevation slightly. In 5 minutes, you'll reach a T-intersection where the Blue Bird Trail drops off to the left, heading northwest. Bear right (east) continuing on the yellow-blazed trail. In a minute or two, you'll come to a Y-intersection, where you should bear left following yellow square and blue diamond blazes. (To the right is the Howell Trail, which descends across the Clove and climbs to meet the Stillman Springs Trail.)

Soon you will encounter hemlock trees, mountain laurel, and little patches of pitch pine as the trail levels for a while, passing two vantage points looking north. It then dips once more into the woods and arrives at Storm King's "summit," an east-facing promontory. Views are spectacular. An ice sheet carved a deep gorge through the Highlands here, one of the few places where a river bisects the Appalachian chain almost to sea level, lending considerably to the savage look of the landscape. Below and to the east is Constitution

A hiker next to the American flag on Breakneck Ridge enjoys superior views of Storm King.

Marsh. Mount Taurus is close across the river, and you can see hikers near the stunning vertical drops of Breakneck Ridge. In the northeast, with many towers, is Mount Beacon. Views taper into the endless, verdant flatlands and the dimple hills and mountains to the northeast. To the southeast you can see into Putnam and Westchester counties.

In the river below is Bannerman's Castle, on Pollepel Island. Francis Bannerman was an arms dealer who bought the island in 1900 and built the castle to serve as an arsenal for most of the surplus arms from the Spanish-American War. The island is said to be haunted by horses and sea captains, goblins, witches, and spirits. It is known that the American Indians and the Dutch genuinely feared the place, probably because of the strong tidal rips and high winds. A fire destroyed all of the buildings in the late 1960s. The island is owned by New York State, and the Bannerman's Island Trust is attempting to create a park there.

Continuing on the yellow- and blue-blazed trail, descend to a T-intersection where the yellow-blazed Stillman Trail goes off to the left (east). Here, you turn right onto the white-blazed By-Pass Trail that leads southwest and descends along a rock-strewn trail, offering several southerly lookouts. In less than 0.5 mile, the Howell Trail leaves to the left. The By-Pass Trail then joins Clove Road (a dirt footpath) and begins climbing. Marking is scarce. After a steep, final ascent, bear left as the trail joins the parking area turnout, and you're back at the trailhead.

For a more challenging hike, you can begin east of Storm King at the lower elevations along the river, where trailheads can be accessed from NY 218/

Storm King Highway. This approach requires significant climbing to reach Storm King's summit. The southerly Howell Trail provides part of a very popular, longer loop hike that connects Pitching Point, on the eastern flank of the beautiful Crow's Nest, to Storm King via the Bobcat Trail and the Stillman Springs Trail. The Stillman Springs Trail climbs through the steep valley of Mother Cronk's Clove, which is also known as Storm King Clove, beginning at 200 feet above sea level.

MORE INFORMATION

The park is open for day use year-round. It is undeveloped with limited parking and no rest rooms; www.nysparks.state.ny.us/parks/152/details.aspx; 845-786-2701.

NEARBY

The Storm King Art Center on Old Pleasant Hill Road in Mountainville is a 500-acre sculpture park, open April 1 through mid-November; www.storm-king.org; 845-534-3115.

THE BIRTH OF THE ENVIRONMENTAL MOVEMENT

When development began in the Hudson Valley in the early twentieth century, the Highlands' valuable rocks—the building blocks of New York's skyline—were heavily quarried. The lack of public ownership and protection allowed private mining industries to dismantle the Highlands piecemeal.

In an effort to meet the energy needs of the greater New York population, Consolidated Edison appealed to the Federal Power Commission in 1963 for permission to build a power-generating plant on Storm King Mountain. People who lived in the Highlands, with the support of hiking clubs and other groups, organized the Scenic Hudson Preservation Conference to fight the plan in court. The 1965 ruling in favor of Scenic Hudson was a legal landmark, the first time that a conservation group had successfully sued on behalf of the public—and on the basis of the aesthetic value of a landmass.

The decision in favor of Scenic Hudson created important legal precedents, leading to the 1970 National Environmental Policy Act (NEPA) and other significant legislation such as the Clean Air Act and the Clean Water Act. During this time, two environmental advocacy groups emerged: the Environmental Defense Fund and the National Resources Defense Council. As a direct result of the fight to save Storm King, the field of environmental law was born.

TRIP 2
POPOLOPEN GORGE AND THE TORNE

Location: Fort Montgomery, NY
Rating: Moderate
Distance: 4.5 miles
Elevation Gain: 1,250 feet
Estimated Time: 3.5 hours
Maps: USGS Popolopen Lake, Peekskill; NY–NJTC Harriman Bear Mountain (northern); Bear Mountain and Harriman State Parks, Palisades Interstate Parks Commission

An easier mountain hike than most in the Highlands, this route leads you through a scenic and rugged gorge to the summit of a low hill (Torne), with 360-degree views of the Hudson Valley and the West Point Reservation.

DIRECTIONS
Take I-87 (the New York State Thruway) to Exit 16. Exit right, take a left onto NY 17 south, then take a left onto CR 6E, following signs for Bear Mountain State Park. At the first traffic circle, take the third exit, following signs for CR 6E. At the next traffic circle (Bear Mountain Bridge Circle), take the third right onto NY 9W north. In 0.5 mile, take a right into the Fort Montgomery visitor parking area. *GPS coordinates:* 41° 19.455′ N, 73° 59.305′ W.

By train, take the Metro-North Hudson Line to Manitou station. Walk south on US 9D, then cross the bridge and walk north on US 9W (3 miles total).

TRAIL DESCRIPTION
Known simply as the Torne (from the Dutch *Torenberg,* for "tower" or "pinnacle"), this small, low-elevation peak (942 feet) provides hikers with unusual views across the eastern Hudson Valley and northwest into the lands of the West Point Military Reservation. Most of the vertical rise in this hike is concentrated into a short, steep ascent from the base of the hill. Though climbing the Torne is not as strenuous as navigating the neighboring Major Welch Trail to Bear Mountain's summit, the Torne is more remote and requires deliberate preparation for a half-day outing. So you won't have to descend the ledgy and steep south face of the mountain, this hike is routed up the steeper side first. The return follows alongside scenic Popolopen Gorge, also known as Hell Hole.

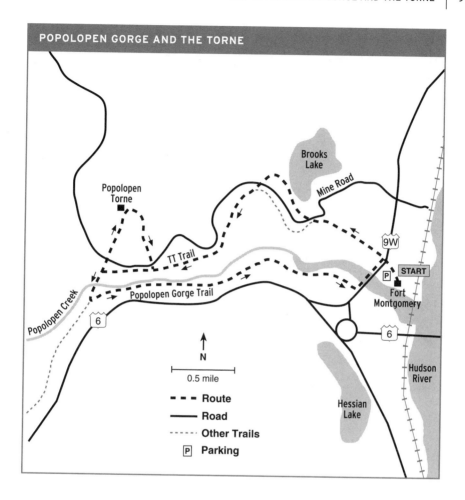

POPOLOPEN GORGE AND THE TORNE

Brooks Lake

Mine Road

Popolopen Torne

TT Trail

Popolopen Gorge Trail

Popolopen Creek

9W

P START

Fort Montgomery

6

6

Hudson River

Hessian Lake

↑
N

0.5 mile

- - - Route

——— Road

----- Other Trails

P Parking

Your route is the Timp–Torne Trail (TT), a blue-blazed loop leading west. The TT climbs the Torne through open woodlands and returns to the Fort Montgomery parking area following the scenic, narrow gorge of Popolopen Creek. From the south side of the parking area, follow the blue 1779 and red 1777 trail signs up a small stone stairway, heading toward the west and the Round Hill redoubt area. This will lead you along the north side of Popolopen Creek (a.k.a. Popolopen Brook). Do not take the suspension bridge. Instead, go under NY 9W, heading west. You will see both the 1777–1779 trail disks and the blue blazes of the Timp–Torne Trail. The trail is wide and self-guiding with interpretive signs. Continue straight ahead, following the red and blue trail disks and the blue blazes of the TT trail through dense hardwoods. Turn left on the single-lane park road, entering the woods at the road's western end, a cul-de-sac. The trail continues in a westerly direction. A spur on the left

Looking southeast from Popolopen Torne provides extensive, sweeping views of Anthony's Nose (east) and the Lower Hudson Valley.

leads to a view of the Popolopen Bridge and the Bear Mountain area. Continue straight ahead.

The wilderness quality of the trail improves as you travel west, but first you have to hike through a few wooded residential areas. Soon you rise to meet the Mine Torne Road (a.k.a. Mine Road), named for the many local iron mines that smelted ore largely for arms and ordnance during the Revolutionary War. Cross diagonally toward Brooks Lake. Bear left as you join the lake trail, but don't take the trail around the lake, which is easy to do if you're not paying attention. As soon as you begin to walk along the lake's south shore after crossing a pair of plank puncheons in a wet area next to the road, look left for the trail disks, which lead you on a moderately steep uphill path, leaving the lake to your right. Passing through a maturing sugar maple and oak forest, the trail turns again toward Mine Road, joining it and following it briefly. Pass the intersection of Mine and Wildwood Ridge roads, and follow the trail to the left back onto Harriman State Park lands. On the steep banks of the creek, hemlocks appear in an area of early settlement, where the woods are strewn with glacial erratics. The creek runs audibly (in high water) downhill to the left.

The roadbed, which once served the Forest of Dean Mine, is wide and can be walked two abreast. Soon you will draw closer to the creek. Mine Road is still visible uphill to the right. You'll be crossing it ahead.

At a Y in the trail, the section of the TT Trail, which forms a loop around the Torne, begins. The right fork heads uphill, to the north. Don't take it; this is your return route. Continue straight ahead, keeping the creek to your left. Watch for the blue TT Trail markers on the right, which will appear several hundred feet beyond the point that you left the Y behind you. Turn right (north), ascending to a nameless dirt road. Cross this and continue to climb on blue markers, soon crossing the guardrail onto the Mine Road. The trail continues just across the road. Now you begin the ascent, which follows a gently rising switchback trail as it winds through hardwoods, trending northeast. Soon the ascent steepens through ledges, and pitch pines appear. The terrain steepens dramatically onto the highest of these ledges, which provide scenic resting points en route to the summit, where a cairn commemorates members of the U.S. military.

Along the north slope of Bear Mountain, you can see the exposed rock that the Major Welch Trail traverses, as well as the road that climbs across the mountain's face to the Perkins Memorial Tower, but you can't see the tower itself. You can also see Hessian Lake directly below, to the southeast.

Continue across the open summit. At the north end of the Torne, before it drops down into hardwoods onto the lands of West Point, the blue trail switches back sharply into the south. There's a double blue marker here displayed on two short stone posts—don't go between them, but just before, bear right and drop downhill back into the south through a maturing hardwood forest, switching downhill to the Mine Road. At the point where the trail meets the road, a private residence sits to the left. Across the street is a hikers' parking area. Follow the trail to the right past a West Point Reservation "restricted area" gate. It is legal to proceed along the trail, which avoids the restricted area 500 feet ahead. Follow blue blazes left as the trail drops downhill to the left toward Popolopen Creek, to the Y you encountered earlier.

Continue west with the creek down to your left. Leave the blue TT Trail to your right, and in several hundred feet cross the metal footbridge. Do not follow the 1777–79 trails once you are across the bridge; instead, bear left onto the red and white markers of the Popolopen Gorge Trail. This pretty woods road follows east along the creek, now to your left, and climbs away from it for a while. The trail switches back and forth down the ravine amid large oaks, tulip trees, locusts, and hemlocks that have been killed or damaged by hemlock woolly adelgid. The many pools of the gorge are visible down to the left. Trail markers may vary in shape and size, but they appear frequently and the trail is self-guiding.

Soon the trail comes back along the creek's edge, and climbs uphill slightly, passing above Roe Pond, where a bridge once spanned the brook over a steep-walled gorge at the site of a 1799 gristmill. Hikers in the area will see references to the West Point Aqueduct. In fact, two aqueducts were built along the sides of the gorge in the early 1900s, one to bring water to West Point and the other (on the south side) to serve Bear Mountain. Both show visible remains.

The trail continues uphill slightly on a wide dirt surface now, rising gently to meet NY 9W. Marking becomes indefinite where herd trails make their way east to the nearby road. Trail markers lead to the road beyond the first herd trail. Once at the road, turn north to cross the 600-foot-long bridge along the sidewalk, remaining on the west side without crossing the highway.

Turn left as you reach the north end of the bridge and, in lieu of crossing this dangerous section of the road, bear left until you reach the 1777–1779 trails that you will recognize from earlier in the hike. Look to your left where a small sign says Visitor Center and go back under the bridge on the 1777–1779 trails. This will bring you back to the Fort Montgomery parking area.

DID YOU KNOW?

The center span of NY 9W's Popolopen Bridge is over 150 feet high—high enough that a parachutist was able to jump from it successfully, though he was later arrested for the unauthorized use of an aircraft (the parachute).

MORE INFORMATION

The Fort Montgomery visitor parking area is open year-round, sunrise to sunset; the visitor center is open Wednesday to Sunday, 9 A.M. to 5 P.M., but call ahead as times may vary; www.nysparks.com; 845-446-2134.

Additional parking is available farther north on the east side (northbound) of NY 9W, from where you can walk the site's foot trails back to the main parking area. The interpretive trails are not suited to people with limited mobility. Dogs are allowed on leashes in the park. Swimming is prohibited.

NEARBY

The Visitor Center and the West Point Museum are open to the public daily at the United States Military Academy at West Point. Guided tours of the academy grounds are available; www.usma.edu; 845-938-2638 (Visitor Center) or 845-938-3590 (Museum).

TRIP 3
BREAKNECK RIDGE TO
SOUTH BEACON MOUNTAIN

Location: Beacon, NY
Rating: Strenuous
Distance: 9 miles
Elevation Gain: 1,400 feet
Estimated Time: 6 hours
Maps: USGS West Point; NY–NJTC East Hudson Trails

This demanding hike up the steepest and most exposed scenic trail in the Highlands offers sustained views from open ridges, with a return through quiet forests.

DIRECTIONS

From the intersection of Main Street and NY 9D in the village of Cold Spring, drive north on NY 9D, passing the Little Stony Point parking area at 0.8 mile, and continuing north. Just as you pass under the tunnel at 2.1 miles, park immediately on the left (west) side of NY 9D. If this very small lot is full, continue north to find two more parking areas at 0.1 and 0.3 mile. (This hike terminates at the parking area 0.3 mile ahead.) *GPS coordinates:* 41° 26.584′ N, 73° 58.660′ W.

By train, take the Metro-North Hudson line to Cold Spring station. Walk north on NY 9D to the trailhead.

TRAIL DESCRIPTION

The steep, windswept spine of Breakneck Ridge is considered the most difficult and rugged ascent in the Highlands. Rising from nearly sea level on the Hudson at Breakneck Point to 1,100 feet on Breakneck's summit in less than 0.5 mile, it is a rock scramble requiring an all-fours approach. Because the sheer southerly face of Breakneck draws very close to the trail in spots, this hike is not advisable in wet or icy conditions, or in periods of high winds. It also is not a good choice for unfit hikers or those with bad knees. This is an intense aerobic workout, and hikers need to ensure they carry enough water. (The Appalachian Mountain Club recommends that participants carry a minimum of 2 quarts on hikes of this nature.) The route described here is a long day hike, but there are several options for shortening the trip.

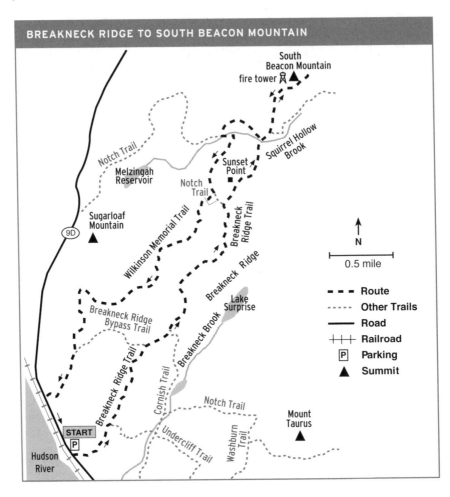

BREAKNECK RIDGE TO SOUTH BEACON MOUNTAIN

To begin, locate the white Taconic Region Trail markers and white paint blazes of the Breakneck Ridge Trail (BRT) immediately north of the tunnel on NY 9D. The trail's initial ascent brings you to a popular rock ledge over the river, directly facing Storm King Mountain, and then turns east, crossing over the top of the tunnel and ascending steeply. After 15 minutes of climbing through ledges, over slabs, and around boulders, you'll find yourself on a rock ledge facing west, with fine views up and down the river. An American flag is planted in a steel stand. Storm King blocks a good deal of the western skyline. You have a good view of Pollepel Island and Bannerman's Castle just upriver.

Resuming the climb, you will follow along the southern cliffs of the ridge, enjoying increasingly good views north to south. If you're lucky, there will be a cooling southwest breeze pouring across the ridge top. You'll see military helicopters from West Point and C5 cargo planes on maneuvers from Stewart Airbase, and you can look down onto the decks of ships moving fuel and freight up- and downriver from the Port of Albany. In fall, many of the large sailing craft you'll see will be heading out to the Intracoastal Waterway to wintering places in the Caribbean.

Sometimes the paint blazes may seem confusing, with alternate routes away from the rock ledges presented here and there. Continue climbing (the alternate markings tend to parallel the main trail). The sparse hardwood forest covering most of the ridge gives way to pockets of pitch pine, where sun-starched clutches of violet asters persist late into October. Hawks and vultures, their wing tips trembling, survey the ledges with the rising air. Pine needles make the rocks slippery, so mind your footholds.

Once on top of Breakneck's main summit (the summit ridge is stretched out in a series of domes), you'll be ready for a break. The ground you've covered to this point is probably the most popular "weekend warrior" hike in the Highlands, and there is obvious impact. The trail would be in much worse condition if it weren't for the erosion- and impact-resistant rock surface. From this point, most day-hikers turn back, so chances are you will have the ridge to yourself from here.

Get a good look at the views again before you continue, descending to a point where the yellow Undercliff Trail departs to the south. Climb northeast on the BRT again to another scenic crest, where you look across the forests of Breakneck Brook at Mount Taurus. The trail continues through grassy oak woodlands. Nearly 2 hours into the hike, you will pass the red-on-white-blazed Breakneck Ridge Bypass Trail on your left. (You can shorten the hike by taking this trail north to the yellow-marked Wilkinson Memorial Trail [WMT] and turning southwest to NY 9D.) Continue straight ahead on the BRT. In 15 minutes or so, the blue-marked Notch Trail joins the BRT from the south and continues with it. Following blue and white markers now, you're headed for Sunset Point. The trail surface is moderately rocky, but soft; it is mostly self-guiding and marking can be sparse in rocky areas. The trail goes through flat, shady woods for a spell.

Arrive at a T and bear left. Don't make the mistake of going off to the right on the informal, blue-blazed trails you'll see—stick to the blue and white Taconic Region disks for now. As you reach another T, bear right with the white markers as the blue-blazed Notch Trail goes left (northwest). (This is another place where you may wish to turn around, following the Notch Trail to the WMT, where you would turn left [southwest] with the option of climbing Sugarloaf Mountain on your return.)

Continue on the BRT, climbing slightly to Sunset Point. Once treeless and scenic, the point is now enclosed by vegetation. A very well-built observation deck appears along the trail, but even it provides little in the way of views,

The rising western slopes of Mount Taurus are seen from Breakneck Ridge.

although you can see South Beacon Mountain's fire tower if you look north-east. If it seems too far away you can backtrack from here or bail out ahead. The BRT heads downhill now through an area crisscrossed with old trails and skid roads, to a point where it intersects with the yellow WMT at a four-way intersection (the unmarked trail to the right leads to private property). This is your last bail-out point. If it's late in the day or your energy is ebbing, consider the additional distance and elevation gain required to ascend South Beacon. (To quit here, bear left and follow the WMT out, as described above.)

Continue straight on a woods road now, following both white and yellow blazes for a few hundred feet and turn left (north) on white to begin the ascent of South Beacon. This is the steepest section of trail since Breakneck. Climb open rock ledges and east-facing flats as the woods turn grassy and sheltered again, and the trail swings gradually into the east. After about 4 hours of hiking, you will summit South Beacon at 1,400 feet, the highest point in the

Highlands. (Your return route is much faster.) You won't see the fire tower until you're almost at its base. The tower is in a dangerous state of disrepair and is closed to the public. The views are excellent from the summit, however, from points north to the Catskills and the Shawangunks (you can pick out Sky Top in the Mohonk Preserve), south across the river into the Highlands, and east into the low hills of Dutchess and Putnam counties and Fahnestock State Park. The tower field of North Beacon Mountain stands close to the north. The Newburgh-Beacon Bridge spans the Hudson 3.0 miles to the northwest.

Turn around now and retrace your steps to the WMT, following it to the right at both intersections, proceeding downhill to a point where it crosses Squirrel Hollow Brook, turns left (east, then south) and rises (with the Notch Trail) along a pleasant old woods road. Watch carefully to the right as the easily missed, yellow-blazed WMT parts company with the Notch Trail (you've gone too far if you encounter the white-and-blue-marked intersection you crossed earlier). Heading southwest, your route takes you through airy woods with a few herd trails to scenic overlooks, and climbs the northeastern shoulder of Sugarloaf Mountain. Views to the north and south from Sugarloaf are the last you'll get. The yellow WMT markers are complemented by white paint blazes here, so don't get confused. Drop down the south side of the mountain and pass the Breakneck Ridge Bypass Trail on your left. The trail is now an old road with a good surface that takes you back to NY 9D. Be careful as you follow this busy stretch of road back to your car.

DID YOU KNOW?

Legend has it that in Colonial times, a farmer's bull escaped its confines and found its way to this steep ridge, where it plunged to its death, resulting in the odd place-name of Breakneck.

MORE INFORMATION

Breakneck Ridge is open daily from sunrise to sunset. Dogs are permitted, but must be on a leash of 10 feet or less; www.nysparks.state.ny.us/parks/9/details.aspx; 845-225-7207.

NEARBY

Exhibits of contemporary art are featured at the Dia:Beacon Museum at 3 Beekman Street in Beacon; www.diabeacon.org; 845-440-0100.

A boat cruise with a walking tour of Bannerman Island (site of the famed Bannerman Castle) is offered weekends from May 1 to October 31, departing from either Newburgh or Beacon; www.prideofthehudson.com; 845-220-2120.

TRIP 4
BEAR MOUNTAIN

Location: Bear Mountain, NY
Rating: Strenuous
Distance: 4.0 miles
Elevation Gain: 1,000 feet
Estimated Time: 3.5 hours
Maps: USGS Peekskill; USGS Popolopen Lake; NY–NJTC Northern
Harriman Bear Mountain Trails

This pretty hike from the famous Bear Mountain Inn in the state park along Hessian Lake goes to Perkins Memorial Tower and its 360-degree views and descends on the Appalachian Trail.

DIRECTIONS

Begin at Bear Mountain State Park, 0.4 mile south of the Bear Mountain traffic circle on US 9W. The traffic circle is located at the northern end of the Palisades Interstate Parkway, at the western entrance to the Bear Mountain Bridge. *GPS coordinates:* 41° 18.771′ N, 73° 59.335′ W.

By train, take the Metro-North Hudson Line to Manitou station. Walk south on US 9D, then cross the bridge and walk south on US 9W (3 miles total).

TRAIL DESCRIPTION

Since its creation in 1913, millions of people have visited Bear Mountain State Park to indulge in founder George Perkins' version of rest and relaxation, but only a fraction of them ever climb its namesake, the scenic "little" mountain lying west of Hessian Lake. Though Bear Mountain isn't especially formidable at 1,305 feet, the steep northerly ascent from near sea level to its summit via the Major Welch Trail makes this hike feel longer than it is, and you should prepare accordingly.

There are several approaches to Bear Mountain, but the Major Welch Trail is the most scenic and interesting, sharing its popularity among hikers with the somewhat easier southerly approach using the Appalachian Trail (AT). (It is also possible to drive to the summit on Perkins Memorial Drive, so expect to see cars and people at the summit picnic area.) Major Welch was the general manager of Palisades Interstate Park from 1912 to 1940. He organized the completion of the first section of the AT, and designed the trail's distinctive

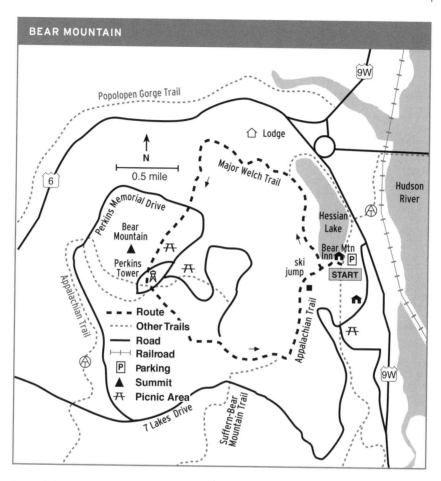

BEAR MOUNTAIN

Popolopen Gorge Trail

⌂ Lodge

N
0.5 mile

9W

Major Welch Trail

6

Hudson River

Perkins Memorial Drive

Bear Mountain ▲

Perkins Tower

Hessian Lake

Ⓐ

Bear Mtn Inn ⌂ P

ski jump

START

⌂

Appalachian Trail

Appalachian Trail

- - - Route
····· Other Trails
—— Road
⊢—⊣ Railroad
P Parking
▲ Summit
� Picnic Area

Ⓐ

9W

7 Lakes Drive

Suffern-Bear Mountain Trail

logo. (The AT Conference believes that the Bear Mountain section of the AT is the most heavily used portion of the 2,167-mile trail.)

Despite the extremely high day-use figures Bear Mountain State Park sustains, it has been kept clean and orderly—a result of the park's careful planning, management, and supervision. You will appreciate this as you stroll through the inn complex, where you'll park. Try to take this hike before the park's swimming pool opens for the season on the first day of summer, or after it closes in early September, when parking is free and visitors are not present in great numbers.

Walk in front of the Bear Mountain Inn and bear left toward the south end of Hessian Lake. Orient yourself at the southern shore, behind the inn on the paved path. Watch for the red circle on a white background as you follow the shore in the company of friendly geese and squirrels. Head toward the boat-rental concession to the west. As you pass a children's playground on your left, the AT joins the paved lake path. (That's your return route.) Leave the AT to your left and walk along the pretty western shore of Hessian Lake. In 15 minutes or so, look left at the location of a bench, where the Major Welch Trail departs to the left (northwest). If you're daydreaming, you might miss it.

The Major Welch Trail is slow in ascending. The first 0.5 mile is forgiving as the trail rises gently and sidehills along the northeasterly hardwood slopes, passing a water tower on the left and the park's Overlook Lodge downhill and north. By the time you're wondering where the vertical rise begins, you've turned south and the trail climbs directly upslope over a rocky surface. These rocks have enabled the trail's direct approach, protecting it from the kind of erosion you'll see on the softer southern slopes. You'll appreciate your poles or hiking staff here. Most of the hike's vertical rise is packed into the next 0.5 mile.

The trail climbs through nearly pure oak/laurel woods among thick mats of blueberry bushes. Underfoot is the bright limestone of the Greenville Series, which is of Precambrian origin—among the oldest surface bedrock of its kind. As you gain elevation, you'll come upon a long, angled slab with a northern exposure. Things get more interesting now as views of the valley open up. Here you will get a close look at Popolopen Torne with its brown, exposed summit. Ahead, the scenery improves as you are treated to views to the north, west, and east, encompassing a good deal of the northern Highlands and the river. You can identify Sugarloaf, Taurus, Storm King, the Black Rock Forest, the lands of Fahnestock State Park, and, down along the river, Garrison Landing. A few pitch pines appear.

The trail cuts across Perkins Memorial Drive and continues to climb, more easily now, flattening out after one more steep pitch. After crossing a gravel road in the picnic area, you will soon pass the true summit, where tower bolts can be seen in the rocks to the right of the trail. Continue straight through the picnic area, following markers past a rest room on your left (with a pair of vending machines outside), and ascending slightly to Perkins Tower. Take a few minutes to view the tower, with its tiled, art deco pictorial history of the park and its four walls detailed with panoramic locator maps of the 360-degree views. Note Anthony's Nose to the east and Dunderberg, Bald, and the Timp to the south. The tower commemorates George Perkins, of the banking firm J.P. Morgan, who envisioned a place where the people of New York City (visible to the south) could find "rest and relaxation." Perkins was an activist instrumental in the long struggle to preserve the Palisades, leading to the effort to protect the entire Hudson Valley from exploitation and development.

The Major Welch Trail ends here. Just outside the front entrance of the tower and across the parking area to the south, your route continues on the

Anthony's Nose provides far-reaching views, including Bear Mountain (left).

AT. In the rocks at the trailside, you'll find the AT next to the bronze plaque honoring Joe Bartha, the trails chairman from 1940 to 1955. Search the rocks for a vague, weathered carving indicating the AT's distance to Arden and to Vogel State Park in Georgia (1,260 miles; the southern terminus has since been relocated to Springer Mountain). Following the AT now, descend through open hardwoods.

In about 10 minutes, you will cross Perkins Memorial Drive. Descending, you'll again reach it at a point where a trail marker reads, Tower, 30 Mins. The word "tower" is stenciled onto a rock to the left, next to the road. Pay close attention, as the trail turns right and follows the road. (It is evident from herd paths that many hikers unwittingly continue downhill into the woods after crossing the road.) Follow the road for 10 minutes until reaching a loop. The AT leaves the loop on the right side over a stretch of broken pavement; marking is good. Within 100 feet it turns hard left (east) and descends. The AT switches and drops into the east, passing through a beautiful grove of white pine before continuing through hardwoods. At the well-marked junction where the

Suffern-Bear Mountain Trail (SBM) comes in, bear left with the SBM and AT. At the head of a gully the trail swings hard to the right, continuing its descent and flattening out at a point where the park complex becomes visible. Avoid the trail to the right, instead continuing on the AT and SBM for a short climb past the old ski jump and tower; piecing together the missing runway and the crowds of spectators, you can imagine what the scene must have looked like.

Now the trail follows the old service road to the ski jump as it switches back and drops to lake level again behind the inn. The SBM trail ends and the AT continues along Hessian Lake, across the Hudson toward Maine's Katahdin. You may ponder, for a moment, the vision of Mary Averell Harriman, wife of Edward Harriman, who gave 10,000 acres of land to the state under the condition that the state discontinue plans for the construction of Sing Sing prison at the base of Bear Mountain. The prison was eventually built downriver, in Ossining, north of New York City, giving rise to the expression "Sent up the river."

From here, follow the short trail back to your car.

DID YOU KNOW?

Perkins Memorial Tower on the summit of Bear Mountain was constructed to take advantage of the scenic Hudson Highlands' views, and was such a hit with the touring public that in September and October of 1935 (the year after the tower was inaugurated), it attracted 9,869 cars from 36 states and two Canadian provinces.

MORE INFORMATION

The park is open for day use year-round. There is a large playing field, shaded picnic groves, a swimming pool, and river access, in addition to the rustic Bear Mountain Inn, the Bear Mountain Zoo, Trailside Museums, and a merry-go-round; www.nysparks.state.ny.us/parks/13/details.aspx; 845-786-2701.

TRIP 5
HESSIAN LAKE AND FORT
MONTGOMERY STATE HISTORIC SITE

Location: Fort Montgomery, NY
Rating: Easy
Distance: 3.25 miles
Elevation Gain: 350 feet
Estimated Time: 2 hours
Maps: USGS Peekskill; Bear Mountain and Harriman State Parks, Palisades Interstate Park Commission; State Park handouts

This easy hike winds through a park and a zoo, around a lake, and through a Revolutionary War site adjacent to the Hudson River.

DIRECTIONS

To reach Bear Mountain from the Bear Mountain Bridge Circle, which is located on CR 6 immediately on the west side of the Bear Mountain Bridge, take NY 9W south. At the first traffic light, bear right and go up the hill. The parking area is on your right at this point. For directions to the Fort Montgomery State Historic Site, see Trip 2. *GPS coordinates:* 41° 18.771′ N, 73° 59.335′ W.

By train, take the Metro-North Hudson Line to Manitou station. Walk south on US 9D, then cross the bridge and walk south on US 9W (3 miles total).

TRAIL DESCRIPTION

This scenic, historic, and zoologic hike gives you the opportunity to walk around Hessian Lake, through the Bear Mountain Zoo (route of the Appalachian Trail, or AT), and across CR 6 to the Fort Montgomery State Historic Site. Although the trails in this hike are interconnected and the hiking time is fairly brief, put aside at least a half-day to wander among these interesting places, especially if you are with children, who will be fascinated by the zoo. Like most of the popular trails in the Bear Mountain vicinity, this one is best taken before the Bear Mountain complex opens for the season in June, when it is often congested with day users. Hiking in the off-season will provide you with more privacy on the trail, and you will not be charged the parking fee. However, if you have children with you and wish to use the full services of the park, such as the swimming pool, merry-go-round, and picnic area, the fee is well worth these amenities.

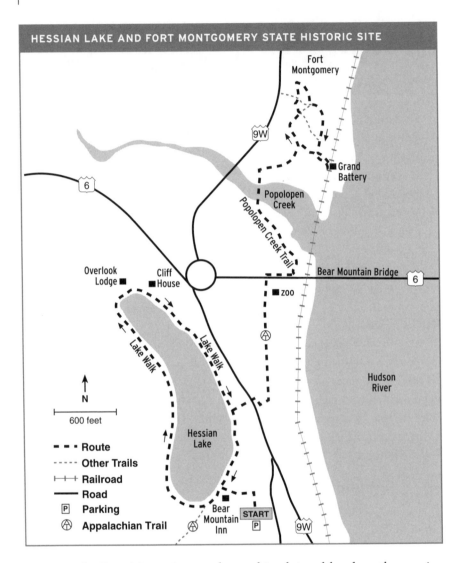

HESSIAN LAKE AND FORT MONTGOMERY STATE HISTORIC SITE

Fort Montgomery

9W

Grand Battery

Popolopen Creek

Popolopen Creek Trail

6

Overlook Lodge
Cliff House

Bear Mountain Bridge
6

ZOO

Lake Walk

Lake Walk

Hudson River

N

600 feet

Hessian Lake

- - - Route
- - - - Other Trails
+-+-+ Railroad
—— Road
P Parking
Ⓐ Appalachian Trail

Bear Mountain Inn

START
P

9W

Leave the Bear Mountain complex parking lot and head north, crossing in front of the Bear Mountain Inn and heading left toward Hessian Lake. The conspicuous mountain visible across the river east of the parking lot is Anthony's Nose, one of the Hudson Valley's most scenic hiking destinations. Immediately to the west across the lake, the slopes of Bear Mountain rise sharply.

The 1.25-mile loop around Hessian Lake makes for a pleasant walk. Follow the paved Lake Walk along the water's edge, bearing left toward the western shore. Pass the boat-rental dock and follow the Lake Walk around the lake's south end and into the north. Along the Lake Walk, you will see the Major Welch Trail markers, which are red dots on white, and nearing the lake's north end you'll see where that trail leaves the Lake Walk to head for Bear Mountain's summit. Continue around the north end of the lake. Uphill to the north you will see Overlook Lodge and the Cliff House, along with the little cottages of the Bear Mountain lodge system. Walk south, remaining on the Lake Walk until you enter the picnic groves. When you see the picnic shelter, leave the Lake Walk and bear left on a path that goes east toward the underpass in the direction of the zoo. Now you're following the Appalachian Trail. (Look for white paint blazes on the trees.)

Continue past the pool house and go through the gate into the zoo (it is free for AT hikers; a $1 donation is suggested). The zoo features mostly species indigenous to the region, many of which are rescues. The zoo trail is very wooded and attractive as it winds its way north past the Walt Whitman statue and into the area of the former Fort Clinton, which was razed so badly by the British during the Revolutionary War that not much of it is recognizable. A short diversion to the west takes you through the redoubt (walled fortification) area. Continue north, heading toward the museums, which are fascinating, featuring rare collections of American Revolution artifacts, many of them excavated from forts Clinton and Montgomery.

On the zoo's north side next to the history museum building, the AT leaves for the Bear Mountain Bridge and points northwest. The trail you want is the Popolopen Creek Trail, which also leaves from here (blue stripes on gray; marking is sparse) and follows along with the AT a bit farther. Both trails cross the pedestrian crosswalk next to the tollbooth. (There is an alternate trail that leaves the zoo to the east, goes under the highway, and joins the Popolopen Creek Trail, but the zoo end of the trail is gated when the zoo is closed.) Cross on the pedestrian crosswalk and turn right (east) as if you intend to cross the Bear Mountain Bridge. (If you have time, walk to the center span for a sweeping view of the river.) Watch very carefully as you walk along the sidewalk; immediately before the bridge guardrail begins, bear left (north) onto the Popolopen Creek Trail (the AT continues across the bridge at this point). At this point the trail is not marked and there is no signage. Follow the trail downhill on a natural stone stairway and bear left at a Y.

Follow the trail downhill into the ravine toward Popolopen Creek, where it crosses the footbridge, an interesting pedestrian suspension bridge that was dedicated in 2002 by Governor George Pataki. Bear right and uphill into the Fort Montgomery Historic Site. Here you will find the visitor center along with many outdoor interpretive signs and maps. The site's trail system begins on the north side of the visitor center. A stroll through the redoubts and associated fortifications will take about a half-hour, allowing time to read the

Visitors will enjoy the western shore of Hessian Lake, part of the easy and pleasant Lake Walk.

interpretive information that's posted in each area of this extensive excavation. Here you will see the foundations of several buildings, among them barracks, redoubts, bunkers, artillery placements, and other, yet-to-be-identified relics. Follow the interpretive trail past the site of the storehouse, the enlisted men's barracks, officers' barracks and commissary, the north redoubt, the guardhouse, and the magazine, finishing with the cannon battery before returning to the visitor center. The Western and Round Hill redoubts can be examined on the west side of NY 9W by following the 1777 and 1779 trails. Go west under the NY 9W bridge, a short detour on your return to the suspension bridge.

Early in the American Revolution, the Continental Congress recognized the need to defend the Hudson River from the British, who sought to take the river and divide the New England colonies from New York. It was believed that the best location for such a defense was at the present site of Bear Mountain, where the river narrowed and the current made navigation slow and difficult. Advancing ships would be easy prey for the cannon battery that was set atop the hill between Fort Clinton and Fort Montgomery. Construction of both forts began in 1776, despite difficulties in procuring supplies and manpower, and the combined fortifications were completed in 1777. After realizing ultimately that Fort Montgomery was vulnerable to attack by land (originally it was felt that the Hudson Highlands' rugged topography would protect it from a land-based assault), colonists fortified it by placing of redoubts along its western line of defense. These were essentially earthworks behind which infantrymen could snipe at the advancing enemy.

Retrace your steps now, back to the zoo and the Lake Walk. If you return after closing time, you will not be able to follow the trail through the zoo and will instead have to walk along the grass strip next to NY 9W, crossing it at the point where a paved spur appears at the north end of Hessian Lake, just south of the entrance road to the Bear Mountain lodge complex (this is the recommended route of the AT when the zoo is closed). Try to avoid doing this, however, as traffic coming off the Bear Mountain Circle moves very fast.

DID YOU KNOW?

During the British attacks on forts Clinton and Montgomery, both the British and American forces suffered heavy losses. The bodies were disposed of in what was originally called Bloody Pond, later renamed Hessian Lake.

MORE INFORMATION

The trailside zoo and museum are open daily from 10 A.M. to 4:30 P.M.; www.nysparks.state.ny.us/parks/13/details.aspx; 845-786-2701.

Fort Montgomery is open year-round, sunrise to sunset; visitor center hours vary Wednesday to Sunday, 9 A.M. to 5 P.M; www.nysparks.state.ny.us/historic-sites/28/details.aspx; 845-446-2134.

NEARBY

For more Revolutionary War history, visit Washington's Headquarters State Historic Site, located in an eighteenth-century stone house at the corner of Liberty and Washington streets in Newburgh. The site is open April through October; www.nysparks.state.ny.us/historic-sites/17/details.aspx; 845-562-1195.

TRIP 6
ANTHONY'S NOSE

Location: Cortlandt, NY; trail begins in Bear Mountain
Rating: Moderate
Distance: 4 miles
Elevation Gain: 700 feet
Estimated Time: 4 hours
Maps: USGS Peekskill; NY–NJTC East Hudson Trails

A fairly steep ascent climbs to an easy woods road leading to Engagement Rock, where you look straight down on the Hudson River and Bear Mountain Bridge.

DIRECTIONS

Bear Mountain State Park is 0.4 mile south of the Bear Mountain traffic circle on US 9W. The traffic circle is located at the northern end of the Palisades Interstate Parkway, at the western entrance to the Bear Mountain Bridge. Park in the Bear Mountain Inn parking lot, or along NY 9D on the east side of the Hudson River, 0.2 mile north of the Bear Mountain Bridge, where there are two very small, legal pull-offs near the AT signage. (Note: This option cuts out the Bear Mountain Zoo and Bridge.) *GPS coordinates:* 41° 18.771′ N, 73° 59.335′ W.

By train, take the Metro-North Hudson Line to Manitou station. Walk south for 2 miles on US 9D (as above, this options cuts out the zoo and bridge).

TRAIL DESCRIPTION

How about a hike that takes you past a parish-green lake, through a zoo, along the lowest-elevation stretch of the 2,169-mile Appalachian Trail (AT), and across the Bear Mountain Bridge to one of the most dramatic scenic destinations in the Hudson Valley? This unforgettable outing begins at Bear Mountain State Park and Inn Complex, where you join the AT as it makes its way across the Hudson River. There are other ways to reach Anthony's Nose (900 feet), but this one is the shortest and most interesting, and easily the most exciting.

From the Bear Mountain Inn parking area, walk toward the inn, keeping the main entrance to your left. To the right, beyond the flagpole and cannon, is Anthony's Nose, 0.7 mile to the east. The highest reach of exposed rock, Engagement Rock on the western face, is your destination.

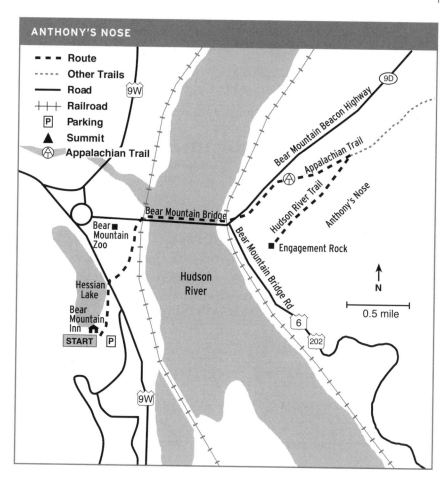

Two paved paths diverge into the picnic area to the north within 100 feet of the inn. Stay to the left, walking with Hessian Lake to your left, and in a few minutes you will intersect with the white-blazed AT (near the rest rooms). Be alert now as the AT bears right (east) and tunnels under US 9W/202, passing the pool and entering the wooded paths of the zoo. (There is a $1 fee for adults, but no charge for AT hikers. Handicapped parking is available.)

The zoo marks the lowest elevation on the AT between Maine and Georgia (124 feet above sea level). The AT is consistently well marked and will bring you to the northern exit at the Bear Mountain Bridge administration building. Bear left as you reach the toll plaza and follow blazes left to the pedestrian crossing just west of the tollbooths. Cross carefully here and walk along the north side of the bridge on the protected pedestrian path. As you reach the east side of the river, bear left onto the shoulder of NY 9D, and follow the AT markers to the point where the white-blazed trail enters the woods on the

Engagement Rock commands a long, sweeping view of the Hudson Highlands.

east side of the road. Be careful here. Although you have only a 0.2-mile walk, traffic moves briskly through this short road stretch of the AT. Follow the trail uphill as it swings northeast to begin a 700-foot vertical rise. Most of this gain is experienced in the first 0.6 mile of the AT as it climbs a good footway on a well-maintained trail with makeshift steps and heavy rock water bars.

At an obvious, well-marked T, the trail relaxes and the AT departs left (northeast) to the Hudson Highlands State Park (Osborne Preserve). Turn right here following the blue-blazed Hudson River Trail onto the lands of the New York State Military Reservation (Camp Smith). This gentler, more enjoyable section of the trail follows an old woods road that rises briefly and levels at 700-feet of elevation, where it passes through open hardwoods, winds past a vernal pond, and gently rises to a T. This point is not signed, and if you didn't know to turn right here, you'd miss the Nose completely.

The blue blazes lead southeast here on a foot trail, but the roadbed you've been walking on continues to the right (west), immediately reaching the open ledges of Anthony's Nose at Engagement Rock. The views are startling, as is the breathless sensation you get from standing over the Hudson that lies at your feet nearly 900 feet below. Freighters, plying the river's channel, pass beneath you, their turbid wakes twisting a half-mile behind them. The hills of Harriman State Park are displayed north to south, from the northern Popolopen Torne to

Dunderburg and the Timp. From here, Haverstraw Bay looks like a vast arm of the sea—which it is—and upriver the Central Highlands lie in a pastel haze of multiple horizons beyond World's End. This section of the Hudson is called the Devil's Horse Race, so named for the high winds and strong tides that funnel through its narrowest point. According to one legend, the Nose is named for the proboscis of a sea captain—one Antony Hogans—whose crew thought the facial and geological phenomena had a great deal in common.

You can see Perkins Memorial Tower on Bear Mountain, and Iona Island, nudged against the western shore of the river. This is a popular spot and you're likely to be sharing it with other hikers. There is another, less spectacular outcropping nearby, just a few feet south on the blue trail from the junction where you turned east to the Nose. There you can find more privacy among the burnished summit rocks facing the southern valley. Directly below is the Bear Mountain Bridge, privately built by the Harriman family in 1923.

Retrace your steps to return to your car.

DID YOU KNOW?

When Earl Shaffer became the first AT hiker to cross the Bear Mountain Bridge in 1948, it cost a nickel. Today, passage is free for hikers.

MORE INFORMATION

Bear Mountain Inn parking lot opens when the park and zoo are open, which is year-round, 10 A.M. to 6 P.M. A parking fee applies from late June through Labor Day (when the zoo and inn are closed, the official route of the AT becomes the shoulder of US 9W); www.nysparks.state.ny.us/parks/9/details.aspx; 845-225-7207.

NEARBY

Nature programs and self-guided trails are available weekends from April to November at the two centers of the Hudson Highlands Nature Museum in Cornwall and Cornwall-on-Hudson; www.museumhudsonhighlands.org; 845-534-5506 or 845-534-7781. Tours and tastings are available at the Brotherhood Winery in Washingtonville, America's oldest winery; www.brotherhood winery.net; 845-496-3661.

TRIP 7
THE HOOK

Location: Nyack, NY
Rating: Moderate
Distance: 5.3 miles
Elevation Gain: 1,200 feet
Estimated Time: 3.5 Hours
Maps: USGS Sloatsburg; NY–NJTC Hudson Palisades Trail Map

This very scenic loop outing begins with a flat walk along the river and then climbs a high section of the northern Palisades.

DIRECTIONS

To reach Nyack Beach State Park from west of the Hudson River on I-87 (a.k.a. I-287, the New York State Thruway), take Exit 11 for Nyack. At the traffic light, turn left onto CR 59 East. This leads you straight onto Main Street. Go under the I-87 underpass and through the intersection of NY 9W. Continue 1.0 mile straight through town on Main Street to its intersection with North Broadway in the center of the village. Turn left (north) and go another 2.0 miles to Nyack Beach State Park.

Coming from east of the Hudson River, take I-87 to Exit 10. This is a large circular interchange. Pass the turnoff to NY 9W and continue to the next right. This is South Nyack. At the stop sign, turn right onto Clinton Avenue then left onto South Broadway. Go straight onto North Broadway and continue to the park entrance, 2.5 miles from the exit. *GPS coordinates:* 41° 7.235′ N, 73° 54.685′ W.

By bus, take Coach USA from Port Authority to Broadway and Cedar Hill in Nyack (call 201-263-1254). Walk north for 2 miles on Broadway to trailhead.

TRAIL DESCRIPTION

The Hook has long been a favorite of Hudson Valley hiking enthusiasts, who enjoy the very high scenic vistas from this easily accessible, moderately difficult trail. The trail is named for Hook Mountain, which at 728 feet is the highest landscape feature on the trail and the second-highest point on the Palisades Ridge after High Tor. The long, flat approach along the river's edge and the high-country feel of the vertical cliffs of the Palisades make this a satisfying hike of contrasts.

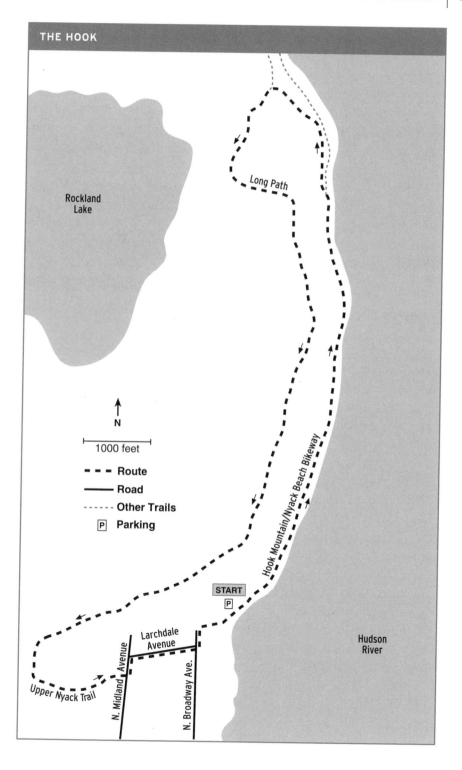

THE HOOK

Rockland
Lake

Long Path

N

1000 feet

- - - Route
——— Road
------- Other Trails
P Parking

Hook Mountain/Nyack Beach Bikeway

START
P

Larchdale
Avenue

N. Midland Avenue

N. Broadway Ave.

Upper Nyack Trail

Hudson
River

Far-reaching views extend north to south from the high, vertical cliffs of the Long Path.

The Hook is a loop hike, beginning and ending at Nyack Beach State Park, a 76-acre parcel managed by the Palisades Interstate Park Commission. This is a part of the Hudson River Greenway Trail, a linear park development project that connects the scenic areas along the western shore of the Hudson River. Hook Mountain and Nyack Beach State Park have been designated a National Natural Landmark by the National Park Service because together they posses exceptional value as an illustration of the nation's natural heritage.

From the entry kiosk, drive downhill to the parking lot, which has become a destination in itself for its scenic appeal. Walk to the north with the river on your right and follow the dirt path along the river's edge. This is a multi-use trail. The path continues along the river for more than a mile, to a point where it rises gently, passing small stone ruins on the left. Just ahead, you'll arrive at a fork. This is the 1.5-mile point. Bear left here.

Proceed along this paved section of road toward Rockland Lake. The forest is dense, consisting of sycamore, maple, locust, and mulberry. Passing a park administrative building on your right, continue uphill. At a point where the road levels out, walk through a barrier of large concrete blocks and look to your left for the Long Path trailhead (aqua blazes), which will take you in a southerly direction over the Hook. There is an interpretive sign at the trailhead describing the ice industry that began here in 1930. Ice was shipped from spring-fed Rockland Lake to New York City via a long conveyor belt to barges at Slaughter's Landing, a settlement that dates from 1711. The best restaurants and hotels preferred the ice because of its purity and clarity.

You will not be walking as far as Rockland Lake, nor will you see much of it except for a brief glimpse from this point or during leaf-out (looking west). From the trailhead, the foot trail now avoids a direct and steep ascent up the north side of the Hook and instead swings around into the west, where you'll see a herd trail. Avoid this trail and bear to the right (west), passing a foundation on your right, and climb along a switchback before turning east again to rise steadily to the ridge top. In 15 minutes or so from the trailhead, you will reach the first open, grassy, and exposed cliffs on the mountain, where views are sweeping and the drop is high and vertical. Use caution here!

Sumac and cherry trees dot the cliff's edge. You look straight across the river at the ominous visage of Sing Sing maximum security state prison, and up to the town of Cortlandt. You can see south as far as the Tappan Zee Bridge, and north into the Hudson Highlands. Directly west is Croton Point. Beneath and all along the eastern face of the escarpment, this area of the Palisades was subject to heavy quarrying, which, as you will observe, has claimed a good part of the mountain nearly to ridge elevation.

Quarrying began as early as 1811 for the highly valued volcanic traprock that surfaces through an upper layer of Triassic sandstone in this location. The rock was used in road building as well as for concrete, most of which went to Manhattan. This industry helped to wipe out the bluestone quarrying industry in the Catskills, which ended very suddenly with the invention of Portland cement. In the late 1800s, dynamite and steam-driven equipment were used here. The rapid deterioration of the landscape attracted public outcry, resulting in the formation of advocacy groups, including the Palisades Interstate Park Commission. By 1915, preservation of lands including the Palisades and the Hook Mountain area was accomplished using public funds and private funds donated by the Perkins family (George Perkins was the head of the Park Commission), the Rockefellers, and the Harrimans.

The Long Path continues along the edge of the cliffs before entering the hardwoods. You'll see old stone walls made of large talus blocks defining abandoned roads through here. You may see deer foraging in the dense underbrush. The terrain is rolling but never very steep at this point. Marking is sparse but adequate (the low-impact presence was the intention of the Long Path's originators, who didn't want a defined, physical trail, only a system of waypoints between which hikers would navigate using map and compass), but the trail is self-guiding and fairly smooth underfoot.

You will never stray far from the river, and although you will not always see it, you will sense the abyssal cliffs to the east. You will soon drop behind a low ridge and descend for a while before rising to your original elevation again. Soon you will reach a point above the parking area where you will look directly down at the beautiful Marydell Faith & Life Center, run by the Sisters of Our Lady of Christian Doctrine. This is the most spectacular cliff on the hike. Don't try to shortcut this hike by descending the cliffs on any herd trails you might see—the only safe way down the mountain is the Long Path.

Continue, and avoid the yellow trail that leaves to the right for Rockland Lake. The trail becomes rocky now. A long, viewless ascent up to the summit of Hook Mountain follows and soon you will hear the traffic on NY 9W. Following an old road lined with boulders (an abandoned attempt to create a road to the Hook's summit), look left for the white-blazed Upper Nyack Trail, which winds through a residential area, passing beneath a lovely young stand of vigorous tulip poplars.

The Upper Nyack Trail ends on Midland Avenue, 500 feet south of the Marydell Center. Turn left toward the center, passing another residential street on your left, then bear right on Larchdale Avenue and go down the hill. Up to your left are the high cliffs of Hook Mountain. Bear left onto North Broadway Avenue and join the park access road, descending toward the parking area. Look to the right just before the small stone office building for a stone staircase that shortcuts the road, taking you through a quiet woods with a few picnic tables along the river.

MORE INFORMATION

Nyack Beach State Park is open year-round for day use. A parking fee ($6) is charged on weekends, April through September. A rest room and telephone are located at the large, unused park building in the parking area; www.nysparks. state.ny.us/parks/156/details.aspx; 845-268-3020.

NEARBY

There are many interesting antique shops and eateries on Main Street and Broadway in Nyack. A number of attractions and activities are located in Tarrytown and Sleepy Hollow, across the river via the Tappan Zee Bridge.

2

THE
SHAWANGUNKS

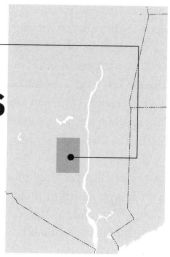

THE ENCHANTING SHAWANGUNK RIDGE (a.k.a. Shongums or Gunks or the Ridge) is the scenic and recreational mecca of the mid-Hudson Valley. It is among the region's most ecologically important landmasses. An extension of the south-lying Kittatinny Ridge of the Appalachian Mountains, the Gunks stretch from the town of Rosendale in the north to Cragsmoor in the south, rising between the Wallkill and Rondout valleys. It is a place of high, wind-swept plateaus and cliffs (average elevation 2,000 feet), remarkably clear "sky" lakes, sheer ledges (the highest vertical drops east of the Mississippi), pellucid streams, robust waterfalls, and diverse natural habitats. The Ridge has been identified as one of Earth's "Last Great Places" by The Nature Conservancy, as well as one of the 40 most important natural resources lying within the North American continent and the Pacific Rim Basin.

The Shawangunk Mountains look a good deal different from the surrounding, younger ranges, such as the Catskills. This is because of the Ridge's prominent, white-quartz conglomerate bedrock and its 450-million-year-old sands and quartz gravels that were deposited at the base of a shallow sea during the Taconic orogeny. Much later, the mountains were eroded, faulted, fractured, and smoothed by a million years of glacial action. The glaciers dragged off the tops of ridges, breaking them into talus blocks and leaving behind vertical cliffs such as Sky Top, the Trapps, and Millbrook Mountain. The resulting bare rock can be seen from great distances. Folding lifted the sandstone into broad, west-tilting slabs, and retreating ice nearly a mile thick scraped and polished the uplands into bright, open promontories such as Gertrude's Nose and Castle Point that are studded with pitch pine and thick with blueberry heaths. This impervious, nutrient-poor rock held water, resulting in the creation of the five sky lakes that are strung across the top of the Ridge. These are among the clearest lakes imaginable (in particular, Lakes Minnewaska and Awosting; see Trip 11), because aquatic plants cannot grow in their thin, acidic, nutrient-poor soils.

Underlying the conglomerate, the softer, older layer of Martinsburg shale is a few thousand feet thick. Hikers will see the shale layer spilling out here and there around the Ridge, where it was mined for building material, as well as crushed and sprinkled on the extensive carriage roads of Mohonk and Minnewaska.

As the glaciers retreated, plants took hold in protected crevices and on the bare rocks, beginning a succession that would lead to today's varied vegetation profile. Hikers will often see oak woods with the mountain laurel understory that is so common in the higher woodlands, along with pockets of hemlock and, less frequently, white pine and red spruce. The northern hardwood group (beech, birch, maple, and associated species) appeared about 8,000 years ago, followed by southern trees (the Carolinian forest types), including oak, chestnut, and hickory. Comprising a good deal of the often dense understory are flowering dogwood, shadbush, striped maple, viburnum, witch hazel, lowbush blueberry, huckleberry, and raspberry.

The southern area of the Ridge is dominated by the widely distributed pitch pine (the Badlands, or Pine Plains), for which the Shawangunks are famous. Although extensive pitch-pine barrens can be found in places such as Long Island and New Jersey, those forests grow on sand—not rock. The naturalist Erik Kiviat points out that the Shawangunks contain "the only extensive high-altitude pitch-pine barrens, and the only bedrock dwarf-pine plains in the world." Hikers will see these forests in patches all around the Gunks, but most intimately in the otherworldly Badlands.

In addition to its alteration by physical forces and soil type, the distribution of the Gunks' vegetation groups was altered significantly by human intervention. Although the Ridge area was not fertile enough to attract anything more than seasonal use by indigenous, valley-dwelling peoples, it is possible that they manipulated the land with fire, opening it up for deer browse and nut trees or berry growth. Resource-extractive industries followed when, by the early 1700s, settlers were using the forests for lumber, charcoal production, tanbarking, barrel hoop and furniture making, and for the production of the very desirable Shawangunk millstones. Particularly in the southern Shawangunks, the Ridge was perennially burned to enhance growth (by removing the competing vegetation) when the commercial berry-picking industry thrived here until the 1930s. Pickers' shacks can still be seen along the trails of the southern Ridge. Ongoing efforts to protect the Ridge from commercial and residential development have been difficult, and several potentially ruinous projects have been defeated, sustaining a broadening plan of protection and acquisition of buffer lands to protect this precious resource.

At this time there are four independent, cooperating management partnerships stewarding the Ridge.

THE MOHONK PRESERVE

The largest member-and-visitor-supported nature preserve in New York State, Mohonk Preserve protects 6,400 acres of the northern Shawangunk Ridge. Established in 1963, its mission to protect and preserve the Ridge includes fostering an "understanding of the relationship between people and nature." The preserve is committed to providing open space for "contemplation and recreation in keeping with the peace and natural beauty of the land."

The Smiley family (who, in 1869, began building what would become today's Mohonk Mountain House resort hotel) initiated the tradition of land stewardship in the Shawangunks. Their holdings grew to 7,500 acres over the next century. The Smileys created the Mohonk Preserve (previously called the Mohonk Trust) to provide a management presence for the public use of preserve lands lying beyond the Mountain House boundaries.

The preserve's recreational resources include 100 miles of multi-use carriage roads and trails for hiking, jogging, mountain biking, cross-country skiing, snowshoeing, and horseback riding. There are an estimated 1,000 rock-climbing routes on the preserve's lands. All of these resources are heavily used; the greatest challenge the preserve faces—next to the preservation of the Ridge itself—is the management of human impact. Those with annual memberships constitute most of the user group.

Take the time to stop at the Mohonk Preserve Trapps Gateway Visitor Center on your trip to the Gunks; you'll go past it on your way to the Trapps trailheads. Here you will find interpretive displays, a gift shop with books and maps of local interest, a kids' corner and butterfly garden, and a self-guiding nature trail. You can purchase day passes and memberships.

Access Fees. You may want to purchase an annual membership (purchasing a membership first will ultimately save you money). While some will consider the day-use fees high ($10 for hikers and bikers), these can be substantially reduced through the purchase of a membership (a basic individual membership costs $55, and additional adults in the same household can be added for $20 each; youths age 13 to 18 can be added for $5 each; children under 12 are free). There are additional fees for mountain biking and rock climbing. As a member, you can enjoy additional privileges and access preserve lands from sunrise to sunset, 365 days a year.

Parking. On peak weekends, the preserve parking areas fill up extremely fast—and early. Try to arrive before 10 A.M. to be assured a spot. Parking is limited to 30 minutes at the Scenic Overlook and Hairpin Turn above the visitor center on US 44/NY 55, and tickets are issued for violations. Although the preserve's Wawarsing and West Trapps parking lots fill quickly on weekends, weekdays are seldom a problem.

Camping and Pets. You must leash and clean up after your pets. Camping and fires are not permitted. There is a very small campsite east of Trapps Bridge for use by rock climbers only. The nearest legal camping area can be found at the unsupervised Shawangunk Multiple Use Area, 0.8 mile east of the intersection of US 44/NY 55 on NY 299. Leave nothing unattended there.

Directions and Information. Mohonk Preserve Trapps Gateway Visitor Center is on US 44/NY 55, 0.5 mile west of its intersection with NY 299 in Gardiner, New York, 6.0 miles west of New Paltz. Contact the Mohonk Preserve at P.O. Box 715, New Paltz, NY, 12561; call 845-255-0919; or visit www.mohonkpreserve.org/visit/.

MOHONK MOUNTAIN HOUSE

Named a National Historic Landmark in 1986, this private, nineteenth-century, Victorian-style castle and the beautiful lands, trails, and carriageways surrounding Lake Mohonk are a separate entity from the Mohonk Preserve. The resort began in 1869 with the Smiley brothers' purchase of 280 acres of the Ridge, on which they built a ten-room boarding house. Subsequent purchases and improvements resulted in today's hotel of 250 rooms, 138 with working fireplaces, and 238 balconies providing world-class lake and mountain scenery. Nightly double-occupancy room fees vary from $510 to $2,500 (for the Mountain View Tower suite), and include three meals and tea. Single occupancy starts at $320 for a standard room.

Day access is accordingly pricey. While a membership with the Mohonk Preserve will allow you access to the Mountain House property and trails, additional fees and restrictions apply. Parking at the Gatehouse is included. Hikers are asked not to enter the hotel, and hotel facilities are reserved for guests only. Hikers purchasing day-use passes at the hotel Gatehouse rather than at the Preserve Visitor Center will be charged $25 per person on weekends, and $20 on weekdays. Preserve members are charged only $5, however. A shuttle-bus ride from the Gatehouse to the hotel trailheads is included. No pets are allowed on the property, even if left in a vehicle. To see the hotel, ask for a 1-hour pass at the Gatehouse, which will allow you to drive to the main entrance.

Directions and Information. From Exit 18 of the NYS Thruway (I-87), drive west through the village of New Paltz on NY 299. As you cross the bridge over the Wallkill River, take the first right onto Springtown Road and set to zero. At 0.5 mile, turn left onto Mountain Rest Road (CR 6), where you'll see signs for Mohonk. At 1.7 miles, go through the intersection of Butterville-Canaan Road. Continue up Mountain Rest Road, and at 4.0 miles you'll pass the Mohonk Mountain House main gate on the left. Contact the Mohonk Mountain House at Mountain Rest Road, New Paltz, NY, 12561; call 845-255-1000 or 800-772-6646; or visit www.mohonk.com.

MINNEWASKA STATE PARK PRESERVE

Encompassing nearly 12,000 acres of forested land on the Shawangunk Ridge, Minnewaska is just as beautiful as Mohonk—but more remote. Originally owned and developed as a rustic resort area by the Smiley brothers, this day-use park is connected to the Mohonk Preserve by the same extensive trails and carriage roads that were built more than a century ago. It contains three lakes—Minnewaska, Awosting, and the remote Mud Pond—as well as the high ledges, cliff-top promontories, and dwarf pitch-pine barrens that have made the Ridge one of the world's most distinctive natural resources.

Recreational use in the park includes cycling, hiking, biking, snowshoeing, cross-country skiing, riding horses and horse carriages, swimming (accessible to people with disabilities), and scuba diving under permit in Lake Minnewaska. Cartop boats are permitted in Lake Minnewaska by permit. Rock climbing is permitted at the Peterskill Area, 1 mile east of the park's main gate on US 44/NY 55. Leashed pets are allowed.

Note: The terms "carriageway," "carriage road," and "road" are used interchangeably on maps, in publications, and in speech in both the Mohonk Preserve and Minnewaska State Park.

Directions. From Exit 18 of the NYS Thruway (I-87), head west through the village of New Paltz on NY 299 for 7.5 miles. Turn right onto US 44/NY 55 and drive past the Trapps Gateway Visitor Center. Continue up the hill and under Trapps Bridge, and go another 3.0 miles to the Minnewaska State Park entrance on your left (a total of 11.4 miles from I-87).

TRIP 8
BONTICOU CRAG

Location: New Paltz, NY
Rating: Moderate
Distance: 3.0 miles
Elevation Gain: 500 feet
Estimated Time: 2.5 hrs
Map: USGS Mohonk Lake; NY–NJTC Shawangunk Trails, Lake Mohonk Area; Mohonk Preserve Trail Map, Northern Section

This carriage road walk is followed by a short introduction to rock scrambling on the Shawangunks' white-quartz conglomerate talus fields, before arriving at a bare summit with vertical cliffs and excellent views.

DIRECTIONS

The most convenient access to the Crag Trail is from Upper 27 Knolls Road, just west of the Mohonk Mountain House main entrance on Mountain Rest Road in New Paltz. From Exit 18 of the NYS Thruway (I-87), drive west through the village of New Paltz on NY 299. As you cross the bridge over the Wallkill River, take the first right onto Springtown Road and set to zero. At 0.5 mile, turn left onto Mountain Rest Road (CR 6), where you'll see signs for Mohonk. At 1.7 miles, go through the intersection of Butterville-Canaan Road. Continue up Mountain Rest Road, and at 4.0 miles you'll pass the Mohonk Mountain House main gate on the left. (Ask for a map here.) At 5.0 miles, turn right onto Upper 27 Knolls Road, and in another 0.3 mile, park in the Spring Farm trailhead parking area. *GPS coordinates:* 41° 47.729′ N, 74° 7.658′ W.

TRAIL DESCRIPTION

This short but rigorous hike includes a stroll through the northernmost Shawangunk forests and on the foot trails and carriage paths of the Virginia Smiley Preserve, plus an invigorating, short rock scramble through the savage, broken talus of the Gunks' conglomerate cliffs. What you get in exchange for a relatively short half-day hike are sweeping views of the Catskills and the southeastern Hudson Valley lowlands, as well as a "hands-on" feel for a remarkable cliff-and-talus environment of dark green pitch pine and white, tilted slabs.

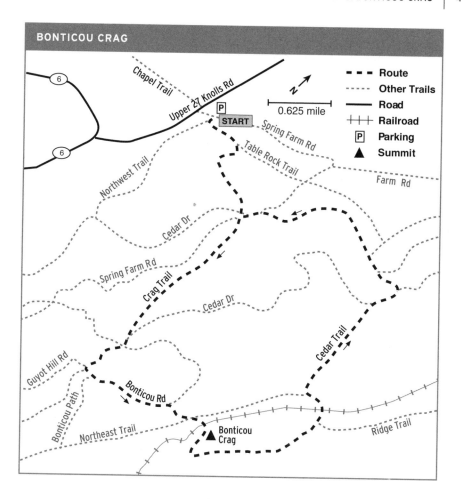

Locate the red-marked Crag Trail across the road from the parking lot kiosk and follow it through open fields past cedar hedgerows. Immediately, you will be treated to views of the Catskills over the Esopus and Rondout valleys, and these views improve dramatically as you ascend the Crag. Cross Cedar Drive and Spring Farm Road, climbing through open hardwoods into the east. At the four-way intersection of Cedar Drive and Bonticou Road, go straight ahead on Cedar Drive. This will bring you to circuitous Bonticou Road again, where you will turn nearly 180 degrees to the northeast. Stay alert here so that you leave the red-marked Bonticou Path to your right (it descends to the Northeast Trail, out of your way), remaining on Bonticou Road. This level carriageway will soon treat you to open views of Bonticou Crag, looming from the north on the easy section of the Bonticou Ascent Path.) There's a flat rock to the right of the ascent where you can adjust your pack, tighten your bootlaces, and prepare for the climb. If you wear a watch, you may wish to remove it to protect it from scrapes—you're going to be using all fours now as you make your way through the tumult of broken, radically angled slabs that have fallen away from the cliff. As a general rule in scrambling high-angle rock faces, keep your body low and close to the rock. Search for good foot-, hand-, fist-, and fingerholds as you head upward, moving slowly and deliberately. The going is generally easy if you're reasonably agile and fit. Follow the yellow paint blazes. There's one challenging point in particular at the upper end of the climb where you'll ascend through a narrow crack. Some members of your party may need assistance. Be careful and stick together.

Feel that cold air coming from the deep crevices of the talus? These moist fissures, some of them appearing endless, may well be one of the last known habitats of the endangered eastern wood rat, which, although once common here, has not been seen on the Mohonk Preserve since 1967. Erik Kiviat, author of *The Northern Shawangunks* and a founding ecologist of Hudsonia Limited, observes that the wood rat, which resembles an "oversized Norway rat (house rat)...with larger ears and longer whiskers," has been found in the Ice Caves Mountain area of the southern Shawangunks, a locale that may be the "most northeastern station in the eastern wood rat's range." Do not be alarmed in the fortunate event that you see a wood rat—they are not aggressive. One thing you will notice is how little soil there is in these crevices, and how little vegetation is able to grow among the blocks of talus, which shift over time. Here and there are trees that are perhaps 20 years old. As you ascend, more appear, along with mountain laurel and, at last, pitch pine, the most dominant and obvious member of this cliff-and-talus plant community.

Very soon after cresting this narrow ridge, bear right (south) following the yellow paint blazes. The scarp opens up and you'll walk across the tilted summit rocks. These open slabs provide you with several choices for relaxing and observing the magnificent views to the west and southeast. You'll also be treated to the antics of curious turkey vultures. Note the two-toned wings, with the flight feathers being lighter in color. This scavenger, nearly the size of an eagle and with up to a 6-foot wingspan, get its name from the bare red heads of the mature birds. They are gregarious, commonly soaring in groups of a dozen or more in search of carrion. As you watch, beware of the extremely high vertical drops of the cliffs.

Follow the spine of the Crag north and recover the yellow paint blazes; go past your ascent point and continue north and downhill. Join the obscure blue-marked Northeast Trail (joined here by the Ridge Trail), where the yellow

The white conglomerate cliffs of Bonticou Crag are seen from the southeast, off Mountain Rest Road.

paint blazes of the Ascent Path end. After 15 minutes, you're down to forest level again. Pass beneath one last ledge and bear right onto the Cedar Trail (red blazes), following through reclaimed fields—now ash groves—and join Cedar Drive in a mature oak forest. Follow the carriageway along an even, northerly contour, passing Spring Farm Road, and then you're back at the point at which the Crag Trail is recognized. Go right to the Spring Farm parking area and your point of origin.

MORE INFORMATION

A self-pay fee collector ("iron ranger") is located in the parking lot for times when the booth is not staffed (during winter and on spring and fall weekdays).

There's a kiosk with map and trail information adjacent to the attendant booth; www.mohonk.com; 845-255-1000.

NEARBY

The village of New Paltz has a variety of interesting shops and restaurants; for details visit the New Paltz Regional Chamber of Commerce site at www.new-paltzchamber.org or call 845-255-0243. The town is also the home of the State University of New York at New Paltz; www.newpaltz.edu.

EASTERN WOOD RAT

The friendly and curious bushy-tailed eastern wood rat was last seen on Storm King Mountain in 1980. Because wood rats proliferate in the kind of rocky slopes found in the Shawangunks, an attempt was made to reintroduce them into the ideal cliff talus habitat of Bonticou Crag in 1991. The rats, introduced from Virginia and equipped with radio transmitters, all perished because of the raccoon nematode, an insidious roundworm parasite that can survive for more than 10 years in dens and remain virulent. Biologists were puzzled by this outcome, since raccoons and wood rats have been sharing the same habitat for thousands of years. At this time the only active population of the eastern wood rat in New York State is in the Palisades—and it has been extirpated from the northern part of even this range.

The disappearance of the wood rat here is an indicator more of unknown negative changes in the local environment than of the potential endangerment of the species. Healthy, reproducing populations of the wood rat survive throughout the south.

TRIP 9
CASTLE POINT, LAKE AWOSTING, AND MARGARET CLIFF

Location: New Paltz, NY
Rating: Moderate
Distance: 10 miles
Elevation Gain: 500 feet
Estimated Time: 6.5 hours
Maps: USGS Gardiner; USGS Naponoch; NY–NJTC Southern Shawangunk Trails; Minnewaska State Park Preserve Hiking Map

An easy though long hike passes two sky lakes along the old Shawangunk carriage roads, with swimming in Lake Awosting and far-reaching valley views from Castle Point.

DIRECTIONS

From Exit 18 of the NYS Thruway (I-87), head west through the village of New Paltz on NY 299 for 7.5 miles. Turn right onto US 44/NY 55 and drive past the Mohonk Trapps Gateway Visitor Center. Continue up the hill and under Trapps Bridge, and go another 3.0 miles to the Minnewaska State Park entrance on your left (a total of 11.4 miles from I-87). From the Gatehouse, drive 0.7 mile to the upper lots. *GPS coordinates:* 41° 43.723′ N, 74° 14.223′ W.

TRAIL DESCRIPTION

Many hikers walk the easy, scenic carriage roads of Minnewaska to Castle and Hamilton points, taking a brief side trip to swim in Lake Awosting's sapphire waters. But few venture beyond Awosting, the point where this hike turns north to approach Castle Point across the lonely rim rocks of Murray Hill, Spruce Glen, and Margaret Cliff.

Plan for a long outing and bring your bathing suit. Try to reach Minnewaska State Park before 9:30 A.M. on nice weekends or you may have to park in the Lower Awosting lot, requiring an additional 1.5 miles of hiking and 400 feet of elevation gain to this already long hike.

There are two levels to the upper (Wildmere) parking area. The trail begins at the southwest corner of the higher lot, at the north end of Lake Minnewaska. A map and an interpretive kiosk are posted on the picnic area lawn

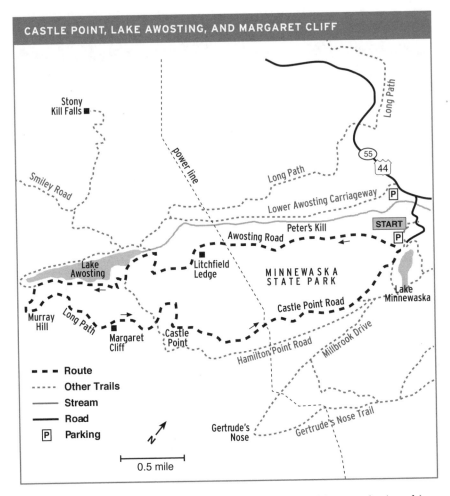

CASTLE POINT, LAKE AWOSTING, AND MARGARET CLIFF

Route
Other Trails
Stream
Road
P Parking

0.5 mile

nearby. Walk toward the lake (the view is terrific) and bear right (south) to find the trailhead.

With Lake Minnewaska to your left, bear left at the first fork (don't take the Sunset Trail), and walk down to the Lake Minnewaska swimming area, where you'll find a map and a battalion of chemical toilets. Bear right onto the green-marked Upper Awosting Road (a.k.a. carriage road). You will be sharing the path with bikers and equestrians. The surface is hard-packed shale with no rocks—those will come later.

Views of the Catskills will appear intermittently to the right (west) as you travel south on the carriage road. Within a half-hour you'll pass a stone stream-bed to the left. Pass under the power line, where you'll get a look at some white conglomerate bedrock. A few ledges offer views of Peter's Kill Valley to the right as Litchfield Ledge begins to build up on your left. Leaving the long ledge behind, climb easily to the intersection where the Lake Awosting Road goes right; you'll bear left here, staying on the green Upper Awosting Road.

Soon, the seemingly long walk (more than 3.0 miles) will begin to pay off as you climb the ramparts of Lake Awosting's north shore. These provide long views of the Catskills to the northwest and south, over the lake. Short spur trails lead to expansive panoramas and vertical pitch-pine ledges as you level out on the carriage road.

At the intersection of Hamilton Point Road and Upper Awosting Road, turn right onto the black-marked Lake Awosting Road. You'll pass through a thick hemlock glen before arriving at Awosting's stone beach, where swimming is allowed only when lifeguards are on duty. There's a comfort station here. Continue along the lake's edge, passing two small peninsulas where people frequently sunbathe.

As you approach the south end of the lake, ledges appear across it to your right. Be alert for a left, unmarked turn here. As this trail departs to the south, two rocks lie across the trail next to a No Bikes sign. Very old blazes are detectable on the trees. Follow this trail and bear left as the blue-blazed Long Path enters from the right. This will bring you uphill easily to the deeply fractured southerly summit of Murray Hill, a ledge outcropping facing southwest with sprawling views of the Badlands that take in High Point and the lands of the Sam's Point Preserve, with the Kittatinnys lying beyond to the south. Peekamoose, in the Catskills, lies due north. As you cross Murray Hill, stay on the Long Path; some spurs lead to dangerous drops that are concealed by low vegetation.

As you work your way north toward Margaret Cliff, views to the northwest and southeast are dramatic, with the Catskills rising beyond the glacially ravaged, pitch-pine tablelands. Battlement Terrace, Castle Point, and Lake Awosting appear ahead. The landscape looks raw and weather-beaten; cairns appear to help you stay on course, and blazes show up more frequently on rocks. Margaret Cliff lies ahead, identifiable by its two deep cracks. Stay with the blue-marked trail as you pass a few established-looking spurs that head east to create a herd connector along the extensive Margaret Cliff. At a third T, bear right. Blue markers are not obvious at this junction until you follow the trail for a moment. This is one of the few areas in the park where red spruce appears in numbers—you can distinguish it from surrounding hemlock and white pine by its pointed, spearlike spires.

Nearly 3 hours into the hike, the trail follows onto an old carriage road. The change in tree type to hemlock is dramatic; at this point, watch very carefully for the Long Path as it climbs left onto a narrow, slightly eroded laurel path.

The viewshed extends in every direction from the precipice of Castle Point, along the designated bike route.

As the trail levels, you will pass a small rock balanced upon a cannonball-sized stone adjacent to a high and dangerous fissure. Shortly after, the trail heads downhill steeply but then soon levels, crossing a talus field among oaks and a moist glen with a few very large hemlocks at the site of a grassy, dead-end carriage road. Climb now, tunneling through the rocks at one point before ascending to meet the intersection of Hamilton Point Road and Castle Point Road. Follow the blue-marked Castle Point Road uphill. Walk under the large overhanging ledges of Battlement Terrace, then wind around to cross the top of it, climbing into the east and enjoying far-flung views from east to west across the Badlands. Soon you will reach Castle Point, a high, white conglomerate ledge forming the eastern-most cliff of the Terrace. The views are the culmination of most everything you've seen so far, only better; to the southeast, you'll see the fertile, agricultural lands of the Wallkill River floodplain with the Hudson Highlands beyond.

Castle Point Road treats you to fine views to the north and east as you continue descending north along the ledges. Perhaps nowhere else is the view of Gertrude's Nose so complete and vivid. The little dimples to the north of it are the backsides of the otherwise dramatic Millbrook Mountain. You can see the white, obelisklike Patterson's Pellet balanced on the ledge next to Millbrook Drive across the Palmaghatt Ravine. In another 45 minutes or so, you will arrive at a T, where Hamilton Point Road goes right. Go left, staying with the Castle Point Road. Lake Minnewaska's high northern ledges appear to the right as you descend, and shortly you'll arrive back at the swimming area for the short climb back to the parking lot.

DID YOU KNOW?

The Badlands, or Pine Plains, in the area west of Castle Point are among the largest dwarf pitch-pine barrens on Earth. The nearest large barrens are in the Hamptons area of Long Island.

MORE INFORMATION

Parking requires a per-car entry fee of $6. For more information, visit www.lakeminnewaska.org.

NEARBY

The gravel-surfaced Wallkill Valley Rail Trail extends for 12 miles from Gardiner to New Paltz. It is dedicated to passive recreational use and passes through woods, fields, and agricultural lands; www.gorailtrail.org.

TRIP 10
MILLBROOK MOUNTAIN AND
GERTRUDE'S NOSE

Location: New Paltz, NY
Rating: Strenuous
Distance: 9.5 miles
Elevation Gain: 850 feet
Estimated Time: 5.5 hours
Maps: USGS Gardiner; USGS Naponoch; NY–NJTC Southern
Shawangunks; Minnewaska State Park Preserve

**A long and fascinating hike passes through glacial cobble fields and
pitch-pine balds next to the sheer cliffs of Millbrook Mountain.**

DIRECTIONS
From Exit 18 off the NYS Thruway (I-87), head west through the village of
New Paltz on NY 299 for 7.5 miles. Turn right onto US 44/NY 55 and drive
0.8 mile up the hill to the Trapps Gateway Visitor Center. Just beyond the entrance, turn right into the Wawarsing parking area. *GPS coordinates:* 41° 44.
224′ N, 74° 11.074′ W.

TRAIL DESCRIPTION
The hike across Millbrook Mountain to the white conglomerate cliffs of Gertrude's Nose is among the longest outings in the Gunks—and easily the most
memorable. These landmarks are frequented less than the popular destinations nearer to the Trapps or Lake Minnewaska. Bring plenty of food and
water, a good map, and boots with enough support to protect your feet from
the rocky trails.

Park at either the Mohonk Preserve's Gateway Center Wawarsing area or
the West Trapps parking area and make your way up to Trapps Bridge. (See
Trip 12 for details.) Turn west, crossing the bridge onto Trapps Road (carriage
road). Watch carefully to the left while still in sight of the bridge, and bear left
(southwest) onto the blue-blazed Millbrook Ridge Trail. As you climb, you'll
see views to the west across Coxing Kill Valley, including the ledges of High
Peter's Kill as well as Dickie Barre and Ronde Barre in Minnewaska State Park.

Signage and blazes are faint at the trailhead. The trail begins by climbing
the low-angle pitch-pine slabs of the Near Trapps and continues southwest

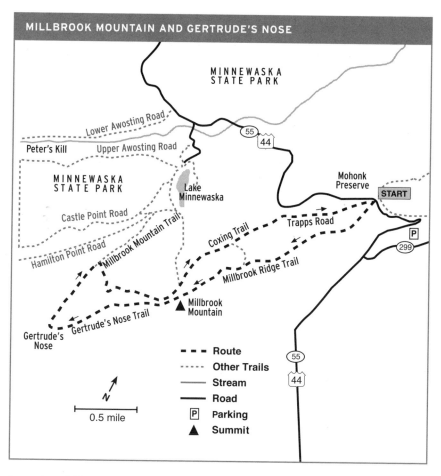

MILLBROOK MOUNTAIN AND GERTRUDE'S NOSE

MINNEWASKA
STATE PARK

Lower Awosting Road

Peter's Kill   Upper Awosting Road   55   44

MINNEWASKA
STATE PARK   Lake   Mohonk
                               Minnewaska   Preserve

Castle Point Road   START

                                    Trapps Road
Hamilton Point Road   Millbrook Mountain Trail   Coxing Trail   P

                                                                   299
                        Millbrook Ridge Trail

                            ▲ Millbrook
Gertrude's Nose Trail   Mountain

Gertrude's
Nose   55

          Route   - - -   44
          Other Trails   · · · ·
          Stream   ————
     N   Road   ━━━━
          Parking   P
0.5 mile Summit   ▲

long the cliffs. Interesting views develop back across the Trapps as the trail winds in and out of the woods over a variety of surfaces—from rocks and soil to pine needles—sometimes coming close to high vertical ledges.

This area of the Ridge is part of the Appalachian hawk migration route. In certain conditions, updrafts and tailwinds allow hawks to soar long distances with little energy expenditure. During fall, the preserve conducts its annual hawk watch along these slabs and cliffs, where you can see hawks, harriers, and vultures moving through the flyway. You will almost always see vultures and hawks here, and sometimes a bald or golden eagle.

You will pass the Bayard Path (red blazes) when you are 25 minutes into the hike. Continue through rolling oak and laurel woods into the southwest. Here and there you'll have a glimpse of Millbrook Mountain ahead of you.

An hour or less into the hike, turn left on blue blazes as the red-blazed Millbrook Cross Path departs to the right. (It's easy to absentmindedly bear right here.) Continue left on the Millbrook Ridge Trail, rising into an open area before descending to a little hemlock glen, where the trail crosses an unnamed, mossy creek that dries in the summer months. From this point, you will ascend consistently along the northern spine of Millbrook's steep ridge. Dramatic views of the Trapps and Sky Top appear as you progress, and the trail walks the lip of a spine-tingling, 350-foot-high vertical cliff to your left (east). Walking below the west-tilted knife edge of the ridge, you will see the red-blazed Millbrook Mountain Trail appearing on the right (west). This will be your return route to the Trapps, so fix this spot in your memory.

Where the blue trail ends, the vegetation changes from oaks over bedrock and blueberry to the white conglomerate, piney summit of Millbrook—not exactly a "summit" in appearance or feel, but the highest point along the ridge. Millbrook Mountain was fractured more or less in two by the Wisconsin ice sheet, so what you're standing on is roughly half of its preglacial shape. (The other half of the mountain can be seen lying in chunks below the cliffs.) Here are extensive views of the ridges to the west, the flatlands to the south and east, the Hudson Highlands and Fishkill Ridge beyond them, and the Catskills to the northwest. You can see both Hamilton and Castle points to the west and the lands of the Mohonk Preserve to the north.

Millbrook Mountain marks the boundary between the Mohonk Preserve and Minnewaska State Park. Adjacent and downhill from the summit of Millbrook Mountain, Millbrook Drive (carriage road) ends in a hairpin turn. Here, the red-blazed Gertrude's Nose Trail begins and the Millbrook Ridge Trail ends. Follow the red blazes, continuing along the ridge to the southwest. For a while, the Gertrude's Nose Trail parallels Millbrook Drive. You will have glimpses of Gertrude's Nose ahead, a diminished version of Millbrook without the rocks. The trail traverses variable terrain, crossing a beautiful, flat-rock pitch-pine barren before descending steeply past a deep hole near a hemlock ledge to the left, and then you'll walk beneath a power line at 1,500 feet. Now you ascend again, following a level contour along the cliffs. The forest type will change several times, from hardwood to hemlock to pitch pine over blueberry heaths. Then, with little warning, you're on Gertrude's Nose, about 3 hours into the hike. The trail curves to the northeast to cross the wind-punished conglomerate flats.

The southwest-facing promontory of the Nose, though lower in elevation, is similar in many respects to Hamilton and Castle points. Each is a high, level plateau of faulted and fractured conglomerate cap rock, the white stone that is the signature geology of the Shawangunks. Long fractures reach from the cliffs' edges back to the woods; some are dangerously deep and can be obscured by

The flat, white sandstone slabs of Gertrude's Nose make for a great resting spot.

a significant snowfall. Signs are posted on the cliffs reminding hikers to move cautiously across the rocks and be mindful not to trample the fragile vegetation off-trail. Below the cliffs are large talus blocks and rubble that have fallen away from the cliff face, forming crevices that are old enough and deep enough to support a significant plant and animal habitat. The rock margins are covered in thick mats of blueberries. As you move west, you'll walk in and out of the woods along the upper northerly edge of wild Palmaghatt Ravine and the Kline Kill (pronounced *kline-ah-kill*). The trail continues next to the cliffs, past scattered erratics (boulders, pebbles) and isolated patches of pitch pine, hemlock, and hardwoods before it rises through an enchanted hemlock forest and up to a high, rocky ledge you can see ahead of you.

Soon you will arrive at Millbrook Drive. Turn right and follow the carriageway back to Millbrook Mountain. You'll recognize the summit area soon. Turn left on the blue-blazed Millbrook Ridge Trail, backtracking on your earlier route a short distance to the red-blazed Millbrook Mountain Trail, where you bear left and descend. After another 10 minutes, make sure to turn right on the blue-blazed Coxing Trail, descending from open pitch-pine slabs with northerly views into dense woods. These westerly slopes of Millbrook Mountain— the boisterous Coxing Kill's watershed—are often wet. Puncheons have been placed in the wettest areas to protect the soft soils. You will pass the Millbrook Cross Path on your right, remaining on the blue Coxing Trail until you reach Trapps Road. Bear right onto Trapps Road and walk northeast, back to Trapps Bridge and your point of origin.

DID YOU KNOW?
Millbrook Mountain has one of the highest sheer cliff faces east of the Mississippi River.

MORE INFORMATION
Arrive prior to 9:30 A.M. on a nice weekend or you won't find a parking spot. If you can't get a spot in the Wawarsing parking area, continue on US 44/NY 55 to the West Trapps parking area (there is a $10 fee for day-hikers; members park free) just beyond Trapps Bridge on the right. For more information, visit www.mohonkpreserve.org.

NEARBY
Historic Huguenot Street is a National Historic Landmark District in the village of New Paltz. On six landscaped acres there are seven unique stone houses dating to the early 1700s, a burial ground, and a restored 1717 stone church; www.huguenotstreet.org; 845-255-1660.

TRIP 11
LAKE MINNEWASKA

Location: New Paltz, NY
Rating: Moderate
Distance: 1.5 miles
Elevation Gain: 230 feet
Estimated Time: 2.5 hours
Maps: USGS Gardiner; USGS Naponoch; NY–NJTC Southern
Shawangunk Trails; Minnewaska State Park Preserve Hiking Map

**This moderate hike provides a walk around a crystal-clear lake,
hemmed by white conglomerate sandstone cliffs, and far-reaching
vistas of the Catskills and the Hudson Valley.**

DIRECTIONS

To reach the Minnewaska State Park Preserve from Exit 18 off the NYS Thruway (I-87), head west through the village of New Paltz on NY 299 for 7.5 miles.
Turn right onto US 44/NY 55 and drive past the Mohonk Gateway Visitor
Center. Continue up the hill and under Trapps Bridge, and go another 3.0
miles to the Minnewaska State Park entrance on your left (a total of 11.4 miles
from I-87). *GPS coordinates (upper parking area): 41° 43.723′ N, 74° 14.223′ W.*

TRAIL DESCRIPTION

This fine, short hike is among the great scenic treks available in the Minnewaska State Park Preserve. The highlight is Lake Minnewaska itself, one of
the clear sky lakes (upper elevation) of the Shawangunk Ridge. In addition to
the lake's striking blue water and bright conglomerate sandstone cliffs, hikers will be treated to far-reaching views of the Catskills in the west and of the
Hudson Highlands to the southeast. The hike around Lake Minnewaska is
short and easy enough to leave time for other activities such as sightseeing, a
visit to the Mohonk Preserve's Trapps Gateway Visitor Center, a swim in the
lake, or perhaps a picnic in the scenic overlook area atop the lakeside cliffs
along the Lake Minnewaska carriage road, former site of the Cliff House.

The trail begins at the southwest corner of the upper parking lot, at the
north end of Lake Minnewaska. Walk toward the lake and bear right (south)
to find the trailhead. Follow the carriage road downhill, with the lake to your
left, (avoiding the Sunset Trail on your right), to lake level, where you will see

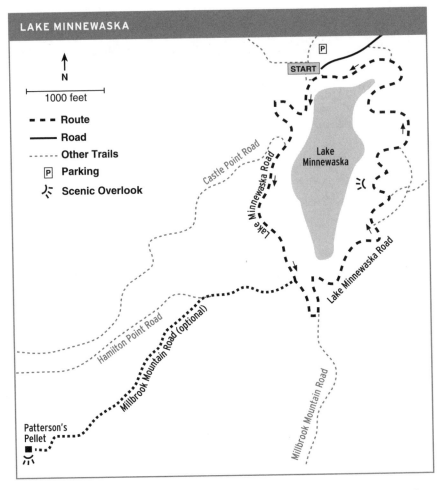

LAKE MINNEWASKA

N

1000 feet

- - - Route
—— Road
----- Other Trails
P Parking
⅄ Scenic Overlook

Castle Point Road

Lake Minnewaska Road

Lake Minnewaska

START

P

Hamilton Point Road

Millbrook Mountain Road (optional)

Patterson's Pellet

Millbrook Mountain Road

Lake Minnewaska Road

the red trail markers of Lake Minnewaska Road (carriageway). Bear left at the bathing beach. There are chemical toilets here. The carriage road ascends slightly, heading south. The vegetation is hemlock and oak woods, and in the spring, shadbush is in bloom. Continue climbing very easily past the junction where Castle Point Road goes off to the right. Avoid it and continue. Soon you will see the yellow-marked Millbrook Mountain Road on your right. If you have the time and wish to extend this hike, consider following the Millbrook Mountain Road for a visit to Patterson's Pellet, a white conglomerate glacial erratic that sits on the lip of the wild Palmaghatt Ravine. This easy side trip is a nearly flat, 1.4-mile round-trip.

The vantage from the Pellet will give you the lay of the land in the west, where the long, high ridges lead to Hamilton and Castle points and into the far reaches of the Shawangunk Badlands (Pine Plains). Patterson's Pellet is marked as such, though the boulder itself can't be mistaken; there are no others like it in the vicinity.

Along Lake Minnewaska Road, you will enjoy isolated views to the north toward Mohonk, including Sky Top (these views will improve ahead). As you hike around the south side of the lake, you'll come downhill and walk along the water's edge. You'll pass Millbrook Mountain Road on your right. A few isolated lookouts present themselves ahead, but the best views will be had as you climb to the picnic area. Continue uphill on the east side of the lake now, still following red diamonds, bearing left at a fork. Suddenly, you arrive at a broad, flat, open field with the vertical ledges of Lake Minnewaska on your left. The views are exceptional in every direction. The Catskills appear in the west, a long array of peaks stretching from the northerly Indian Head wilderness area through all of the high peaks in the south. Sky Top is immediately to the east over the Trapps. The Hudson Valley sprawls away to the southeast. In the near northwesterly realms of the state park preserve, you can see beyond Napanoch Point, Pulpit Rock, and Four Mile Camp on the Tombstone Trail.

You are standing on the former site of the Lake Minnewaska Cliff House, also known as the Minnewaska Mountain House. Built by Alfred H. Smiley (of Mohonk fame) in 1879, the Cliff House could accommodate 225 guests and enjoyed immense popularity during the years of its operation. In 1972, the cost of maintaining Cliff House caused it to be abandoned, and it burned down in 1978. The barn still stands to the north of the site, which you will see as you descend toward the lake again. Smiley built another hotel, Wildmere, which stood near the lake at the site of the present upper parking lot. It too was abandoned, and it burned in 1986. For years the future of the property was in question. The Marriott Corporation wanted to build a hotel there, but a succession of lawsuits blocked the plans and the state purchased the property, establishing the Minnewaska State Park Preserve in 1993. It is managed today by the Palisades Interstate Park Commission.

Perhaps Lake Minnewaska itself, with its remarkably clear and colorful water, will fascinate you as mush as the sweeping views of the high ledges. The 34-acre, 78-foot-deep Lake Minnewaska is so clear and beautiful because its acidic water and rocky shoreline cannot support aquatic vegetation—it is, in essence, "dead." This is not to say that vegetation is absent, but it is limited to the minimal presence of water lilies, pipewort, and milfoil. The last recorded fish caught in the lake was in 1922. Collectively, the upper-elevation Shawangunk lakes are known as sky lakes. The lakes serve to fill the surrounding streams with spring-fed waters—the entire volume of the Coxing Kill depends on Lake Minnewaska. During droughts, conditions can lead to fish kills on the creek.

Rugged vertical cliffs and pure viridian waters greet the hiker at Lake Minnewaska.

While the waters of Lake Minnewaska may be nutrient poor and provide only a marginal vegetation profile, the forests surrounding the lake are diverse, and many significant biological features exist in the area. Peregrine falcons, which live in nesting sites on Millbrook Mountain, hunt over the lake. Unusually old pitch pines grow in the former Cliff House area, and are believed to have lived longer than most pitch pines on the ridge due to the presence of open rock, which acts as a natural fire barrier. (Larger pitch pines are also naturally fire resistant.) Rare plants such as broom crowberry and mountain spleenwort grow near Lake Minnewaska, but some species have been locally extirpated, including yellow lady's slipper and maidenhair fern. There are rhodora, pink lady's slipper, nodding ladies' tresses, slender ladies' tresses, and rattlesnake plantain in the area. Minnewaska State Park Preserve is also the only known area where the noctuid moth, *Zale curema,* exists.

From the high cliffs along the lake's east shoreline, continue north, following the trail as it winds its way downhill above the lake. You may follow either the trail or the carriage road from this point back to the parking lot, passing a private inholding on your left (west) as you descend slightly. Leaving the barn to your right, you will pass beneath a pretty pedestrian bridge that spans the carriage road. Bear left with the red markers back toward the parking area for one last look at the lake at a low ledge.

Even if hikers coming to Lake Minnewaska go no farther than the lake itself, they will become acquainted with some of the northern Shawangunks' significant geologic, physiographic, and biological communities. The varied aquatic, cliff-and-talus, slab rock, and pitch-pine habitats that will be encountered on this hike are a microcosm of what hikers can expect on the longer, more involved forays across the fascinating Shawangunk Ridge.

DID YOU KNOW?

The former owner of Lake Minnewaska, Alfred Smiley, was a temperate Quaker who was distressed over the presence of a rum tavern near Minnewaska's main entrance. Smiley was able to purchase the property after the owner's death, and when he had the tavern cleaned out, he found many tools—spades, picks, and shovels—marked with his name. Smiley surmised that his employees had given the tools to the owner of the tavern in exchange for drinks.

MORE INFORMATION

Arrive at the gate before 9:30 A.M. on weekends or you may have to park in the Lower Awosting lot, which will add 1.5 miles of hiking and 400 feet in elevation to this hike. There are two levels to the upper (Wildmere) parking area. A map and an interpretive kiosk are posted on the picnic area lawn between the parking lot and the lake. Pets are permitted on a leash of no more than 6 feet. A yurt near the edge of the trail provides a nature and activity center for visiting school groups. Other activities allowed on and near the area include scuba diving, boating (car-top boats only), biking, swimming, horseback riding, cross- country skiing, hunting (in designated areas), and fishing (though there are no fish). For more information, visit www.lakeminnewaska.org.

NEARBY

The Samuel Dorsky Museum of Art, located on the campus of SUNY-New Paltz, specializes in twentieth-century works, Asian and pre-Columbian art, and artifacts and metals. The museum is open Wednesday-Sunday, year-round; www.newpaltz.edu/museum; 845-257-3844. The village also has several interesting shops and restaurants and a state university, SUNY-New Paltz. Many seasonal orchards and wineries are nearby.

TRIP 12
THE TRAPPS

Location: New Paltz, NY
Rating: Moderate
Distance: 5.0 miles
Elevation Gain: 400 feet
Estimated Time: 2 hours
Maps: USGS Gardiner; USGS Mohonk Lake; NY–NJTC Northern
Shawangunk Trails; Mohonk Preserve Trail Map

**An easy, enchanting hike along carriage roads passes under high
cliffs, where rock climbing is very popular.**

DIRECTIONS
From Exit 18 off the NYS Thruway (I-87), head west through the village of
New Paltz on NY 299 for 7.5 miles. Turn right onto US 44/NY 55 and drive
0.8 mile up the hill to the Trapps Gateway Visitor Center. Just beyond the
entrance, turn right into the Wawarsing parking area. *GPS coordinates:* 41°
44.224′ N, 74° 11.076′ W.

TRAIL DESCRIPTION
The century-old Undercliff and Overcliff carriageways (gravel roads) form a
loop around the famous cliffs known as the Trapps, creating one of the most
popular scenic hikes (and bike rides) in the Shawangunks. The route travels
beneath, then above, the high vertical cliffs of bright conglomerate that are
unique to the Gunks. Here, you will become intimately acquainted with the
diverse cliff, talus, and slab rock communities that have made the Trapps not
only the most fascinating scenic attraction of the mid-Hudson Valley, but an
ecological preserve of global significance.

Both the Undercliff and Overcliff roads are multi-use, so you will encounter many cyclists, hikers, and joggers, as well as the knowledgeable preserve
rangers who patrol the cliffs and carriage roads. (You may be asked to show
or purchase your day pass at this point.) These carriage roads are also popular
cross-country skiing routes, their surfaces carved into dual, diagonal striding
tracks by local skiers the moment there is a 4-inch snowfall. But by far, the
Trapps are most renowned for the world-class rock-climbing routes that have
been pioneered along their eastern face. As you hike, you'll get to see climbers
in action on the vertical walls, some as high as 250 feet.

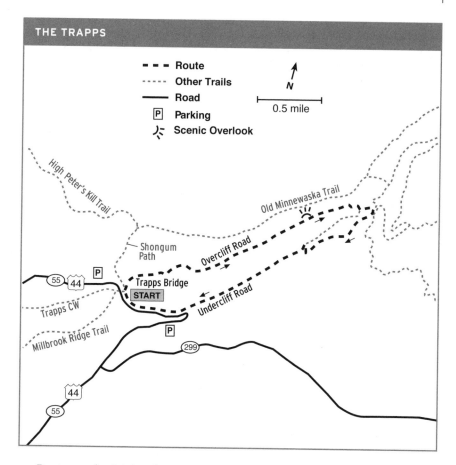

Begin at the Mohonk Preserve's Trapps Gateway Visitor Center. Take the short but steep East Trapps Connector Trail from the north end of the Wawarsing parking area up to Undercliff Road. Catch your breath after climbing the Connector Trail's 250 stone steps and turn left (southwest) on Undercliff Road. Signage is good. From here, the hike remains fairly level.

In a few minutes, you will arrive at the wooden hut and information kiosk, (with a rest room) in the general meeting area known as the Uberfall. The carriage road continues directly under the sheer cliffs here, where dozens of climbers can be seen top-roping (a method by which an anchor, or protection, is placed above the climber, who is then held on belay from below by another person, thereby protecting the climber in the event of a fall). It will amaze you to see how some climbers are able to scale a vertical wall that seems to have no handholds or ledges on it; for a non-climber, difficulty is hard to judge. Some of these very difficult climbs are in many cases adjacent to very easy ones. You'll find yourself enthralled, maybe even eager to give this thrilling sport a try. Although climbers are a friendly bunch, many of those who are "on belay" are in close vocal contact with their partners and can't risk being distracted. The atmosphere is somewhat solemn, and highly focused. The white stains on the rock are from chalk, which is used by climbers to keep their hands dry and maximize friction. Chalk has an erosive effect on sandstone.

Continue, ascending slightly past a southerly view and rising to Trapps Bridge. Don't cross the bridge. Turn right here where the Overcliff Road departs to the west. Shortly, the flat carriage road turns northeast and views to the west appear, slowly revealing the Coxing Valley and the broad lowlands of the Rondout Valley and the southern Catskills beyond. The viewshed expands as the carriage road cuts through sunny, low-angle pitch pine and oak-covered slab rocks. The entire east-facing silhouette of the Catskills, from Ashokan High Point in the south to Overlook Mountain in the north, forms the western horizon. Continue into the woods as the road descends slightly and curves past ledges on the left, passing an unmarked connector road on the left (avoid it) to Laurel Ledge Road. Within minutes you'll arrive at Rhododendron Bridge, a shaded five-way intersection in the densely wooded heart of the Mohonk Preserve. Bear right on Undercliff Road, winding below the massive cliffs of the Trapps as the road turns south. Soon you will enjoy views of the broad, flat Wallkill Valley and its little hamlets and farms, and the Fishkill Ridge and Hudson Highlands beyond the village of New Paltz. On the talus alongside the carriage road, climbers will be "bouldering," practicing overhang holds and relaxing between routes. The yellow spur trails lead through the labyrinths of talus to reach climbing routes. On days that are not busy, it is not unusual to see copperheads sunning themselves in the middle of the road. Give them space. You'll be pleased to know that there have been few, if any, incidents involving hikers and snakes here.

From time to time, the cliffs may be closed to hikers in order to protect a peregrine falcon nest or black vulture nest; often you will see observers set up along the carriageway with telescopes trained on the nests. Most are volunteers and enthusiasts who help with census and tracking studies. If you've never seen a raptor up close, this is your chance to study the head of a falcon completely filling the view field of a high-power telescope—a surprising and unforgettable image. Soon you will come upon the East Trapps Connector Trail junction you used earlier. Descend to return to your car.

Undercliff Road was built by hand and steam power in 1903. The area became a climbing destination when Fritz Wiessner, a climber scaling the cliffs around Breakneck, spotted the white cliffs of the Gunks. He pioneered the first routes on Millbrook Mountain (the so-called Old Route), and then moved to Sky Top.

The scenic Trapps cliffs are among the world's most popular rock-climbing destinations.

DID YOU KNOW?

In 1941, renowned climbers Fritz Wiessner and Hans Kraus established the route known as High Exposure in the Trapps. This is considered by many world-class climbers to be the best technical rock-climbing pitch in the world. Today there are an estimated 1,000 climbing routes in the Shawangunks.

MORE INFORMATION

Arrive before 9:30 A.M. to find a parking spot. If you can't get a spot here, continue on US 44/NY 55 to the West Trapps parking area (there is a $10 fee for day-hikers; members park free) just beyond Trapps Bridge on the right. Walk east up the gravel path to Trapps Bridge. For more information, visit www. mohonkpreserve.org.

NEARBY

To find out more about climbing in the Gunks, visit Rock and Snow on Main Street in New Paltz. There are many shops and restaurants in town.

BLACK VULTURE

The black vulture, *Coragyps atratus*, is an exciting recent addition to the Shawangunks' bird population (along with the clay-colored sparrow and the peregrine falcon). This large southern scavenger has been expanding its habitat into more rugged areas farther north due to warming trends. The first documented nest in the state appeared near Bonticou Crag in 1997. By 2004, there were three confirmed nesting sites on the Mohonk Preserve, now the bird's northernmost known breeding area in the United States. Eggs, two to a clutch, take from 38 to 41 days to incubate. The birds fledge at around 70 days.

It is likely that the black vulture will do well in the Shawangunks, and in similar areas of moderate-to-intensive human use, because it is not overly sensitive to human presence during its breeding season. From time to time, the Trapps cliffs have been closed to protect falcon and vulture nesting sites from disturbance by rock climbers. The increasing populations of turkey vultures and now, smaller black vultures, often confuse observers. Black vultures have a short, square tail, with whitish patches toward the wing tips. They have a black head (as opposed to the adult turkey vultures' easily identified bald, red head) and a smaller wingspan. They tend to flap vigorously and glide in short intervals.

TRIP 13
SKY TOP

Location: New Paltz, NY
Rating: Moderate
Distance: 6.0 miles
Elevation Gain: 650 feet
Estimated Time: 4 hours
Maps: USGS Mohonk Lake; NY–NJTC Shawangunk Trails, Lake Mohonk Area 10A; Mohonk Preserve Trail Map

A boulder scramble from Mohonk Mountain House through a deep and exciting crevice leads to a 360-degree view from Sky Top Tower, with an easy walk back.

DIRECTIONS

From Exit 18 off the NYS Thruway (I-87), drive west through the village of New Paltz on NY 299. As you cross the bridge over the Wallkill River, take the first right onto Springtown Road and set to zero. At 0.5 mile, turn left onto Mountain Rest Road (CR 6), where you'll see signs for Mohonk. At 1.7 miles, go through the intersection of Butterville-Canaan Road. Continue up Mountain Rest Road and at 4.0 miles you'll enter the Mohonk Mountain House main gate on the left. *GPS coordinates: 41° 46.727′ N, 74° 8.150′ W.*

TRAIL DESCRIPTION

This historic, scenic hike to Sky Top is perhaps the Shawangunks' most popular outing; the hike winds to the crowning glory of the Mohonk Mountain House property that adjoins the 6,400-acre Mohonk Preserve. The walk, as described here, begins at the Gatehouse parking lot. (You can save distance by taking the shuttle directly to the trailhead.) Follow the Huguenot Trail at the southwest corner of the parking lot to Whitney Road (these are carriage roads). Follow scenic North Lookout Road to a point at which you will see signs for Picnic Lodge (where you can find food, rest rooms, and phones). From Picnic Lodge, walk across Garden Road, past the greenhouses, and up through the gardens to the Mountain House. (The estimated time from the Gatehouse is 40 minutes.)

For casual visitors and Mountain House guests, the main attraction of Sky Top is the views it affords of six states (some say seven). Hikers have the

SKY TOP

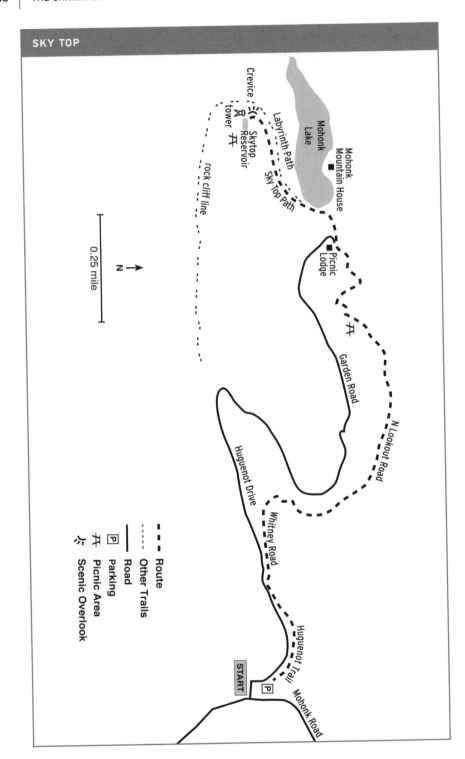

bonus of actually tunneling their way through the white conglomerate talus fields below the cliffs, then scaling the cliff face on rustic ladders and bridges following the cool, dark path known as the Labyrinth. The two most popular approaches to Sky Top are the Labyrinth Path, your ascent route, and Sky Top Path, your descent route. The designated, well-traveled Labyrinth Path is a serious rock scramble requiring all-fours agility, a good share of gumption, and, in some instances, raw courage. This trail is recommended only to the strong and adventurous, and not to anyone who is unsteady or afraid of heights. Sky Top Path, on the other hand, follows a graded, easily managed footway and takes half the time to climb although it requires the same 350-foot ascent from Mohonk Lake to the tower's base as the Labyrinth does. Many parties split up at the Mountain House's East Porchere and rendezvous at the tower. Make certain that younger children are closely supervised. Both hikes approach and in some cases traverse high vertical ledges and crevices.

While your party is getting organized, have a look at the huge, stocked rainbow trout that swirl around Mohonk Lake under the East Porchere, waiting for food pellets that you can buy from dispensers near the archway. (Fishing is reserved for Mountain House guests only.) With the East Porchere at your back, follow the path along the edge of the lake (Lake Shore Road), go under a footbridge, through a crevice, and join Sky Top Path. (Follow Sky Top Path if you do not wish to take the Labyrinth Path.) Cross a boardwalk and go a short distance to Sentinel Rock, where the Labyrinth Path to the Crevice (a.k.a. Lemon Squeezer) and Sky Top appears to your left. Signage is good. Follow the red paint blazes into the Labyrinth.

Immediately, you will make your way through holes and crevices, stooping, crab-walking, and crawling under house-sized boulders. You'll climb ladders, cross catwalks, and scale the tops of tilted slabs. You will pass connector trails to both Spring Path and Sky Top Path, where you continue straight ahead toward the Crevice. Within a half hour of beginning your hike, the trail breaks out onto the sunny, treeless scree slopes west of Sky Top, with rugged views of the Hudson Valley to the south, as well as the Trapps, Millbrook Mountain, and Eagle Cliff.

Follow the paint blazes carefully now as you rock-hop your way below the cliffs toward the Crevice. (Stay alert so that you do not continue past the Crevice onto the Staircliff Path.) The Crevice appears in the cliff on your left as a high, narrow fissure. A series of wooden stairways ascends through several dark, damp pitches. The final climb out of the Crevice is a challenging, 10-foot vertical wall (be sure of your foot- and handholds, and assist younger hikers here) that brings you out to a flat slab with high, vertical drops, overlooking the

The Sky Top Tower offers some of the most far-reaching views in the Hudson Valley.

preserve lands. (You can see the top of Sky Top Tower from here if you look up and north.) Walk back over the top of the Crevice on a wooden bridge, following the blazes for a short distance up to Sky Top Road. Go left, pass the Armstrong Seat, and turn right onto the tar-paved walkway (note that Sky Top Path meets Sky Top Road here—this is your descent route), and walk a short distance to Sky Top Tower. The tower is open and you can climb to the observation deck, where you'll enjoy 360-degree views, from the Green Mountains of Vermont over to New York's Taconics, the Catskills, the Hudson Highlands, and New Jersey's Kittatinnys. Below are the Mountain House and Mohonk Lake. The tower, which stands over Sky Top Reservoir, was originally constructed for fire control. There is a picnic table next to the map kiosk on Sky Top. Return via the Sky Top Path for the fastest descent (25 minutes) to the Mountain House.

There are several choices for return routes to the Mountain House. Many hikers opt for the longer, gentler Sky Top Road, or the Reservoir, Pinkster, or Bruin paths. Often, Sky Top hikers who have parked at the Gatehouse return by way of Sky Top Road and the Fox Path, crossing Garden Road onto the Glen Anna Path, North Lookout Road, Whitney Road, and the Huguenot Path.

DID YOU KNOW?

Built in 1921, the internationally famous monument of Sky Top Tower commemorates Albert K. Smiley (1828-1912), who founded the Mohonk Mountain House with his twin brother, Alfred.

MORE INFORMATION

The Labyrinth is not recommended as a descent route. Carry as small a pack as possible and bring a first-aid kit. For more information, visit www.mohonk-preserve.org.

NEARBY

The Shawangunk Wine Trail takes in 11 wineries between the Shawangunk Mountains and the Hudson River, extending from New Paltz in Ulster County to Warwick in Orange County. There are many other attractions, activities, and restaurants along the route. For details visit www.shawangunkwinetrail.com or call 845-256-8456.

PEREGRINE FALCON

Probably the most successful wildlife reintroduction effort in the United States has been that of the peregrine falcon, *Falco peregrinus*, or duck hawk. Before the 1950s, the birds bred from the southern states as far north as the high arctic islands. Peregrines were nearly wiped out by the use of the pesticide dichloro-diphenyl-trichloroethane (DDT), and were extirpated from the area east of the Mississippi River by 1964. When DDT was banned in North America in the early 1970s, the birds were reintroduced through a captive breeding program, the Cornell Recovery Program, to places where it was believed they would thrive—especially bridges and skyscrapers. Because of this, and to the surprise of many people, their reappearance occurred around large population centers.

Peregrines are common migrants and can be observed in increasing numbers along the Appalachian Highlands and into the upper Hudson Valley. One of the most popular places to watch them is from the Trapps area of the Shawangunks, where the Mohonk Preserve conducts an annual hawk watch. Often you will meet volunteer observers tracking nesting pairs of falcons along the Undercliff Carriageway. The birds are sensitive to disturbance, and parts of the Trapps have been closed to rock climbing from time to time in order to protect their breeding sites.

TRIP 14
EAGLE CLIFF AND MOHONK LAKE

Location: New Paltz, NY
Rating: Easy
Distance: 6.0 miles (2.0 miles if you begin at the Mountain House)
Elevation Gain: 625 feet
Estimated Time: 3.5 hours
Maps: USGS Mohonk Lake; NY–NJTC Shawangunk Trails, Lake Mohonk Area; Mohonk Preserve Trail Map

A carriage road walk from Mohonk Mountain House heads to the gazebos and cliffs overlooking the Shawangunks and the Catskills, with a walk around Mohonk Lake.

DIRECTIONS
From Exit 18 off the NYS Thruway (I-87), drive west through the village of New Paltz on NY 299. As you cross the bridge over the Wallkill River, take the first right onto Springtown Road and set to zero. At 0.5 mile, turn left onto Mountain Rest Road (CR 6), where you'll see signs for Mohonk. At 1.7 miles, go through the intersection with Butterville-Canaan Road. Continue up Mountain Rest Road and at 4.0 miles you'll enter the Mohonk Mountain House main gate on the left. *GPS coordinates:* 41° 46.727′ N, 74° 8.150′ W.

TRAIL DESCRIPTION
Rivaled only by Sky Top for dramatic views, this short, easy hike reveals the kind of bewitching and far-reaching landscapes for which Mohonk is famous. It ranks as a Mountain House favorite, and perhaps because of its gentle, easy grades and scenic payoffs, it may be the most popular hike on the hotel property. The easy jaunt to Eagle Cliff, with views of Sky Top, the southlands, and the Victorian "castle" of the Mountain House along the shores of Mohonk Lake, will be among the stateliest and most alluring easy hikes you'll have ever taken.

Eagle Cliff is an east- and south-facing escarpment of vertical white conglomerate. Its rugged beauty is due in part to the jumbled tonnage of talus that has broken away from Eagle Cliff and lies glistening among moss- and tree-clad pockets below. The serpentine route of the carriage road will introduce you to an awe-inspiring series of panoramic surprises, from the Catskills in the west through the southerly rolling hills of western New Jersey, Minnewaska

EAGLE CLIFF AND MOHONK LAKE

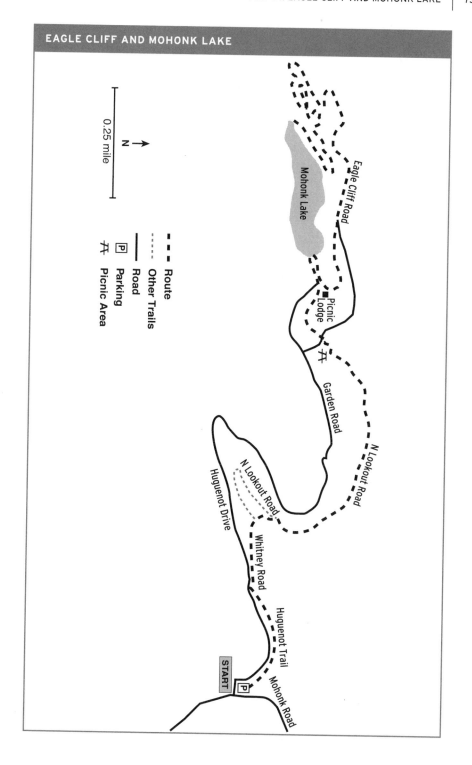

0.25 mile

N →

- ■ ■ Route
- ∷∷∷ Other Trails
- —— Road
- P Parking
- 🌲 Picnic Area

Mohonk Lake

Eagle Cliff Road

Picnic Lodge

Garden Road

N Lookout Road

N Lookout Road

Huguenot Drive

Whitney Road

Huguenot Trail

START

P

Mohonk Road

State Park, and the Hudson Valley Highlands. In the foreground, the jagged rocks of the Mohonk Preserve form a fitting picture frame for some of the east's most startling vistas and one of the world's most enchanting carriage roads, created by the Smiley brothers to delight their guests.

The walk, as described here, begins at the Gatehouse parking lot. (You can save distance by taking the shuttle directly to the trailhead.) Follow the Huguenot Trail at the southwest corner of the parking lot to Whitney Road (these are old carriage roads). Follow scenic North Lookout Road to a point at which you will see signs for Picnic Lodge (where you can find food, rest rooms, and phones). From Picnic Lodge, walk across Garden Road, past the greenhouses, and up through the gardens to the Mountain House. (The estimated time from the Gatehouse is 40 minutes.)

Begin at the front entrance of the hotel and turn left onto the main service road (Garden Road). Follow the road a few hundred feet to the apex of the hairpin turn. Here you will find Eagle Cliff Road. Follow this cinder carriage road, leaving the tennis courts to your right. Entering the forest, you're surrounded by moss-frocked boulders sticking out of the ground like fuzzy emeralds. Amid the hemlock and laurels, ascend easily, passing a small bench on a slab of stone to your right, with limited views to the west. Keep climbing, and soon you will come upon a small pair of gazebos with views of the Trapps and Millbrook Mountain. The trail turns through the south now, passing another west-facing gazebo with views of the Catskills.

Soon you will reach an H-intersection. Bear right now, and, although you can't sense it just yet, you're climbing the tilted northwest slopes of Eagle Cliff and Huntington Ledge. Red and white oak appears, along with hemlock, white pine, and pitch pine. Suddenly, you arrive at Huntington Lookout, a stunning tableau across the preserve lands and beyond. Beneath you are the pristine lands of the Trapps and Millbrook Mountain, and rising to the west are the retreating folds of hills that reach up across the Rondout Valley to Ashokan High Point. The south is enveloped in the scrubby pitch pines of the Badlands. At your feet is the thin valley of Rhododendron Brook, which you can "locate" by pouring an imaginary torrent of water between you and the Trapps, and following its course eastward, downhill.

Humpty Dumpty Road is just below you, amid the dizzying, bright chunks of talus rock. Continuing the hike, the next gazebo is the magical Artist's Rock, and more follow as you turn toward the south. On your right you'll pass Eagle Cliff, a rough path that shortcuts down to Short Woodland Drive and Humpty Dumpty Road.

Peaceful carriage roads and quiet forests characterize the path to Eagle Cliff.

Eagle Cliff Road now heads north, and suddenly the vertical cone of Sky Top comes into view. The carriage road threads in and out of the woods, walking the cliff's edge past a collection of the world's finest handmade cedar gazebos, constructed by the Mountain House's rustic builders. From here are sweeping valley views and close-ups of the Mountain House and its terra cotta roof, with Sky Top on your right, perched on its monolith of bright conglomerate. Mohonk Lake, shimmering in deep shades of viridian, lies beneath you. Views to the northeast are striking, with the hotel imposed before the northern lowlands of the Hudson Valley.

Views don't get much better than from Arthur's Seat gazebo,, and surely you will think that this stretch of carriageway ranks as one of the finest short walks in the world. The carriage road curls into the forest again, passing Cuyler Castle gazebo. Pass the H-intersection you saw earlier, bearing right toward the Mountain House, and just after crossing a wooden bridge, turn right and descend Lambdins Path, turning left under the bridge and descending a three-pitched flight of stairs to join the Undercliff Path. Bear right, walk around the southwest shore of Mohonk Lake, and follow along the lake's edge on the Shore Path, joining Lake Shore Road (east) back along the water's edge to the Mountain House.

Return to the Gatehouse by the route you came.

DID YOU KNOW?

The Mohonk Preserve (founded in 1963), which surrounds the Mohonk Mountain House property, is the largest membership-supported nature preserve in New York State. It was the first land trust (originally the Mohonk Trust) established to protect the Shawangunk Ridge, which was created by guests of the Mountain House and the Smiley family.

MORE INFORMATION

Maps are available at the Gatehouse parking lot. For more information, visit www.mohonkpreserve.org.

NEARBY

The SUNY-New Paltz School of Fine and Performing Arts presents music concerts and theater performances during the spring and fall semesters, and "Piano Summer," an international summer institute and festival. For performance schedules visit www.newpaltz.edu/artsnews or call the box office at 845-257-3880.

3

THE EASTERN MID-HUDSON REGION

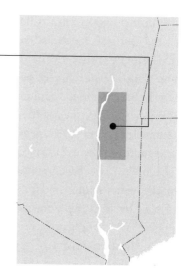

THE HUDSON VALLEY DEVELOPED SLOWLY in comparison with the English settlements of New England and Virginia. The Dutch East India Company lost interest after Henry Hudson determined that what would later be called the Hudson River was not the sea route to the Orient. (On his return to the Netherlands, the British seized his ship, the *Half Moon;* Hudson's last expedition to the Northwest Passage in 1610 would be under the British flag in the ship *Discovery.*) Hudson did, however, interest a powerful group of private investors in the region's lucrative fur trade, and this group formed the Dutch West India Company, which was chartered in 1621 with a 21-year trading monopoly.

The company established trade connections with the colonies, built forts in Albany and New York City, and introduced patroonships as an inexpensive means of encouraging colonization. A patroonship was, in essence, a land grant given to a patroon (a lord or feudal master), who could establish a colony of 50 settlers within a 4-year period. Because patroonships were so large (8 miles square), and because those who farmed the land could not own it, the system prevented permanent settlement on both sides of the river. Ultimately, the patroonships failed. Most farmers found that life was better in the Netherlands, where land could be privately owned. The best-known patroon was Peter Minuit, who is remembered for the purchase of Manhattan Island from the Canarsie tribe. Only one patroonship, Rensselaerwyck, survived the transition to British rule intact.

After the patroonships, much of the open land remained unsettled until the German Palatines (religious refugees from the Electoral Palatinate of Germany's Rhine Valley) arrived in 1710. Fleeing persecution in their homeland, 3,000 refugees relocated to America after seeking asylum in Britain. Robert Hunter, appointed as first governor of the New York province, oversaw the Palatines' settlement. They were "encamped" in the vicinity of Germantown, on both sides of the river (in an East Camp and a West Camp), and employed by the crown for the manufacture of naval stores, such as tar. The lands on the east bank were purchased from Robert Livingston; the west banks were the queen's lands. In spite of a concentrated effort, the production of naval stores was unsuccessful and the Palatines disbanded. Later, marble, slate, and iron mining contributed to the region's prosperity. Eventually, the area took part in the lucrative world trade, a development made possible by proximity to the Hudson River.

The eastern mid-Hudson Valley is bounded in the east by the Taconic Range, in the south by the Fishkill Ridge, and in the west by the Hudson. Substantial open space exists along the river's edge in the eastern mid-Hudson region, where most of the hikes in this guide are located.

OLD CROTON AQUEDUCT

The Old Croton Aqueduct was built to supply New York City with water, and it did so from 1842 to 1955. Around the beginning of the twentieth century, when Manhattan started to expand north of Wall Street as its population exploded, the city began the construction of reservoirs in the Catskill Mountains (see Trip 35). But the Old Croton Aqueduct, an impressive feat of engineering referred to as simply "the aqueduct," was the one by which all others would be measured. Thirty-five million gallons of water flowed into the city daily through the aqueduct from Croton to two reservoirs, one in today's Central Park, the other in the present location of the New York City library.

Neither reservoir exists today, but the 26-mile-long aqueduct does, along with many of its disused aerators and weir chambers. The aqueduct still provides the village of Ossining with drinking water. Its combined length and width have been designated as one of the Hudson Valley's longest linear parks, with a surface that has been improved along its full length, from Croton Gorge Park in Cortlandt to the Bronx. Here and there the trail is interrupted by development, but it is still a continuous, marked trail with a flat dirt surface.

TRIP 15
OLD CROTON AQUEDUCT

Location: Croton-on-Hudson, NY
Rating: Moderate
Distance: 4.75 miles
Elevation Gain: 420 feet
Estimated Time: 3 hours
Maps: Westchester County (road map); Old Croton Aqueduct State Historic Map and Guide

This easy, flat walk through deep woods is ideal for children.

DIRECTIONS

To reach the park, take NY 129 (Maple Street) east from US 9. Go 2.4 miles to the park entrance on the right. Follow the park road past the dam into the parking area. *GPS coordinates:* 41° 13.493' N, 73° 51.499' W.

By train, take the Metro-North Hudson line to Croton-Harmon station. (Hike ends near Ossining station.)

TRAIL DESCRIPTION

Many hikers feel that the most attractive section of the Old Croton Aqueduct Trail (OCA) is the one described here, which connects Ossining to Croton Gorge Park. Each end of the trail has attractions, and in between are 5 miles of quiet woodlands, with one or two diversions through the surrounding communities. It is best to leave a shuttle car at either end of the hike described here, but you can also hike from the north end to the south end and back (a total of 10 miles), or hike from one end to any point at which you may wish to turn around. It would be a mistake, however, to miss either the Heritage Community Visitor Center in Ossining, which features an exhibit on the aqueduct's construction (as well as original cells and an electric chair from neighboring Sing Sing prison), or the remarkable Croton Dam.

Begin the hike from the north end, at Croton Gorge Park. With this choice you get to walk across the dam; on the other side, walk southwest into Croton Gorge Park, where you'll meet the trail. This will allow you the option of seeing New Croton Reservoir, but you can also walk the dam after you've done the hike from below.

The dam is just as impressive from ground level, where you can see the spillway up close. From the Croton Gorge Park picnic area, go to the south

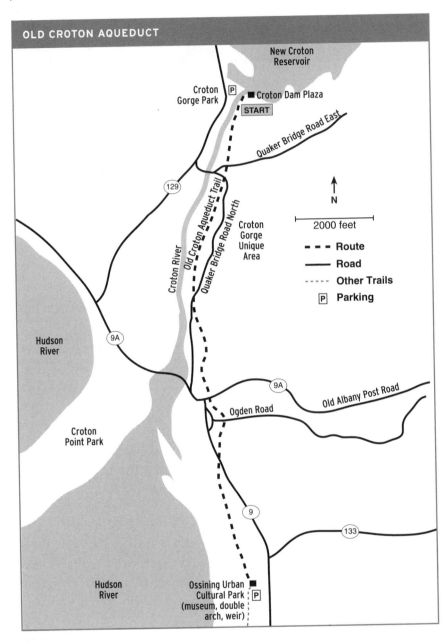

OLD CROTON AQUEDUCT

side of the parking lot and follow the trail to the south as it walks between rows of tall, thin white pines. Soon you will be presented with the option of walking along the River Trail, which lies between the Croton River and the OCA Trail. However, because the markings (blue paint and assorted disks) are poor and the trail is not well managed, it is confusing. There are no maps posted or available. Continue straight ahead on the Old Croton Aqueduct access trail.

Pass beneath a large power line. Soon, large oaks and poplars appear and you will see some trail signs. The trail is flat, hard-packed sandy loam, about 18 feet wide. After walking for 20 minutes, you will reach Quaker Bridge Road, which you cross. You're moving away from the river now, and have risen above it. Barriers across the trail prevent its use by motorized vehicles. Once again, cross the road. Pass the 19-acre Croton Gorge Unique Area (DEC owned), which lies between the trail and the river. Some herd trails, which lead downhill to the river's edge, are evident.

Continue along the OCA. Soon a 10-mile-long vista opens up to the southwest, showing Hook Mountain (the Palisades) and Haverstraw Bay across the Hudson River. Where there are no trees, OCA Trail markers are posted on green stanchions. Soon you'll circumvent the perimeter of the beautifully landscaped General Electric Management Center, walking next to a chain-link fence. This is a residential area you will escape as you cross Albany Post Road and follow blue blazes under US 9. The trail turns left onto Ogden Road and goes uphill about 500 feet, where you bear right onto the OCA again. The low, cylindrical stone towers you will see along the route are ventilators that act to equalize the pressure in the aqueduct and to aerate the water.

At the Ossining welcome sign, cross US 9 on the pedestrian crosswalk, where signposts identify the trail. You'll pass through the property of the Mearl Corporation, on the sprawling grounds of the historic Crane House (1843). The white post on the lawn identifies the center of the aqueduct.

Now you will cross several streets in the village of Ossining. Descending a flight of stone stairs at the south end of a paved green strip, you will arrive at the Double Arched Bridge. On the north side, before you cross, you'll come upon the stone weir chamber, which controlled the flow of water through the aqueduct. When the tunnel needed to be emptied for repair, the weir chamber would release water into the Sing Sing Kill.

Cross the bridge, leave the OCA Trail, and follow an informal trail to the observation platform to look at the Double Arch. You're nearly in the center of Ossining. Go back and cross the OCA again to the Heritage Visitor Center (part of the Joseph G. Caputo Community Center and the Ossining Visitor Center), where there are outstanding displays recounting the aqueduct's history.

Ossining's original name of Sing Sing came from the Sinck Sinck ("stone upon stone") tribe, who sold the land in 1685. The name survives in the Sing Sing Kill and was given to the infamous Sing Sing state prison, which stands just to the west on the Hudson's banks. The historical exhibit at the visitor center contains reconstructed original prison cells, dating from 1826. There are also photos, personal effects, and dioramas of prison life. Sing Sing was

The New Croton Dam created reservoirs that provide New York City with drinking water.

considered a model prison because it earned a profit for the state of New York, as no prison had done before. The prison houses about 1,700 prisoners today.

When you've finished, find your shuttle car in the parking lot.

DID YOU KNOW?

The expression "sent up the river," meaning "to be in prison," is in reference to Sing Sing state prison in the village of Ossining, 30 miles upriver from New York City. The phrase dates from 1891.

MORE INFORMATION

The entry fee for Croton Gorge Park varies year to year. To begin this hike from the south, take the Tarrytown exit (Exit 9 from the NYS Thruway) and go north on South Broadway 7.2 miles. Take the first left after Main Street into the Caputo Community Center. You can also use local street parking.

Maps can be ordered from Friends of the Old Croton Aqueduct; www.aqueduct.org; 914-693-4117. For more information about Croton Gorge Park, call 914-827-9568. For more information about the Caputo Community Center and Ossining Heritage Visitor Center, call 914-941-3189.

NEARBY

Rockefeller State Park Preserve, located on NY 117 in Sleepy Hollow, is a 1,400-acre preserve with an extensive network of carriage roads available for walking. It is open year-round, sunrise to sunset; www.nysparks.state.ny.us/parks/59/details.aspx; 914-631-1470. The Preserve is adjacent the Sleepy Hollow Cemetery and the Kykuit (John D. Rockefeller) Estate.

TRIP 16
STISSING MOUNTAIN

Location: Pine Plains, NY
Rating: Moderate
Distance: 3.0 miles
Elevation Gain: 1,000 feet
Estimated Time: 2 hours
Map: USGS Pine Plains

A steep ascent to a fire tower overlooking the mid-Hudson Valley's agricultural lands leads to views of the Southern Taconic Plateau and the Catskills.

DIRECTIONS

From the Taconic State Parkway, take Exit 44 to NY 82 north. Watch for the firehouse on the left; turn left here onto Lake Road, where you will see Stissing Mountain and its fire tower ahead. (From the center of Pine Plains, go south on NY 82 for 0.4 mile and turn right on Lake Road.) At 1.6 miles, pass the Thompson Pond Preserve trailheads (there is one on each side of the Stissing Pond outlet). At 2.2 miles, park at the trailhead, on the right. The trail begins across the street. This parking area is also a Friends of Stissing Landmarks (FOSL) trailhead that you can take to reach the Thompson Pond trailhead, rather than walk the road. *GPS coordinates:* 41° 58.192′ N, 73° 40.933′ W.

TRAIL DESCRIPTION

Choose a clear, sunny day for this short hike to Stissing's summit (1,403 feet) and fire tower, leaving time to hike the loop trail around Thompson Pond. They make an unforgettable outing to a diverse 507-acre preserve located midway between the Hudson River and the Southern Taconic Mountains.

The area's natural value was recognized by a group of local citizens whose dedication led to the involvement of The Nature Conservancy (TNC) in 1957, and finally to the preserve's designation as a registered National Natural Landmark in 1973. FOSL continues to act as liaison to the conservancy.

The trail to Stissing summit, although short, is steep and rocky. Especially during spring and fall, come prepared for high winds and chill factor if you plan to climb the fire tower, which is not on the true summit of Stissing but on its northerly slope. From the FOSL trailhead, cross the street to the Stissing trailhead, identified by a preserve sign and diamond/oak leaf TNC arrow

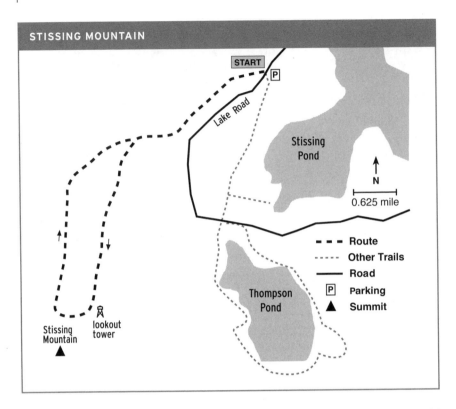

markers. Climb immediately up the rocky, steep trail as it bears left onto an old fire access road that's posted to the right (north). A seasonal brook sometimes shares this roadway that served the fire tower, but soon you will climb above it. At a Y, where as of this writing there was a pile of stones but no trail markers, bear left for the most direct and steepest route to the summit.

The incline relaxes only slightly as the trail cuts east across the northerly side of the mountain, then it climbs stiffly as it turns south toward the summit. Now you will begin to see open farmlands to the east, through a second-growth hardwood forest that was originally clear-cut for charcoal production. Just as you're wondering where the tower could be, it appears. As you top out on the summit, you'll see the foundation of an old observer's cabin. Now, the tower is 200 feet to your left. It is open and maintained by FOSL. The fire tower is so tall that the squeamish may be content with the limited views from below. The tower has a cab (a waist-high steel enclosure) and a roof but no windows, so you're going to feel the full force of the wind here.

Stissing Mountain is isolated within a relatively flat, peripheral plain of softer sandstones. Its Precambrian gneiss is erosion resistant, representing some of Earth's oldest surface rock.

Stissing Mountain rises above the Thompson Pond marshes to create a scenic mountain setting.

The views from Stissing's heights are expansive, taking in a 360-degree panorama of the north and east farmlands of Columbia and Dutchess counties; and of the Southern Taconic Ridge stretching from North Egremont and Mount Washington State Forest in Massachusetts to Bash Bish, Alander, and Brace Mountain as the ridge tapers down to the flatlands around Millerton, New York. At your feet, north to south, are Twin Island Lake, Stissing Pond, and Thompson Pond. To the southwest, you see the long Shawangunk Ridge sweeping across Minnewaska State Park from Sam's Point all the way to Sky Top Tower in the Mohonk Preserve. With binoculars, you can see High Point tower in northwestern New Jersey and the jagged Kittatinnys.

In the west, you can take in the entire Catskills: from Peekamoose and Table through the Burroughs Range (the high-peaks area of Slide, Wittenberg, and Cornell mountains) and into the vast northerly wilderness areas to the "Big Three" of Thomas Cole, Black Dome, and Blackhead mountains. Beyond these are the Helderbergs, and to the north and east on a good day you may see the southern Adirondacks and the Green Mountains of Vermont. Your compass will not function in the steel tower, so map orientation and peak identification present a challenge.

For the return trip, follow the longer but more relaxed trail that completes the loop. Proceed past the tower that straddles the trail, following downhill into the west, where you'll soon see the arrow markers. Pay attention to the arrows on these markers, which indicate the trail's many switches. Don't get discouraged by the herd trails and washed-out gullies. The marking is sufficient if you're patient and observant. Winding your way around and down, bearing right, note that the trail widens and improves as it turns east through the notch between Stissing and Little Stissing mountains in a healthy oak forest. Bear right at a Y where postings appear, and soon you will have reached the first Y and rock pile where you went left up the mountain. Bear left now, returning to the FOSL trailhead parking area, marked with plain yellow disks. This trail will lead you to the Thompson Pond trailhead (see Trip 17).

MORE INFORMATION

For more information, contact The Nature Conservancy's Eastern New York Chapter by visiting www.nature.org or calling 914-244-3271.

NEARBY

The village of Rhinebeck, New York, has many shops and restaurants. The Clermont State Historic Site in Germantown preserves the longtime home of New York's prominent Livingston family. The grounds are open year-round, with guided house and garden tours available April to November; www.nysparks.state.ny.us/historic-sites/16/details.aspx; 518-537-4240.

THE GOLDEN EAGLE

Visitors to Stissing Mountain and Thompson Pond are likely to get a glimpse of the majestic golden eagle, *Aquila chrysaetos,* wheeling overhead in search of food. This large bird is capable of hunting animals as big as house cats, foxes, turkeys, geese, and similar game. Considered a threat to livestock in the western states, at one time the golden eagle had a bounty issued on it.

Though they look similar to bald eagles from a distance, you can distinguish adult golden eagles by their darker, obscurely banded tail. Immature golden eagles have a white tail, similar to the bald eagle's. The hindneck appears copperish or "golden," but don't expect to get close enough to see it!

Although golden eagles have lived in this area for many years, their range in New York is shrinking. Once common breeders in the Adirondacks, the eagles' range has moved south, to an area that is threatened by habitat degradation and reduction. Golden eagles need as much as 35 square miles of uninterrupted hunting and breeding ground, and even under ideal circumstances, juvenile mortality can be as high as 75 percent. Though at one time considered a pest, these endangered birds are now protected under the Migratory Bird Treaty Act.

TRIP 17
THOMPSON POND PRESERVE

Location: Pine Plains, NY
Rating: Easy
Distance: 3.0 miles
Elevation Gain: 50 feet
Estimated Time: 2 hours
Maps: USGS Pine Plains; Nature Conservancy, Thompson Pond Nature Preserve

The pond and surrounding wetlands of this excellent family hike are a National Natural Landmark where golden eagles and king rails nest.

DIRECTIONS

To reach Pine Plains from the Taconic State Parkway, take Exit 44 to NY 82 north. Watch carefully for the firehouse on the left; turn left here onto Lake Road, where you will see Stissing Mountain and its fire tower ahead. (From the center of Pine Plains, go south on NY 82 for 0.4 mile and turn right onto Lake Road.) At 1.6 miles, you'll see the Thompson Pond Preserve trailheads (there is one on each side of the Stissing Pond outlet). If these are full, continue to 2.2 miles and park at the Stissing Mountain trailhead, on the right. Walk back along the road or on the FOSL Trail to the Thompson Pond trailhead. *GPS coordinates: 41° 58.192′ N, 73° 40.933′ W.*

TRAIL DESCRIPTION

Thompson Pond lies east and directly beneath Stissing Mountain in the town of Pine Plains. You can hike both destinations for a scenic day outing. The pond was named for Amos Thompson, who in 1746 was among the earliest white settlers in Dutchess County. During King George's War (1744–1748, one of the French and Indian wars), a Moravian mission also existed nearby, ministering to the Mahican group that was soon disbanded by settlement and by the king's dissolution of the mission.

The trailhead is reached from the same parking lot as the Stissing Mountain trailhead (see Trip 16). Ideally, you should wear waterproof boots for the hike around Thompson Pond, which forms the soggy headwaters of Wappingers Creek. If the water table is high, you might find yourself ankle-deep or more in standing water at the pond's south end, where a series of boardwalks

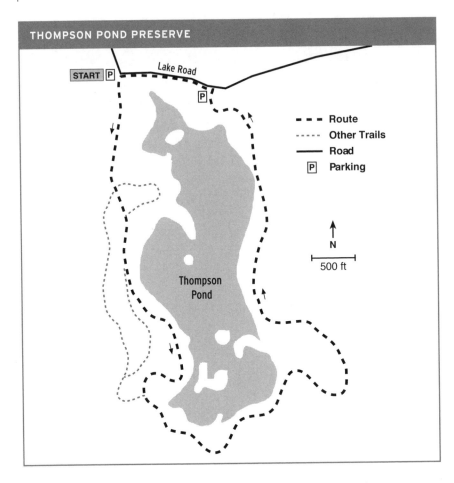

THOMPSON POND PRESERVE

Lake Road

START [P]

[P]

Route
Other Trails
Road
[P] Parking

N
500 ft

Thompson
Pond

are sometimes submerged. These conditions exist mostly in early spring, usually the best time to observe the bird life for which this area is known. Many
naturalists consider Thompson Pond the best location for viewing water birds
in the entire central Hudson Valley area. Nesting golden eagles are found here,
something not mentioned in most of the literature about the preserve. You'll
have a very good chance of seeing them if you arrive early in the season before
hikers have appeared in numbers.

If you're parked at the Stissing Mountain trailhead (FOSL trailhead) and
want to leave your car there, you can either walk 0.2 mile south along the road
to the Thompson Pond trailhead (where there's also a small parking lot) or
walk the FOSL Trail (yellow disks) that begins opposite the Stissing Mountain
trailhead. If you do take the FOSL Trail, bear right at the first junction you
reach (unmarked), which will bring you directly to the Thompson Pond trailhead. (The left turn is a short spur leading to the edge of Stissing Pond.)

The peaceful winter woods surrounding Thompson Pond offer an attractive setting for showshoeing on flat terrain.

Equipped with a bird guide and binoculars (you might also want a staff to help you safely ford the high water and slippery boardwalks), set out along the preserve's yellow-marked trail. This is a road-wide dirt path. Up to your right are the steep eastern slopes of Stissing. To the left is Thompson Pond. The forest is full of sweet birch here (a.k.a. black or cherry birch), identifiable by the thin, horizontal lines on its trunk. This aromatic tree is the traditional source of birch beer, fermented from its sap, and was the source of oil of wintergreen, which is now chemically manufactured. The buds and seeds of this tree provide browse for rabbits, deer, and ruffed grouse.

Soon you will arrive at a kiosk with maps and information describing the details of this calcareous limestone wetland. What makes the preserve so unusual is the high biological diversity in a relatively small space of 507 acres: 300 species of plants, 162 of birds, and 20 of mammals. The exquisite, small, orchidlike milkwort called fringed polygala (a.k.a. gaywings) is also found here in the damp woods, blooming in late spring.

There is another trail (blue markers) that approaches the pond at this point and forms a loop around the main trail. Remain on the yellow trail, continuing south through pockets of hemlocks past a pair of stone commemorative benches. Follow along the pond's western fringes, passing a cornfield and descending to a swampy section of trail with a long boardwalk at the south end.

As you turn north to cross the Wappingers' headwaters, you'll walk adjacent to a farm over several sections of boardwalk. Some sections are covered with chicken wire to provide traction. Walk carefully across the slick surface of the pressure-treated boards. This area is muddy and low. At a culvert where the ponds drain, you may see schools of good-sized smallmouth bass.

Views to the west reveal Stissing's fire tower. The trail rises above the pond now and remains dry. In the dense cattails, look for large, rust-colored king rails, a critically imperiled waterbird species in its northernmost habitat limits, which are now substantially farther north than the range mapped out by naturalist and ornithologist Roger Tory Peterson in 1980.

As you reach the trail's northern terminus, a stand of Norway spruce grows beside an open cornfield at the edge of a new housing development. As the desirability of scenic home sites in this area increases, we should appreciate the efforts of FOSL and The Nature Conservancy that have led to the preservation of this remarkable place. Hunting, trapping, fishing, camping, bicycling, motorized vehicles, and fires are prohibited in the preserve, which is why it is still pristine. Cross-country skiing and canoeing are allowed.

Bear left as you reach the road and cross the outlet of Stissing Pond. The trail entrance appears to the left as you complete the loop.

DID YOU KNOW?

With 162 bird species, Thompson Pond is considered to be the best location for viewing waterbirds in the Hudson Valley region.

MORE INFORMATION

For more information, you can contact The Nature Conservancy's Eastern New York Chapter by visiting www.nature.org or calling 914-244-3271.

NEARBY

Montgomery Place, a 380-acre historic Hudson Valley estate in Annandale-on-Hudson, is a National Historic Landmark. On the grounds of the estate, open year-round, are wooded trails, waterfalls, gardens, and orchards; guided house and grounds tours are available May to October; www.hudsonvalley.org/content/view/16/46/; 845-758-5461.

TRIP 18
NORRIE POINT

Location: Staatsburg, NY
Rating: Moderate
Distance: 5.0 miles
Elevation Gain: 200 feet
Estimated Time: 3 hours
Maps: USGS Hyde Park; Staatsburgh State Historic Site (Mills-Norrie State Park) Trail Map

This shoreline hike along the Hudson River is a great family outing that highlights a fine example of a Hudson River mansion and estate.

DIRECTIONS

Take Exit 19 of the NYS Thruway (I-87) at Kingston. Bear right out of the toll pavilion and set your odometer to zero. Cross over the Thruway and bear right onto NY 209, heading north toward the Kingston–Rhinecliff Bridge. At 5.5 miles, cross the bridge (toll), and as you enter Dutchess County, NY 209 becomes NY 199. At 7.9 miles, turn right (south) at River Road (CR 103). Bear right at the fork you reach after 8.6 miles. At 11.2 miles turn left onto Rhinecliff Road. At 12.4 miles, you're in the center of Rhinebeck. Set to zero here. Turn right onto NY 9G (south), and at 4.3 miles, turn right onto Staatsburg Road. At 5.3 miles, turn right into the Staatsburgh State Historic Site. *GPS coordinates: 41° 51.502′ N, 73° 55.760′ W.*

TRAIL DESCRIPTION

What distinguishes this hike from others in the Hudson Valley is its proximity to the river. For more than 2.5 miles you walk next to the water, enjoying far-reaching views. When you've finished the hike, you can take a look at the Mills Mansion ($5 admission fee) or just sit on the open sweep of lawn above the Hudson and ponder the opulent lives of one of the Gilded Age's wealthiest couples, Ruth Livingston and Ogden Mills. The area consists of two parks joined together—Margaret Lewis Norrie State Park and Ogden Mills and Ruth Livingston Mills State Park—comprising more than 1,000 acres. You will walk through both. There is a campsite and marina at the south end of Norrie Park.

Drive through the grounds. The mansion appears on your left. Take the first right into a shady parking area adjacent to the beautiful old brick carriage houses that serve as the grounds maintenance buildings. This is the designated

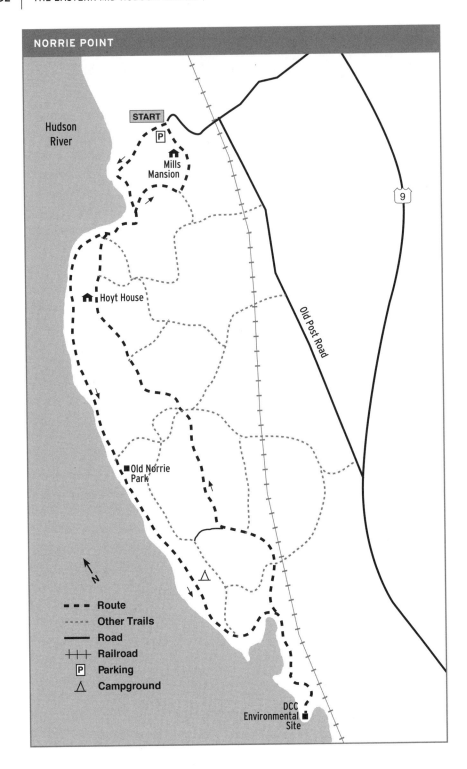

NORRIE POINT

Hudson
River

START

P

Mills
Mansion

Hoyt House

Old Post Road

9

Old Norrie
Park

N

DCC
Environmental
Site

- - - Route
.... Other Trails
——— Road
+++ Railroad
P Parking
△ Campground

parking area for hikers and sledders (sledding is popular on the long, sloping hillside in front of the house). Take Gardener's House Lane from the southwest corner of the lot and head for the river between rows of elegant sugar maples.

As you walk down the road toward the river, you'll pass a stone boathouse on the right that you can explore. Continue past the gardener's house—the large, elegant brick homestead on the left—and you're at water level, looking north toward the Esopus Meadows Lighthouse. Just as the road begins to rise, watch carefully to your right and follow the white trail markers into the woods along the river's edge. You will rise to Dinsmore Point as the trail turns south over the craggy hemlock-shaded path and provides several open vantage points. The trail is rooty and rocky, so watch your footing. In icy conditions, be careful—there are spots where the ledges drop vertically into the river. Continue, passing an abandoned pump house; keep your eyes on the white markers, as they become sparse. You'll notice a few fire pits dating from the park's origins in the 1920s. Shortly, you will arrive at a grassy spot with several picnic tables that is enclosed by old stone foundation ramparts.

Follow to the right on a paved road along the river next to a large gazebo with a fireplace in it. This area is accessible by car, and in season many people drive down for a look at the river. The white trail continues on the south side of this cul-de-sac, making its way into secluded woods again. At a point where the riverbank becomes steeper, the trail veers uphill and east, goes through a hardwood forest of large, mature oaks, and climbs gently above the river to the cabin camping area. Keep the cabins to your left and continue with the river on the right. Markers momentarily become scarce here.

At the rear of the last cabin, the white trail turns right, dropping downhill toward the park road. Cross a small wooden bridge and turn right at the road, leaving the Indian Kill to your left. Continue along the road (yellow markers appear), very shortly passing the marina, and head to the Norrie Point environmental research station that you will see straight ahead. Consisting of an aquarium, a museum, and a field station belonging to Dutchess County Community College, it is open to the public (hours are posted). Treat yourself to a rest amid the far-reaching southerly views across the river from the dock on the south side of the building and watch for harbor seals, which have been seen sunning themselves off the northern tip of Esopus Island.

Return to the stone bridge and go north on the road beyond the white trail, to an intersection. Go left at the blue/yellow trail junction, and in 50 feet go right on red markers, following the multi-use trail (also marked as a horse trail). Ascend gently through a young sugar-maple woods and cross the park road, continuing on the red trail through secluded woods. At the next road,

The Catskills' Indian Head Wilderness Area is seen beyond the Esopus Meadows Lighthouse.

which leads to the river gazebo you passed earlier, turn left and very soon after go right (north) on the blue-marked carriage path. The blue trail will take you past the Hoyt House and its reclaimed gardens, barn, and carriage house. This parcel of land on Dinsmore Point was given to the Mills' daughter, Geraldine, and her husband, Lydig Hoyt. The large cedars and runaway ornamental Norway spruce trees hint at what the place must have been like in the mid-1800s. To get a better idea, continue to the park road (Gardener's House Road) where you were earlier, turn right, and, leaving the gardener's house to your right, follow the green trail along the south side of the mansion grounds to the garden complex. To the north, a footpath crosses the lawn to the mansion, a gift shop, and offices, and leads back to your starting point.

DID YOU KNOW?
Darius Ogden Mills, Ogden Mills' father, found wealth in the California gold rush and became one of the richest men in the business. He bequeathed his fortune to his son Ogden, who married into the Livingston family. At one time the Livingstons owned more than a million acres in the Hudson Valley.

MORE INFORMATION
Guided tours of the Staatsburgh State Historic Site are available April 1 to October 31, Tuesday through Sunday, and on weekends during the winter. There are extended hours during the holiday season; www.staatsburgh.org; 845-889-8851.

NEARBY

The Franklin D. Roosevelt National Historic Site, located in Hyde Park, is open year-round (see Trip 21). This is the site of Springwood, FDR's estate, and the FDR Presidential Library and Museum; www.nps.gov/hofr/index.htm; 845-229-5320. The Eleanor Roosevelt National Historic Site, where her retreat, Val-Kill, was located, is also nearby. The "Roosevelt Ride," a shuttle service between these sites and the Vanderbilt Mansion, is available May to October.

SCENIC HUDSON

Scenic Hudson is the grandparent of all Hudson River environmental watchdog groups. The mission of this member-supported organization is to "protect and restore the Hudson River, its riverfront, and the majestic vistas and working landscapes beyond as an irreplaceable national treasure for America and a vital resource for residents and visitors." Scenic Hudson formed in 1963 to oppose electric company Con Edison's Storm King pumped storage project, which would have been the world's largest hydroelectric plant. The organization was successful and has since added to the inventory of publicly protected open space in the valley through an aggressive acquisition policy. Scenic Hudson's precedent-setting battle against Con Edison continues to serve as a model and cornerstone for federal environmental law.

Through a separately incorporated land trust and a sizable endowment, Scenic Hudson acquires and protects lands, and in many cases creates easements and marked trails providing public access to scenic properties adjacent to the Hudson River. Scenic Hudson also partnered with other organizations and townships to pioneer the creation of the Hudson River Valley Greenway. Many of the parks and preserves described or referenced in this book were created by, funded by, or formed in partnership with Scenic Hudson. Additionally, the organization spearheaded the campaign that led to the Hudson Valley being designated a National Heritage Area by the National Park Service (1996), and the Hudson River being named a National Heritage River (1998). These designations provide the Hudson Valley with a wider range of protection and more funding on a national level.

In addition to ongoing local advocacy and community development and improvement programs, Scenic Hudson promotes its smart growth principles in the river towns of Yonkers, Haverstraw, Hyde Park, and Beacon. Scenic Hudson is active on the state level as well, promoting energy plans and environmentally friendly technologies for power plants.

TRIP 19
POETS' WALK ROMANTIC
LANDSCAPE PARK

Location: Red Hook, NY
Rating: Easy
Distance: 2.0 miles
Elevation Gain: 200 feet
Estimated Time: 1.5 hours
Maps: USGS Kingston East; Scenic Hudson, Poets' Walk Romantic
Landscape Park Map (available on-site and online)

**A fun family river walk among open fields and stone walls with
rustic gazebos provides unforgettable views of the Catskills.**

DIRECTIONS

Take Exit 19 off the NYS Thruway (I-87) at Kingston; bear right out of the
toll pavilion and set your odometer to zero. Cross over the Thruway and bear
right onto NY 209, heading north toward the Kingston–Rhinecliff Bridge. At
5.5 miles, cross the bridge (toll), and as you enter Dutchess County, NY 209
becomes NY 199. From the center span of the bridge you will see the Rondout
Lighthouse a few miles to the south, on a small island off the western shore.
To the north, along the east shore are the marshes of Tivoli Bays. Closer to the
bridge and just beneath you as you approach the east shore are the fields of the
old Astor and Delano estates, the location of Poets' Walk. Take the first left off
the bridge onto River Road, which is also known as CR 103 (you're 7.8 miles
from the Thruway now), and at 8.5 miles, turn left into the Poets' Walk parking area. *GPS coordinates: 41° 58.902′ N, 73° 55.102′ W.*

TRAIL DESCRIPTION

This scenic park, located within a few minutes' drive of Tivoli, Red Hook, and
Rhinebeck villages, offers one of the prettiest, easiest walks in the valley. It is
regarded by many as the crown jewel of Scenic Hudson's open-space preservation efforts. At just over 2 miles round-trip, the walk can be done in an easy
hour by almost anybody. Plan to stay longer if you can, to ponder what Scenic
Hudson rightly calls the "breathtaking, unparalleled vistas" of the Hudson
Valley and the Catskill Mountains. The park has proven to be very popular
with locals, who visit the grounds and its rustic pavilions to cavort, picnic,
walk, write, paint, or simply relax and do nothing.

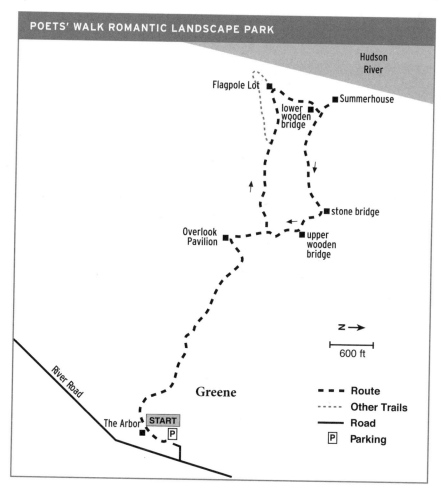

POETS' WALK ROMANTIC LANDSCAPE PARK

Hudson River

Flagpole Lot

Summerhouse

lower wooden bridge

stone bridge

Overlook Pavilion

upper wooden bridge

N →

600 ft

River Road

Greene

- - - Route
····· Other Trails
—— Road
P Parking

The Arbor START
P

Orient yourself at the information kiosk at the trailhead and get onto the path, heading west into open fields that are cloistered by mature hardwood forests. At the next rustic kiosk (the Arbor), there are interpretive notes and a box containing maps. Help yourself to a trail map and a copy of *Scenic Hudson's Adventure Guide to Parks, Preserves, and Trails.* Don't worry if the trail maps are gone; the trail is self-guiding and well posted (you can also print out a map from Scenic Hudson's website ahead of time). Continue along the gravel path.

The sunny fields of the park offer a warm western exposure. There are benches along the path as it winds in and out of the hardwoods over gentle terrain. The theme of the park—the Romantic "sublime," a notion that captured the imagination of the valley's early poets and writers—commemorates Washington Irving (1783–1859) and his friend/mentee, the Knickerbocker writer Fitz-Greene Halleck (1790–1867). The period takes its name from

This west-facing view shows the Kaaterskill Wild Forest.

Irving's fictitious character Diedrich Knickerbocker, the sobriquet under which Irving penned *A History of New York* and *Rip Van Winkle*. Also a satirist and a lesser-known poet, Halleck served as John Jacob Astor's personal secretary, a position that brought him to these grounds. It is unlikely that Irving frequented this same area.

At approximately 0.65 mile, you'll arrive at the Overlook Pavilion, an elegant rustic gazebo and the focal point of the park. Here you can sit back and enjoy views of the Catskills' eastern escarpment. The long wall of ridges and peaks that forms the northeast headlands reaches from Overlook Mountain (325 degrees) at the edge of the Indian Head Wilderness Area north past Kaaterskill High Peak and Round Top to the North Mountain Wild Forest. You see the Catskill High Peaks as well, from Peekamoose and Table in the south all the way through the Burroughs Range, including Slide (284 degrees), Wittenberg, and Cornell. Countless other peaks and low hills invite your curiosity and stir your romantic imagination.

Continue along, arriving at a signed trail junction. Go left (west, toward the river) and descend gently to the Flagpole Lot, where three rustic benches overlook the river. After a brief respite, proceed to the right and downhill, descending a flight of steps into the woods. Cross a tiny creek and ascend easily through a wooded glen, arriving at a T. Turn left to see the Summerhouse, a large cedar gazebo facing west. We can imagine artist Frederic Church having mixed feelings to learn that the cedar used in the structures at Poets' Walk came from Olana, his picturesque estate nearby. The trees in this wooded glen are junipers, or eastern red cedars. The Summerhouse is the most secluded space along the trail. Retrace your steps to the T and ascend easily into the east along the northern edge of the grounds, crossing a pretty stone bridge and another wooden one before arriving back at the trail junction below the Overlook Pavilion. From here, the trail retraces its steps to the parking area.

MORE INFORMATION

Dogs are allowed in the park but you must leash and clean up after them. Closing time varies by season; www.scenichudson.org; 845-473-4440.

NEARBY

The Vanderbilt Mansion National Historic Site in Hyde Park is a magnificent Gilded Age country place with formal gardens. The grounds are open daily year-round; the mansion is also open daily for guided tours; www.nps.gov.vama/index.htm; 845-229-9115 or 845-229-7770.

TRIP 20
OLANA

Location: Hudson, NY
Rating: Easy
Distance: 3.5 miles
Elevation Gain: 250 feet
Estimated Time: 3 hours
Maps: USGS Hudson South; Olana State Historic Site Trail Map

A stroll along the carriage paths surrounding Frederic Church's Persian-style castle winds through picturesque landscapes of pond, gardens, and woods created by this Hudson River School painter.

DIRECTIONS

From Exit 21 off the NYS Thruway (I-87) in Catskill, turn left onto NY 23B and set your odometer to zero. At 0.5 mile, turn left (east) after going under the NY 23 overpass and onto NY 23 itself, heading toward the Rip Van Winkle Bridge. At 2.2 miles, at the intersection of NY 23 and CR 385, go straight. (At this intersection, look diagonally across CR 385 to the right, or southeast, and you can see Thomas Cole's yellow house, Cedar Grove, which is open to the public. Built in 1815, it is where Cole resided from 1834 until his death at age 47.) As you cross the bridge, you can see Olana up on the hill ahead of you. At 3.8 miles, bear right (south) onto NY 9G. In just under a mile, turn left onto the Olana entrance road and travel uphill to the ticket booth. It is 1.0 mile from the entrance to the upper parking area next to Olana. *GPS coordinates: 42° 13.084′ N, 73° 49.743′ W.*

TRAIL DESCRIPTION

Primed by Frederic Church's predecessor and mentor Thomas Cole (and first-generation Hudson River School painters such as Asher Durand), the public received Church's debut full-length landscape, *Niagara* (1857), with celebratory awe. Exhibited "in the flesh," such paintings were the visual blockbusters of the times—nineteenth-century viewers went to see them just as today we go to a movie premiere. At its unveiling, *Niagara* was the only painting on display in New York's Corcoran Gallery. It sold for $12,500 in 1859, and the artist's growing prosperity enabled him to conceive, design, and build Olana on the rolling lands and dense forests that became his personal vision of the "living

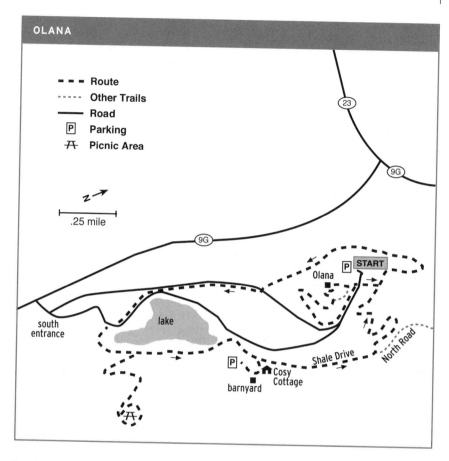

OLANA

- - - Route
----- Other Trails
—— Road
P Parking
Ⓣ Picnic Area

N →

.25 mile

23

9G

9G

P START

Olana

south
entrance

lake

P

barnyard

Cosy
Cottage

Shale Drive

North Road

Ⓣ

landscape." Today, the grounds of his Moorish-style castle are surrounded by a series of carriage paths and trails that were created by Church in the picturesque style of landscape design.

Olana's carriage paths provide only a few miles of trail suitable for walking and cross-country skiing—but what miles! Although the ornate house (one of very few intact artists' residences and workplaces in the country) attracts more than 30,000 people a year, the trails seem to get little use. Because they are fairly flat, they make for easy winter walks and ski tours. The trails can be muddy in springtime, when views of the river and the Catskill Mountains are at their best, though hardly as spectacular as in Church's day, when he "cut" the forest in order to create scenery to set against his favorite points around Olana.

From the parking lot, descend the large brick stairway. There's a visitor center on your right, and the trail loops begin to your left (north). Cross the entry road and go through a cedar gate to a T. There are trail markers on a tree at the T, but they may be the last ones you'll see. Reference the map and

Hikers can glimpse Olana, Frederic Church's picturesque Persian-style castle, from the scenic trail that winds throughout the grounds.

you won't have a problem. This is a wide, flat cinder path, ideal for families with children. Turn left onto Ridge Road. This road was Church's pride and joy—the (1878) route from which he showcased the Hudson Valley for his family and friends, and the vantage from which he painted *Autumn View from Olana*. At one time, the area before you was open fields, but the views are limited today. The path bends north and then south, traveling to the west of the house through evergreen forests with the Hudson on your right. Interpretive signs (with maps and helpful You Are Here stars) are along the entire carriageway system. On your right is an obstructed overlook with a sign illustrating a Church oil sketch from 1870, hardly representative of his earlier, more realistic Expansionist phase, because the artist's right arm had been rendered almost useless by rheumatism at this point. Church contented himself with using nature as his palette, creating scenes not with brush and canvas, but through the manipulation of the living landscape.

Continue, passing beneath the house through a sugar-maple/oak woods, ignoring an unmarked trail that descends to the right (north). Arriving at a gate on the approach road, turn right and descend. Views of the lake will be on your left; beyond, in the southeast foreground, are Blue Hill and extensive farmlands. Leave the ticket booth to your right and follow the road to the end of the lake. Take the Park and Lake carriageway; it isn't identified in the field, but you can't miss it. Bear left here and ascend slightly to a vantage point of the "castle" with an interpretive sign (a trail going off to the south here leads off the property). Proceed north along the lake, and within a few minutes arrive at a Y, with (unmarked) Crown Hill Road (1885) on the right. This spur path climbs very gently to a picnic table overlooking a cut view of the house and buildings. But the "historic" view doesn't seem worth the trees that were sacrificed—there is no shortage of house views on this property, and the cut area looks ragged and unnatural. Return to the Y. Proceed right to the lower lot and the barn complex, where a little picnic area leads to the quaint Cosy Cottage (Church's 1860–72 dwelling during the years of Olana's construction).

Leaving the cottage to your right, climb Shale Drive, which has become grassy, and look to the east at the extensive farmlands and woods of Claverack, Taghkanic, and Gallatin townships, with the Taconic hills in the tri-state area visible on a good day. This is perhaps the most interesting view from Olana, but it receives the least praise. The path enters the woods and arrives at a Y with the intersection of North Road, which leads, as you might expect, north—and off the property. It provides a bit more of a walk, but the hemlock trees Church praised so lavishly in his day are no more; storms in the 1970s and 1980s destroyed the remnant climax forest, and the resulting understory is second-growth hardwood, though with some fine specimens of oak.

From the Y, climb easily back to the first T and the upper parking lot.

DID YOU KNOW?

Frederic Edwin Church became a student of Thomas Cole at age 18, and became the world's best-known living artist between 1850 and 1860.

MORE INFORMATION

The grounds at Olana are open year-round. There is an entrance fee on weekends and holidays, April to October; www.olana.org; 518-828-0135.

NEARBY

The Firemen's Firefighting Museum in Hudson houses one of the largest collections of firefighting apparatus, equipment, gear, and memorabilia in the world. It is open year-round; www.fasnyfiremuseum.com; 877-347-3687. The city of Hudson is noted for its antique shops and fine restaurants.

TRIP 21
ROOSEVELT WOODS

Location: Hyde Park, NY
Rating: Moderate
Distance: 5.0 miles
Elevation Gain: 200 feet
Estimated Time: 2.5 hours
Maps: USGS Hyde Park; National Park Service, Hyde Park Trail

A shore-and-forest walk on easy carriage roads leads to points along the Hudson River, beginning at the museum, library, and home of Franklin D. Roosevelt.

DIRECTIONS

The Franklin Delano Roosevelt National Historic Site is located on the west side of US 9 in Hyde Park. Drive into the main entrance on FDR Drive, heading straight back to the visitor parking area past National Park Service headquarters. *GPS coordinates:* 41° 46.223′ N, 73° 56.077′ W.

By bus, take Coach USA from Port Authority to FDR Home (call 201-263-1254).

TRAIL DESCRIPTION

The beautiful trails of Roosevelt Woods, lying within the heavily wooded estate of the Franklin D. Roosevelt Home, Library, and Museum complex, are patrolled and maintained by the National Park Service (NPS). On this hike you are introduced to each loop in the woods (the Cove, Forest, and Meadow trails), with a short side trip to Crum Elbow Point on the Hudson River's banks.

These trails are unlike many of the foot trails you may be familiar with in the valley; they are wide, well marked, and immaculately maintained "carriageways." Today, they are footpaths only (bicycles are not allowed). Because the elevation change is minimal and the trails are generally flat and wide, this is a walker's paradise, leading you through parklike woods in a peaceful, wild setting with views of the Hudson. These paths are ideal for children and seniors.

The Roosevelt Woods trail system is a part of the Hyde Park Trail (HPT), a cooperative effort among several organizations, including the NPS, the town of Hyde Park, Scenic Hudson, Winnakee Land Trust, and several private landowners. With the exception of the trail to Val Kill, it is a model trail system under continued development with the help of the Hudson River Greenway.

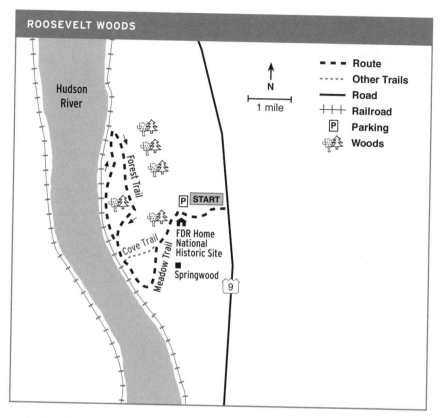

Before heading into the woods, take a look at the visitor center and request a trail map. Curiously, the map (Hyde Park Trail) provided by the NPS is far from ideal for navigation on the trails, but it does provide a helpful overview of the area. Trails are accurately designated and well marked, however, so there's little chance of getting lost or even disoriented. The Hyde Park Trail is a long, linear trail which is still being developed. You will be walking only a short section of it here.

Begin your hike on the paved walkway to the south of the visitor center that runs next to the museum, a long, fortresslike, hand-laid stone building. A small sign near a cluster of Norway spruce trees indicates the Hyde Park Trail to your right. From here you are led a short distance to the trailhead, where there's a signboard and map with information. Follow the paved path downhill. It soon turns to dirt at the point where you'll follow the Meadow Trail south, while the Hyde Park, Cove, and Forest trails go straight ahead.

Immediately you will note the fine, mature forests of red oak, hemlock, poplar, hickory, and sycamore, most of them planted and managed by Roosevelt and his father, who imported many varieties from Europe to beautify the grounds of Springwood. Roosevelt continued his boyhood interest in forestry,

Springwood, Franklin Delano Roosevelt's birthplace, is shown from one of the beautiful trails of Roosevelt Woods.

making it a matter of national interest when he later formed the Civilian Conservation Corps (CCC). Many of the regional plantations we enjoy today—and the trails that run through them (such as those of the Catskills)—were CCC projects. You'll pass a pond and a seasonal waterfall to your right as you descend through a shady glen.

Bear right at the first trail junction, where the Cove Trail goes left (south). Now you're on the Forest Trail. The HPT goes north, beyond the NPS boundary, to the Vanderbilt Mansion (signed at 2.4 miles from this junction), but that is a trip for another day. Unfortunately, the HPT follows paved roads for some distance once it leaves these woods, and you may not find it appealing. Continue, passing the return loop of the Forest Trail on your right (you'll emerge from that trail later). Within 15 minutes or so, you will arrive at a junction where the Forest Trail departs to the right. Bear left here, remaining on the HPT. This is the NPS boundary. Bear left, and within a few hundred yards, bear left again. This will take you across the Metro-North train tracks on a trestle bridge, directly to the river's edge at Crum Elbow Point. There's a large, bright navigation day-marker here to help ships make their way up the channel. You'll have close-up views of tankers and tug barges, most of them carrying oil to the Port of Albany. This is a fine spot to sit on the grassy point and while away the day, and aside from the estate grounds, is the best place to have a picnic.

Retrace your steps to the junction of the HPT and the Forest Trail. Follow left onto the latter as you curve around into the north and east along the park boundary. Following a knoll of red pines on the north side of the trail, bear right once again onto the Forest Trail, walk amid stately hemlocks and very tall white pines, and join the HPT, bearing left now. Walk back to the Cove Trail junction and follow the Cove (and Meadow) Trail to the right (south). The Meadow Trail continues south, while the Cove Trail goes west (right). This very short (0.2-mile) spur trail takes you along the fringes of a pretty, tidal cattail marsh and dead-ends at the railroad tracks. The large building you see on a hill to the south is the Culinary Institute of America. More interesting yet are the bright yellow blooms of marsh marigold you see everywhere in early spring, their flowers submerged by the incoming tide.

Now retrace your steps to the Meadow Trail, bear right, cross the stream on a wooden bridge, and enter a hemlock wood. The trail turns east soon, and then north along the edge of a broad meadow where Springwood comes into view. You are soon back at the first junction, where you turn right to the trailhead and estate grounds. Take a few moments to look at Springwood and the magnificent, soft hues of the Hudson's hills, and walk through the rose garden and the Roosevelt gravesite. Treat yourself to a look at the sculpture of two figures, cut from the thick concrete of the Berlin Wall and fashioned into art by Winston Churchill's great-granddaughter, Edwina Sandys. Follow your way back through the grounds to the parking area to complete the walk.

DID YOU KNOW?

One of the most popular programs of the New Deal was the Civilian Conservation Corps (CCC), Roosevelt's personal favorite. The program employed more than 250,000 young men nationwide. (See page 137.)

MORE INFORMATION

You can enter the grounds and visitor center year-round, free of charge; however, there's a fee for the museum, library, and house tours. Dogs must be leashed at all times. For more information, visit www.hydeparkny.us/Recreation/Trails/TrailsRooseveltWoods.html or www.nps.gov/hofr.

NEARBY

The Culinary Institute of America, billed as the world's premier culinary college, is located in Hyde Park. Visitors can choose from five restaurants at the institute; reservations are recommended. Public tours are also offered; www.ciachef.edu/visitors/hp/; 845-471-6608.

TRIP 22
CRANBERRY LAKE PRESERVE

Location: North White Plains, NY
Rating: Easy
Distance: 2.0 miles
Elevation Gain: 200 Feet
Estimated Time: 2 Hours
Maps: Cranberry Lake Preserve Map, Westchester County Parks

This easy and interesting outing through bogs and wetlands is ideal for children and bird-watchers.

DIRECTIONS
Take Exit 6 off I-287. Follow NY 22 toward North White Plains/White Plains, and bear left onto NY 22 North. Stay alert as you pass the Kensico Reservoir on your left (you may wish to visit the site after the hike), and turn right onto Old Orchard Road. Drive a couple of hundred feet and turn right at the Cranberry Lake Preserve entrance. Continue 0.3 mile to the Nature Center and trailhead parking area. *GPS coordinates:* 41° 04.919′ N, 73° 45.360′ W.

TRAIL DESCRIPTION
This is a delightful and diverse short walk tucked amid the protected watershed lands of the Kensico Reservoir, which lies to the east of the preserve. Only a loop trail is described here, though considerably more distance is available in the preserve's modest but wild 165-acre parcel of oak/hickory forest and wetland habitats. Because distances are minimal and elevation gain is not great, this is an ideal outing for young children or those who need an easy introduction to hiking. The preserve also offers interpretive programs, which are led by trained environmental educators and are available to school, scouting, and community groups year-round. You will be impressed by the preserve's attractive nature center and by the friendly, on-site staff who answer your questions and provide you with program and interpretive materials.

This hike begins at the Nature Lodge. Have a look around the lodge and help yourself to a park map at the trailhead kiosk. Be advised that there is a complex matrix of trails here, and many have been re-marked in recent years, which may at times prove confusing. This is common with smaller preserves, which make an effort to display as many topographic features and wildlife

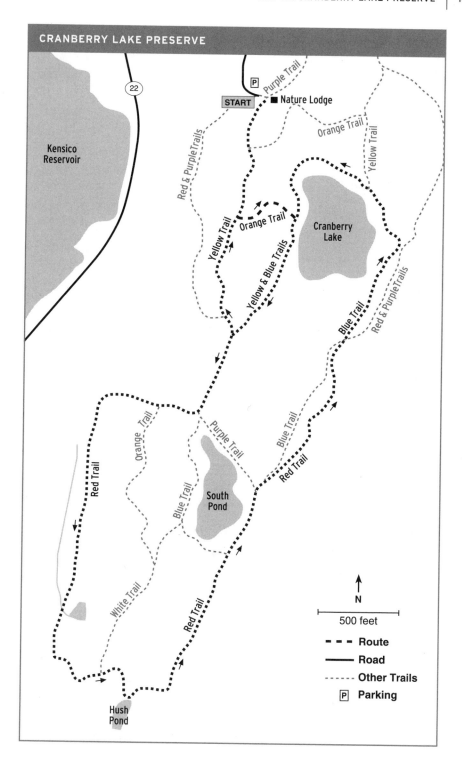

CRANBERRY LAKE PRESERVE

22

Kensico
Reservoir

P

START

Nature Lodge

Purple Trail

Orange Trail

Yellow Trail

Red & Purple Trails

Yellow Trail

Orange Trail

Yellow & Blue Trails

Cranberry
Lake

Blue Trail

Red & Purple Trails

Orange Trail

Purple Trail

Blue Trail

Blue Trail

Red Trail

South
Pond

Red Trail

White Trail

Red Trail

Hush
Pond

N

500 feet

- - - Route

——— Road

· · · · · Other Trails

P Parking

The wetlands of Cranberry Lake are popular with bird-watchers.

habitats as possible. The route of this hike has been chosen to minimize guess-work. Though the trail system's marking may become daunting, you can rely upon the map.

Leaving the Nature Lodge to your left, follow the Yellow Loop Trail in a southerly direction. Large oaks shade the wide gravel trail. Walk for 5 minutes until you see a blue sign that says Lake. Turn left onto the Orange Trail here, follow it to the Blue Loop Trail, and turn right. After following Cranberry

Lake for a while, the trail climbs some low ledges on the left, close to the lake. Crossing a small bridge, you'll arrive at a junction. Follow the Blue and Red Loop trails at this point. Ahead, bear left on the Orange Trail and cross the bog at Bent Bridge. The trail continues through an old settlement area where there is a sparse hemlock grove. This is the site of the Stone Chamber, an old root cellar to the left of the trail. At a T intersection at the end of the Orange Trail, turn right onto the wide Purple Loop (you may also see green paint). You may also see a purple circle with the number 10 on it. At the next junction, follow the Red Loop Trail to the left. Avoid any other turns now as you follow an old stone wall on your right. You are walking uphill slightly, and beech trees appear. Avoid the Orange Trail to your left, continuing on the Red Loop Trail. The wall continues on your right, improving in quality as you progress. At the end of the wall stands a large tulip poplar. Continue on the Red Loop Trail and soon you will notice a residential area some distance to your right. Avoid the White Trail to the left. Your trail heads back into the heart of the preserve at this point, walking the eastern margins of a bog.

As you approach South Pond, note that the Blue Trail leads across its southern edge. Follow the Blue Loop Trail a short distance to the Bird Tower, an elevated observation platform looking north over the pond. The adjacent boardwalk is a good place to watch for butterflies and frogs. As you continue on the Red Trail, you will also see green, blue, and red squares. To the right are some low, vertical ledges. The trail is wide and flat. Against the ledge in one spot is an old concrete façade. This was the site of a stonecutter's shed, where large stones were mined and transported to the Kensico Dam (completed in 1917). Small stones found their way to the crushers and were ground into gravel. To learn more about the subject, ask for the *Cranberry Lake History Trail* brochure.

At a point where you come upon a bench (this location is called the Cascade, where water flows over a small ledge), the Purple Trail departs to the right toward a quarry. This, along with many other quarries in the vicinity, supplied most of the stone and gravel for the construction of the Kensico Dam. If you wish to add an interesting diversion to your hike, visit the quarry as well. (A few steep grades are involved.)

Cross the little creek by the bench and proceed on the Blue Trail now (the Red Trail goes into the quarry). The Blue Trail is heavily grown-in for a spell, but soon opens up. The lake is to your left, but you can't see it at this point because of the heavy vegetation. Rhododendrons are profuse. The trail becomes rocky and rooty underfoot. Large tulip trees appear. At a point where Red and Purple join in on the right, bear left onto a boardwalk, now following blue, red, and purple markings. Within a few hundred feet, the Purple Trail and Red Trail depart to the right again. Bear left, following the lakeshore now. Remain on Blue, though you may see some green paint blazes along the way. The retreating Wisconsin ice sheet formed Cranberry Lake about 18,000 years ago. It is named for the cranberry bogs that are most abundant on its southern shore.

Walk along the edge of a rock outcropping with the lake to your left, passing a commemorative bench on the right, courtesy of Scout Troop 73. The Red and Purple loops join in on the right as you continue left on the Blue Loop. Now you descend to lake level, walking through a forest of huge tulip poplars where some maturing beech trees also appear. The Yellow Trail comes in from the right. Crossing a boardwalk among the ferns and the tulip trees, you are now following blue and yellow markers. Soon you walk directly along the water's edge. Pass the White Trail to your right, continuing to the Orange Trail, where you will turn right. Follow this a short distance uphill and bear right at a Y, crossing some puncheons, to regain the Yellow Trail and, bearing right, return to your point of origin.

DID YOU KNOW?

Butterflies smell with their feet, taste with their antennae, cannot bite or chew, make no sounds, and (except for one species) cannot hear. They are the second-largest group of pollinators, after bees.

MORE INFORMATION

The preserve is open 9 A.M. to 4 P.M. (if you arrive later, you can walk the Red Loop Trail to the Nature Center from the small parking area just outside the gate); www.parks.westchestergov.com/index.php; 914-428-1005.

NEARBY

Several interesting attractions are located in the area, including Lyndhurst, the Gothic revival country estate of railroad magnate Jay Gould, in Tarrytown; the Jay Heritage Center, the boyhood home of founding father John Jay, in Rye; the Donald M. Kendall Sculpture Gardens at Pepsico headquarters in Purchase; and the Caramoor Center for Music and the Arts in Katonah.

4

THE SOUTHERN TACONICS

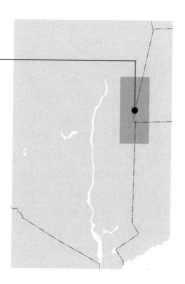

THE NATURE CONSERVANCY HAS NAMED the South Taconic Range of New York, Connecticut, and Massachusetts one of Earth's Last Great Places because it is among the largest and healthiest contiguous forests in the Lower New England Ecoregion (Maine to Virginia). It is also considered one of the most diverse forests in southern New England, supporting rare natural communities like the scrub oak and pitch-pine woods found on cliff and talus slopes, as well as the rare species that inhabit them, such as Gerhard's underwing moth and the purple clematis. Both the North and South Taconic ranges are heavily forested with northern hardwood species and dense hemlock woods in wet ravines.

The Taconics get their name from the ancient continental collision known as the Taconic orogeny, or mountain-building process. Formed near the location of today's Costa Rica, the Taconic Island chain moved northward to collide with Proto North America about 470 million years ago. This event marked the beginning of a mountain-building episode that lasted for 35 million years and stretched from the Canadian Maritime provinces to North Carolina. (The Taconic orogeny was distinct from the east- and north-advancing Acadian orogeny that created the Northern Appalachian Mountains.) At the time, the Iapetus Ocean covered most of North America. Achieving an elevation of about 4 miles, the Taconics were eroded during the Mesozoic and Cenozoic eras, and in the Quaternary Period, the mile-high glaciers of the Great Ice Age finished the billion-year process by sculpting the Taconic landscape we see today. These two distinct ranges define the Taconic Mountains from Williamstown, Massachusetts, to the borders of New York and Connecticut.

Protection of the Taconics began around 1920 with the acquisition of lands that eventually became Taconic State Park on the New York side of the range, the Mount Washington State Forest and Bash Bish Falls State Park in Massachusetts, and the Mount Riga State Park in Connecticut.

The Southern Taconics is a 36,000-acre mountain range that is bounded in the north by Hillsdale, New York, and South Egremont, Massachusetts, and in the south by Millerton, New York, and Lakeville, Connecticut. The plateau's highest peak is Mount Everett (2,602 feet), and the average elevation of the ridge is 2,000 feet above the surrounding valley, or 2,700 feet above sea level. Two major trails cross the Southern Taconic Plateau. The Appalachian Trail enters the ridge in the south, at Salisbury, Connecticut, and follows its eastern edge along the Housatonic watershed, crossing Bear Mountain, Mount Race, and Mount Everett before leaving the range in Egremont. On the west side of the range is the South Taconic Trail (STT), a 15-mile scenic ridge trail with its southern trailhead in the town of Northeast, New York. The STT traverses South Brace Mountain, Brace Mountain (passing west of Mount Frissell and the highest point in Connecticut), Alander Mountain, and Bash Bish Falls before descending to Taconic State Park and continuing north to Mount Fray and Hillsdale. Several trails join the ridge from the east and west sides, providing a number of access options.

MORE INFORMATION

For more information about the Southern Taconics, contact the following organizations:

Rensselaer Land Conservancy, www.rtlc.org.

Berkshire Natural Resources Council (South Taconic Range and Greylock maps), 20 Bank Row, Pittsfield, MA, 01201; 413-499-0596; www.bnrc.net.

New York State Office of Parks, Recreation and Historic Preservation/Taconic Region, P.O. Box 308, Staatsburg, NY, 12580; 845-889-4100; www.nysparks.state.ny.us.

For inquiries about Northwest Camp, contact the Appalachian Mountain Club, Connecticut Chapter, www.ct-amc.org.

TRIP 23
BRACE MOUNTAIN

Location: Ancram, NY
Rating: Moderate
Distance: 3.8 miles
Elevation Gain: 1,300 feet
Estimated Time: 4 hours
Maps: USGS Copake; Berkshire Natural Resources Council, South Taconic Range; NY–NJTC South Taconic Trails

A short, very steep climb followed by a ridge walk across the scenic Southern Taconic Plateau features valley and mountain views.

DIRECTIONS

From Millerton, New York, follow NY 22 for 5.4 miles to Whitehouse Crossing Road and turn right. At 6.1 miles, turn left on CR 63. At just under 0.2 mile, turn right onto Deer Run Road, then left onto Quarry Hill Road. Go an additional 0.5 mile and look for the small (obscure) trailhead parking area on the left. A sign identifies the Taconic State Park Brace Mountain Area. *GPS coordinates: 42° 1.940′ N, 73° 30.286′ W.*

TRAIL DESCRIPTION

Brace Mountain (2,311 feet) and its sister peak, South Brace (2,304 feet), are the southernmost trailed peaks in Taconic State Park. This is the tri-state highlands area of New York, Massachusetts, and Connecticut (nearby Mount Frissell, at 3,453 feet, is Connecticut's highest point), the watershed divide of the Hudson and Housatonic rivers. Climb Brace on a very clear day, when the exceptional views include points from Mount Greylock and northwest through the Helderbergs and the Catskills, south along the Shawangunks, and as far away as the Hudson Highlands.

Like most of the western approaches to the Taconic Plateau, the South Taconic Trail is steep, and because of its rocks and ledges, this trail is not recommended under icy conditions. Though steep, the climb is short and you'll reach ridge elevation of 1,800 feet from the trailhead elevation of 1,000 feet in about one hour.

Begin hiking along an open field, following the white-blazed trail. These blazes (and ridge cairns) may be the only trail identification you'll see—signage,

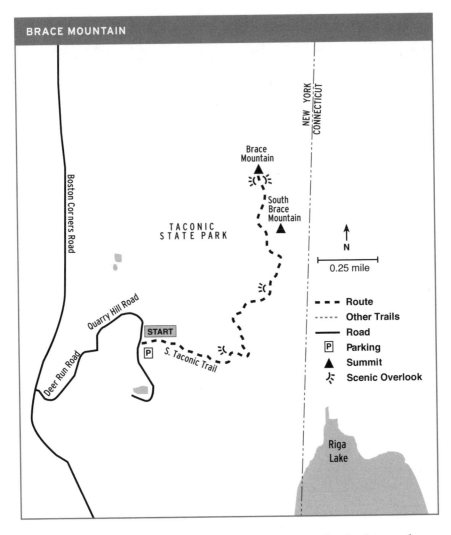

BRACE MOUNTAIN

Brace
Mountain

South
Brace
Mountain

TACONIC
STATE PARK

NEW YORK
CONNECTICUT

Boston Corners Road

Quarry Hill Road

START

P | S. Taconic Trail

Deer Run Road

Riga
Lake

N

0.25 mile

- - - Route
- - - - Other Trails
——— Road
P Parking
▲ Summit
Scenic Overlook

typically sparse in the Southern Taconics, is scarce here. The climb is gentle until, at 1,200 feet in elevation, a shallow gorge appears to the right. Now the trail
climbs steeply through magnificent red-oak woods, following the scoured and
exposed boulders of this once much larger stream course. As the trail steepens,
you'll encounter a high-angled cascade of about 60 feet. Now the trail veers
north, away from the falls, and requires an all-fours approach for the next 10
minutes as you vault your way upward through ledges with increasing views
west and southwest. The trail relaxes at 1,700 feet, and arrives at a flat spot on
the ridge, where you turn left. This was the junction with the red-blazed trail to
the high ledges of New Point, which you can see just to the south, but the blazes
have disappeared and the trail has vanished. You can still follow the vague
footpath to the right a little way to take a look at a fairy glen, where a tiny falls

creates a clear pool beneath a small, thick hemlock stand. Hunters have left fire rings and evidence of makeshift bivouacs here.

The South Taconic Trail heads north now and is well marked with white blazes. You face some additional climbing, but it is spread out as the trail walks level for a while along the western ridge, then climbs through oak woods and scattered laurels. Soon you will cross a small, grassy slab with sweeping views south over Riga Lake and South Pond. Climb a bit farther and you'll arrive on South Brace, its summit identified by a cairn. Here, your views to the west develop into a wider panorama of the Hudson Valley, while you begin to see more in the east as well, including Mount Frissell, Round Mountain (2,298 feet), Gridley Mountain, and Bear Mountain. On the other side of that ridge, the Appalachian Trail corridor runs up over Lion's Head and Bear Mountain, and through Sage's Ravine to cross Mount Everett. From here you can see the burnished open balds of Brace. As the trail makes its way north again around the scenic, windy western side of South Brace, it dips down into a sheltered saddle, then climbs gradually up the south slopes of Brace. The summit is identified by a more impressive rock pile than on South Brace. This broad, open, grassy summit looks directly at Mount Frissell and across nearby Alander Mountain to the north, in Massachusetts. Hidden behind Mount Frissell is Mount Everett, but lying in the northeast like an inverted molar is the unmistakable Mount Greylock (Massachusetts' highest peak at 3,491 feet), pale gray in the haze, with Mount Prospect forming the left part of the tooth.

The viewshed is spectacular and complex, and in order to fully identify surrounding mountain ranges and river valleys you will need USGS metric topographical maps in the 1:100,000 scale. The westerly Catskills skyline is the most comprehensive, including most of the prominent peaks from the Blackhead range to the southern Sundown Wild Forest area. A dizzying complex of mountains and unnamed peaks dissolves across Berkshire County in the direction of Great Barrington and Lee and away to the north-northeast. The north-northwest flatlands rise imperceptibly to the low Helderbergs, and to the east across Litchfield County you can see Housatonic State Forest and the bumpy hills of Canaan. No matter what point of the compass you sit and face, you will enjoy extensive open space.

At one time, this hike could have been fashioned into a loop using the blue-blazed trail to Riga Lake and an informal trail back to the South Taconic Trail. However, private lands to the west prevent this. Several of the maps still in use for this area are no longer accurate, so be careful. For example, note that the blue-blazed trail from South Beacon to Lake Riga has been erased, covered with tree paint and posted by the Mount Riga Corporation.

Return by the route you came.

The northern Catskills can be seen from the westerly ridges of Brace Mountain.

DID YOU KNOW?

Charcoal makers who supplied the iron furnaces and manufacturing needs of the Revolutionary War effort denuded the countryside around Mount Riga. The Riga blast furnace, the last such furnace in Connecticut, stands at the southeast corner of South Pond, north of Mount Riga. It supplied raw product for the ironworks in nearby Lakeville, Connecticut, that were owned in part by Revolutionary War leader Ethan Allen. When large steelmakers began to use bituminous coal for smelting ore, the charcoal industry disappeared and the Southern Taconics began their slow process of reforestation.

MORE INFORMATION

To get a good feel for the spectacular Southern Taconic Range, take a drive north along Mount Riga Road from Salisbury, Connecticut, to Mount Washington Road and the Mount Washington State Forest area, where you can camp for free, though you have to hike in. (The headquarters has relocated, but the area is maintained by the state. You can get maps here at the kiosk north of the maintenance building.) The Connecticut Chapter of the Appalachian Mountain Club maintains a rustic camp (Northwest Camp) on its property just west of the Appalachian trail on the Massachusetts–Connecticut line, making for an ideal alternate staging point for climbing Brace from the east. For more information on Taconic State Park, call 518-329-3993 or visit www. nysparks.state.ny.us/parks/83/details.aspx.

NEARBY

The Norman Rockwell Museum in Stockbridge, Massachusetts, is dedicated to the enjoyment and study of Rockwell's art and contributions to popular culture. The collection includes more than 500 of his original paintings and drawings. The museum is open daily year-round; www.nrm.org; 413-298-4100. Stockbridge also has many antique shops and galleries.

THE APPALACHIAN TRAIL

Conceived in 1921 and completed in 1937, the Appalachian Trail (AT) is a 2,167-mile, National Park Service–protected trail corridor stretching from Springer Mountain in Georgia to Maine's Katahdin, passing through fourteen states.

The first section of the AT was built in Bear Mountain State Park in an effort led by Major William A. Welch, the general manager of the Palisades Interstate Park from 1912 to 1940 (hikers to Bear Mountain will use the Major Welch Trail). He was the first chairman of the Appalachian Trail Conference and designed the AT logo. Hikers will see few if any of the original logos marking the trail; however, the AT is marked with its standard rectangular white paint blazes.

Hikers bound for Bear Mountain and Anthony's Nose will use sections of the AT and stand a good chance of meeting a thru-hiker, who has walked nearly 1,400 miles to reach Bear Mountain. The trail is most often hiked from south to north, beginning in April and taking about six months to complete. Using the south-to-north approach, a hiker who begins in Georgia amid freezing temperatures and heavy snow will be walking toward spring. The Appalachian Trail Conference oversees the trail, and a partner group, the Appalachian Long Distance Hikers Association, promotes the trail. Visit its website at www.aldha.org.

TRIP 24
ALANDER MOUNTAIN

Location: Mount Washington, MA
Rating: Moderate
Distance: 8.0 miles
Elevation Gain: 600 feet
Estimated Time: 6 hours
Maps: USGS Copake; Berkshire Natural Resources Council, South Taconic Range; NY–NJTC South Taconic Trails

A gradual climb to the central Taconic Ridge combines views east over the Hudson Valley and the Catskills with free camping.

DIRECTIONS

From the hamlet of Copake Falls, east off NY 22 (13 miles north of Millerton and 20.5 miles south of Exit B3 off I-90), set your odometer to zero. Take NY 344 east 0.3 mile to Taconic State Park and continue uphill past Bash Bish Falls, into Massachusetts. At 3.2 miles, bear right onto West Street. Turn right onto Cross Road at 4.3 miles and follow to its end on East Street at 5.3 miles. Bear right and go 0.2 mile to Mount Washington State Forest headquarters. Turn right into the entrance and park next to the maintenance building at the trailhead. *GPS coordinates: 42° 05.181′ N, 73° 27.726′ W.*

TRAIL DESCRIPTION

Alander Mountain forms the watershed divide between the Hudson and Housatonic rivers, along the high scenic borderlands of Massachusetts and New York. Although at 2,250 feet it may not seem a formidable peak, its position in the Taconic Range allows for generous views westward, giving it the look and feel of a much bigger mountain. Be aware that the open balds and rocky, unprotected ridge trails are subject to rapid changes in the weather. This increased exposure should be considered as carefully here as in any upper-elevation setting. Be prepared with water, food, warm clothes, and rain gear.

The Taconic Ridge is very popular with backpackers, among them hiking groups from the Appalachian Mountain Club (AMC), many of whom begin at the Mount Washington State Forest trailhead. There are several reasons for approaching Alander Mountain (or any point on the ridge) from the east, in Massachusetts. First, you get to choose from several trailheads, all of them

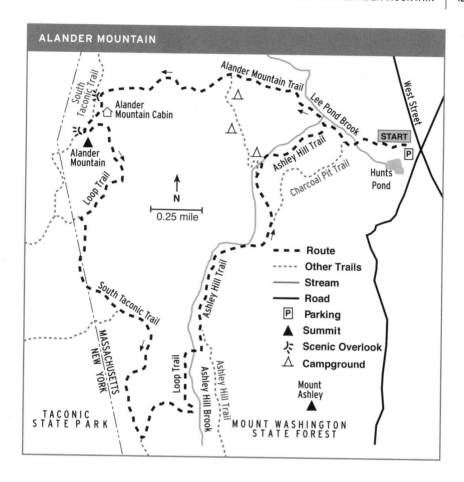

beginning at considerably higher elevations than the single western trailhead in New York State off Mountain Road (750 feet). In contrast, the Alander Mountain trailhead, in Massachusetts' Mount Washington State Forest, begins from the middle of the Taconic Ridge at 1,700 feet, so right away, you've saved considerable climbing. The time you would have spent ascending is time you can spend on the ridge. Consider the other advantages: Camping (walk-in) is permitted free of charge in Mount Washington State Forest. You can plan a side trip after your overnight to the Sage's Ravine primitive camp on the Appalachian Trail or take a quick walk up to Guilder Pond in the Mount Everett State Reservation. And you can drive the fascinating, lonely backroads of the Mount Riga area—as wild as it gets in the tri-state area of New York, Massachusetts, and Connecticut. But the best part is that with some planning and preparation you can stage from rustic Northwest Camp of AMC's Connecticut Chapter off East Street, 2.3 miles south of the trailhead. Seldom will you see a cabin as appealing as this one. (There is also a cabin near Alander's summit that is open all year and is available to hikers on a first-come, first-served basis. It has sleeping platforms that comfortably hold six hikers, plus a woodstove.)

Begin at the state forest headquarters. The trail departs just north of the maintenance buildings. There's a kiosk with handout maps, but they are not reliable for way-finding or navigation. Head west into open bluet fields, threading your way in and out of the woods on the blue-blazed Alander Mountain Trail. The trail is well defined and frequently traveled. Marking is good. Pass the Charcoal Pit Trail and then the Ashley Hill Trail on your left as you walk in proximity to enchanting Ashley Hill Brook. Cross the brook at an idyllic spot on a hand-hewn stringer bridge, and climb easily into a patch of hemlock trees where a sign indicates the primitive camping area at 0.5 mile. The trail assumes the character of a garden path as it passes a blue-blazed connector trail leading to the primitive camping area. Continue straight ahead, remaining on the Alander Mountain Trail. Spring-blooming wildflowers appear in profusion—common blue violets, downy yellow violets, and, notably, the critically imperiled, Audubon Blue-Listed (the early warning list for population or range reduced North American species) milkwort known as fringed polygala, or gaywings. Its little orchidlike purple bloom looks like a tiny airplane, complete with propeller.

Climbing to a point next to a small brook, you may notice a tin strip on a tree, perforated with the statement Last Water In Dry Period. The trail turns hard right (keep your eye on the blue markers) and climbs more steadily now. At the appearance of the cabin—remaining from the days when Alander had a fire tower—you arrive in a shallow saddle cleaving Alander's ridge.

Continue on blue markers to the four-way intersection with the white-blazed South Taconic Trail (STT), which goes west. Don't take it, but bear left on the blue Alander Loop Trail and cross the true summit and the subsequent open ridge rock of Alander. Views to the west are far-reaching, including the Catskills from north to south, Stissing Mountain, the Hudson Valley lowlands, and points southwest. Variations of this view continue as you make your way south in a setting not unlike the Scottish Highlands.

Dropping down off the ridge into a col, the trail makes a sharp right turn, descending briefly west before turning south again below the ridge to join the white-blazed STT. Bear left on the STT at a place identified by a weathered, unofficial sign that says Gentz's Corner and climb easily and steadily thereafter on an old grassy tote road that led to a bygone farmstead. The atmosphere is airy and remote; the forest floor is covered in ferns. The trail takes you around the west side of a hill and gradually up to ridge elevation again (avoid the unmarked trail to the left), where fine views appear from a solitary rock. As you descend this ridge, watch carefully to your left; take the blue trail that departs northeast over a small rise and then descends. As you hike through the upper elevations of the Ashley Hill Brook headwaters, join the Ashley Hill Trail as the terrain levels out. After 20 minutes or so, leave the Charcoal Pit Trail to your right (without the trail sign you'd miss it), and continue on the Ashley Hill Trail, where you turn right (east). You may be surprised to see a latrine here. It serves the primitive campsites below, along the creek. If you look down the hill across from the outhouse, you'll see a fire ring on the creek's edge. Follow the level Ashley Hill Trail along the lip of a magnificent, steep hemlock ravine. This will bring you to the junction of the Alander Mountain Trail, which you'll recognize. Bear right and follow the trail back to the parking area.

MORE INFORMATION

The Mount Washington State Forest is open year-round, sunrise to sunset; access is free; www.mass.gov/dcr/parks/western/mwas.htm; 413-528-0330.

NEARBY

More than 3,000 species and varieties of plants can be viewed at the 15-acre Berkshire Botanical Gardens at the junction of Routes 102 and 183 in Stockbridge, Massachusetts. The public display gardens are open May 1 through Columbus Day; www.berkshirebotanical.org; 413-298-3926.

TRIP 25
BASH BISH MOUNTAIN

Location: Mount Washington, MA
Rating: Moderate
Distance: 3.0 miles
Elevation Gain: 1,200 feet
Estimated Time: 3 hours
Maps: USGS Copake; Berkshire Natural Resources Council, South Taconic Range; NY–NJTC South Taconic Trails

This trail is rugged, rocky, and steep, with a stream crossing and a spur trail to Bash Bish Falls.

DIRECTIONS

From the hamlet of Copake Falls, east off NY 22 (13 miles north of Millerton and 20.5 miles south of Exit B3 off I-90), set your odometer to zero. Take NY 344 east 0.3 mile to Taconic State Park and continue a short distance past the park entrance to the Bash Bish Area parking lot on the right. Cross the creek on the cabin access road. *GPS coordinates:* 42° 07.026′ N, 73° 30.461′ W.

TRAIL DESCRIPTION

One of the most picturesque and desirable wilderness destinations of the nineteenth century, Bash Bish Falls, its gorge, and the sky-clear Bash Bish Brook remain very popular today. Although only a small percentage of the falls' visitors hike the loop using the South Taconic Trail (STT) and the Blue Trail, this hike is the best way to get a complete feel for this unusually rugged and special place.

This hike is a loop that begins and ends at the Bash Bish Area parking lot on Bash Bish Mountain Road (NY 344). Before heading out, read the historical information at the kiosk in the parking area, where there is a comprehensive map. Adjacent to the parking area and just out of sight on the other side of Bash Bish Brook, the Taconic State Park Commission maintains a number of rustic cabins. From the parking area, follow the cabin access road, cross the bridge, and walk along the south side of Bash Bish Brook among several large Norway spruces until you see the first cabin. Watch carefully to the right, where the white-blazed South Taconic Trail appears next to the cabin; follow this trail. Signs indicate Bash Bish Mountain at 2.0 miles. Immediately, the trail ascends, following a small brook through a hemlock forest. The trail switches

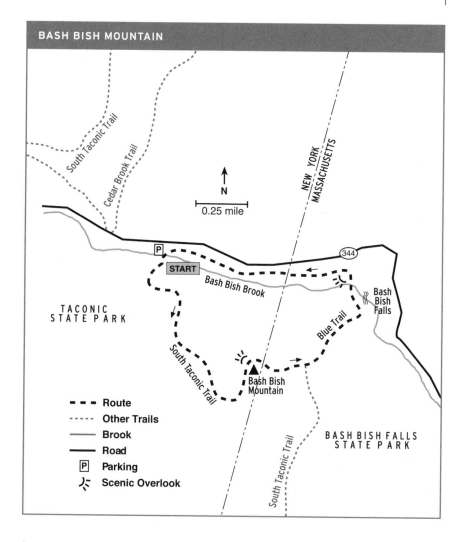

BASH BISH MOUNTAIN

back a few times as it climbs the steep northwest shoulder of the mountain through northern hardwood forests.

Just under a mile into the hike, at 1,500 feet in elevation, look for a faint, blue-blazed spur to the left (northwest) of the STT. This is easy to miss and you'll be given few clues. (At the head of the spur, the trail flattens out only slightly before turning east and climbing again.) You've ascended nearly 900 feet at this point and will welcome a break. Follow the spur downhill slightly to a small rocky lookout, where you look straight down into a bowl of pastoral land between Washburn Mountain (1,642 feet) and the ridge you're standing on. You see nearly the entire Catskills Range, from Windham High Peak in the northwest, along the Escarpment north to south, and beyond Overlook

Mountain into the Burroughs Range (Slide, Wittenberg, and Cornell) and farther south. If you continue a little farther on the blue-blazed spur, you'll discover a pitch-pine outcropping where a limited exposure to the north allows a taunting peek at the north wall of Bash Bish Gorge. This spur provides the hike's best views—don't miss it. You're right at the New York–Massachusetts border. Backtrack to the STT and continue into Massachusetts.

At 1,600 feet, the forest type changes suddenly into a pleasing montage of hemlocks, mountain laurel, and thick blueberry heaths. Hardwoods appear to the right, conifers to the left. The trail flattens, and suddenly you're at a (once again) vague junction where the STT leaves south to Alander and Brace mountains. An old Taconic Trail sign is nailed to a tree to the left of the trail here. The sign Alternate Route to Bash Bish is intended for those coming north on the STT, who could go either left or right here, depending on the season. The sign also advises Must Ford Stream—Use Only When Water Is Low. This is a judgment call on your part. You will ford above the falls, where the brook is relatively tame and shallow, but it is wide, and when the water table is very high or flooding, you may get wet. However, even late in a wet May, you might be able to cross and keep your boots dry. (You can always take your boots off first.)

Continue straight ahead on the well-marked Blue Trail, descending gradually then steeply into the ravine. The trail turns east as it approaches the safety perimeter. A cable provides a convenient handrail. An engraved rock on the trail (you may step over it without noticing) was carefully inscribed by one John Williams, '46. Judging by the style and script, this stone was carved in 1846. Be very careful as you descend; hemlocks cling tenaciously to the slope. You'll be using them—and sometimes be on all fours—to steady yourself. The vertical drops into the cataract beyond the fence are a nerve-wracking 200 feet. Due to the many fatalities here (a good number connected with alcohol and associated acts of derring-do), observers, under threat of a fine, are not permitted beyond the fence. This descent ends at the brook above Bash Bish Falls.

From the small gravel apron at the edge of the brook, the trail continues on the other side, bearing right along the bank. The falls are not in view. Walk upstream to find a good crossing point. (This is where a hiking staff comes in handy.) Once you arrive safely on the brook's northeast banks, look around for the blue blazes and follow the trail up to the parking area of Bash Bish State Park in the Mount Washington State Forest of Massachusetts. The cluster of rock to the left is not worth exploring and offers only obstructed views. Your route continues downhill on the Blue Trail, well identified on the west side of the parking area. Descend past the trailhead kiosk and walk on a storybook section of trail through a hemlock ravine. As you hear the sounds of falling water, the trail jogs hard left and joins the dirt service road that comes up from the parking area where you began. Bear left to look at the falls, and then descend the stone steps to their base. Here a rock protrudes from the lower falls, split by centuries of falling water, the cascade ending in a viridian pool of remarkable clarity. Bash Bish is the highest falls in Massachusetts, falling in multiple tiers to a final drop of 80 feet. Many casual visitors content themselves with painting, writing, photographing, and meditating here; however, few have really seen the whole picture, as you have.

Return to your starting point, 0.75 mile back along the Blue Trail (service road) heading west, keeping the brook to your left until you reach the parking area again. Bash Bish Brook continues without you, to join the Roeliff-Jansen Kill and go on to dissolution at the Hudson River.

DID YOU KNOW?

John Frederick Kensett (1816–1872), a leading figure among the second generation of Hudson River School painters, made field sketches for a series of five paintings of the falls, most notably his first *Bash Bish Falls* (1851). Other versions followed, leading to his 1855 masterwork by the same name.

MORE INFORMATION

Bash Bish Falls State Park is open sunrise to sunset, and access is free; www.mass.gov/dcr/parks/western/bash.htm; 413-528-0330.

NEARBY

The Ventfort Hall Mansion and Gilded Age Museum in Lenox, Massachusetts, is an imposing Jacobean Revival-style mansion built in 1893 for the sister of J.P. Morgan. It is open year-round and offers many lectures, concerts, and other events; www.gildedage.org; 413-637-3206. Also in Lenox is the Mount Estate & Gardens, the home of novelist Edith Wharton; www.edithwharton.org; 413-551-5100.

TRIP 26
HARVEY MOUNTAIN

Location: Austerlitz, NY
Rating: Moderate
Distance: 3.0 miles
Elevation Gain: 480 feet
Estimated Time: 2.5 hours
Maps: USGS State Line; Harvey Mountain State Forest

This little-known trail features views of the Southern Taconics from a blueberry knoll and free camping.

DIRECTIONS

From NY 22 in Austerlitz, New York, 5.5 miles south of Exit B3 off I-90, turn left (east) onto East Hill Road, where you'll see a post office. Go 2.5 miles to the Harvey Mountain trailhead parking area on the left. *GPS coordinates:* 42° 19.569′ N, 73° 26.392′ W.

TRAIL DESCRIPTION

Few scenic vantage points in the Southern Taconics' tapering northern hills offer such unusual views of the Taconic Plateau as Harvey Mountain (2,065 feet). From the east and west as it is viewed from the valley, the range looks like a long, low ridge with minimal relief, but from the north the plateau is seen longitudinally, and the fact that the Taconics are a "real" mountain range—the result of tectonic collision and uplift, not just a dissected plateau from which the shallow seas of the postglacial period receded—becomes strikingly apparent.

Harvey Mountain State Forest (HMSF) is a fairly recent addition to the state forest system (added in the 1990s). Along with the Harvey Mountain Trail and its connector trails to the Beebe Mountain fire tower and Barrett Pond, HMSF offers ten primitive, no-fee, drive-up campsites. Camping permits are required for more than three consecutive nights or for groups of ten or more. Come prepared—there are no water sources, fire pits, or pit privies, and on-site management is limited to occasional ranger patrols, mostly on weekends. Hunting is permitted here as it is in most state forests; dress accordingly.

Die-hard hikers may take umbrage with the fact that there is a road to the summit of Harvey Mountain. However, both the summit road—a washed-out four-wheel-drive route—and the HMSF's dead-end campsite access road get

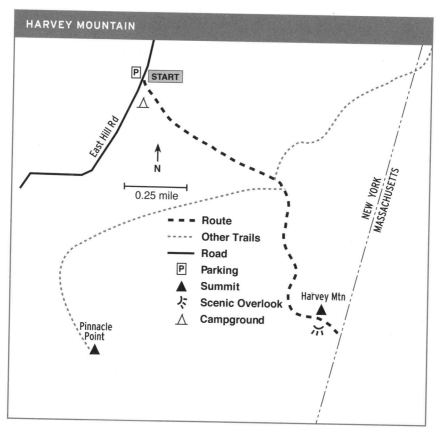

HARVEY MOUNTAIN

East Hill Rd

P START

N

0.25 mile

- - - Route
...... Other Trails
——— Road
P Parking
▲ Summit
Scenic Overlook
△ Campground

NEW YORK
MASSACHUSETTS

Harvey Mtn

Pinnacle
Point

very little use from the sightseeing public. Parking is provided in the well-identified lot on East Hill Road. The Harvey Mountain trailhead is located diagonally across East Hill Road from the parking area, on the northeast side of the Harvey Mountain camping area access road opposite Campsite 1. Follow blue markers.

The trail begins with a sharp ascent, then levels out through hardwoods over a smooth, wide dirt surface. Within 0.3 mile, the trail register appears at the junction of the red-blazed trail to Barrett Pond and the fire tower in Beebe Hill State Forest. Bear right, following the blue markers into a vigorous young sugar-maple forest on this flat and pretty section of trail. Within 15 minutes of the trailhead, the trail departs left at a Y (where a rough road continues straight ahead), soon becomes a narrow path, descends slightly adjacent to a steep ravine where Harvey Mountain can be spotted ahead, and crosses Big Moon Brook. Now the trail rises consistently but never very steeply, as it sidehills up the western slopes of the mountain. Soon after ascending through a white-pine stand, the trail rises to an open blueberry heath. Though not the highest point on the mountain, this spot is, for all practical purposes, its summit. The views to the south are the most interesting, showing the long, thin Taconic Ridge with its dramatic eastern slopes pitching steeply down from Mount Fray into Egremont, Massachusetts, followed by the cluster of peaks around Mount Everett. The highest point of the eastern ridge defines the route of the Appalachian Trail as it makes its way from northern Connecticut through the Southern Taconics, then drops sharply off the eastern shoulder of Jug End heading for the Greylock Range. You can see the Beebe Hill fire tower at 310 degrees. Continue up the hill to the east side of the summit, where a herd trail leads across a field and into the woods. Look left along a stone wall for the New York–Massachusetts state-line marker. The state forest ends here. Return by the route you came.

DID YOU KNOW?

The town of Austerlitz's historian, Sally Light, has identified several home-stead foundations in the state forest dating from 1755, when an iron industry flourished here.

MORE INFORMATION

The Pinnacle Point Trail lies to the west of the campsite area, and offers lean-to camping in a remote location. Significant trail work has been done in the Harvey Mountain and neighboring Beebe Hill state forests, and these trails merit investigation. For general information on state lands in the area, visit www.dec.ny.gov/outdoor/7801.html or call 518-357-2234. For information on the Beebe Hill fire tower, visit www.beebehill.info.

NEARBY

Just outside Harvey Mountain State Forest, on East Hill Road along the upper fringes of the Steepletop Estate, is the Millay Poetry Trail, a short walk posted with selections of Edna St. Vincent Millay's nature poetry written from 1917 to 1935. (Millay won a Pulitzer Prize for her collection *The Harp Weaver and Other Poems* and was noted for her sonnets.) This short trail (about 0.4 mile) leads through quiet woods to her grave. The trailhead is 0.2 mile west of the Harvey Mountain trailhead parking area.

The nearby Millay Colony for the Arts, established by the poet's sister Norma, is an active artist-in-residence colony and writers' retreat; www.millaycolony.org; 518-392-3103.

5

THE NORTHERN TACONICS

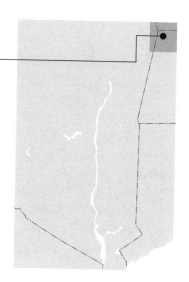

THE PART OF THE TACONIC RIDGE THAT LIES ALONG the border of eastern New York and northwestern Massachusetts is commonly known as the Berkshire Hills. To the north are the Green Mountains of Vermont; to the east is the Greylock massif. In the west, the ridge is referred to as the Taconic Range, although geologically it is known as the Greylock Range because the Berkshire Hills have the same origins. These hills drain eastward into the Hoosic and Hudson rivers. Of interest to long-distance hikers is the Taconic Crest Trail (TCT), a 35-mile scenic ridge trail beginning in Pittsfield, Massachusetts, that links several state forest areas, sanctuaries, and conservation lands (including White Rocks and the Snow Hole); the multiple peaks of Misery Mountain; Berlin Pass; and the scenic summits of Berlin and Petersburg mountains, before ending in Petersburg, New York.

The Taconic Hiking Club (THC) initiated the TCT in 1932. The trail is maintained and/or managed by several groups, including the Taconic Trails Council, the Taconic Hiking Club, the Appalachian Mountain Club, the Williamstown Rural Lands Foundation, and the National Park Service.

Of major interest to most hikers visiting the area is Mount Greylock State Reservation (established in 1898, it was Massachusetts' first state park), at the confluence of the Green and Hoosic river valleys. (Note: In New York, the spelling is "Hoosic"; in Massachusetts, the common spelling is "Hoosac." As such, in New York, it is the Hoosic Valley, while in Massachusetts it is the Hoosac Valley. However, the spelling of Hoosic River does not deviate from state to state, nor do the spelling of Hoosac Ridge and Hoosac Range. For convention, we have used "Hoosic" here for instances when both spellings are acceptable.)

Greylock (3,491 feet) is the highest point in Massachusetts and is surrounded by several peaks in the 3,000-foot range. Originally named Grand Hoosuc(k), and later, Saddleback, its present name appeared in 1918 but only came into regular use in the 1930s. It is believed to derive from the name of the American Indian chief Grey Lock, or from the summit's cloud-shrouded appearance. About 12 miles of the Appalachian Trail passes through the reservation, crossing Greylock's summit, and there are 70 miles of additional trails within the reservation. Fantastic 360-degree views greet you on Greylock, and you will also want to climb the War Memorial Tower and visit Bascom Lodge, where meals and lodging can be enjoyed at reasonable prices between May and October. Between 1933 and 1939, the Civilian Conservation Corps worked on Mount Greylock, at the site of today's campground on Sperry Road. In recognition of their contribution, the area above 3,100 feet on Greylock was designated a National Historic District by the U.S. Department of the Interior.

A good way to begin your exploration of this fascinating area is with a trip to the reservation's new visitor area in Lanesborough, or with a driving tour to Greylock's summit (mid-May to mid-October). Hikers should obtain the excellent *North Berkshire Outdoor Guide,* the authoritative text on the area, produced by the Williams College Outing Club. Included with the book is a pocket map of North Berkshire trails, which identifies the trails around Williamstown, the Greylock Reservation, and the Northern Taconic Range.

MORE INFORMATION

The Taconic Hiking Club is a small club of about 150 hikers that publishes a guidebook and a seven-map series for the Taconic Crest Trail. For more information about the Northern Taconics, contact the following organizations:

Williamstown Rural Lands Foundation; 413-458-2494; www.wrlf.org.

Williams Outing Club, 39 Chapin Hall Dr., Williamstown, MA, 01267.

Mount Greylock State Reservation Visitor Center 3, 30 Rockwell Rd., Lanesborough, MA, 10237; 413-499-4262/4263; www.mass.gov/dcr/

Department of Conservation and Recreation (DCR), 251 Causeway St., Boston, MA, 02114; 617-626-1250; www.mass.gov/dcr/; email: Mass.Parks@state.ma.us.

Taconic Hiking Club; taconichikingclub.blogspot.com

TRIP 27
MOUNT GREYLOCK

Location: Williamstown, MA
Rating: Strenuous
Distance: 8.2 miles
Elevation Gain: 2,300 feet
Estimated Time: 7 hours
Maps: USGS North Adams L; AMC Mount Greylock Reservation; Williams Outing Club, North Berkshire Trails; Department of Conservation and Recreation, Mount Greylock State Reservation and Greylock Glen

This long hike showcases the Greylock massif, Bascom Lodge, and the memorial tower, follows a section of the Appalachian Trail, and descends through a sugar-maple forest.

DIRECTIONS

From Williamstown at the corner of MA 2 and CR 43 (Water Street/Green River Road), go south on CR 43, leaving the Green River linear park to your left. At 2.5 miles, turn left into Mount Hope Park. Go 1.4 miles to a fork and turn left onto Hopper Road. Go 0.7 mile to the Haley Farm trailhead. (You can also come in from South Williamstown on US 7, turning right onto CR 43 and going 2.5 miles to Hope Park.) *GPS coordinates: 42° 39.320′ N, 73° 12.313′ W.*

TRAIL DESCRIPTION

There are many ways to approach Mount Greylock, but the Hopper Trail is the traditional route of serious hikers, along with the Appalachian Trail (AT). According to the Williams Outing Club's *North Berkshire Outdoor Guide,* the Hopper Trail was created in May 1830 by a group of more than 100 people, most of them Williams College students and faculty members. The Greylock trails are still heavily used by college students and Williamstown residents, who have served as trail stewards for more than 100 years.

To the early farmers and romantics of the Hoosic Valley, the steep, narrow gash cleaving Greylock's southwest face resembled a grain hopper. Your route takes you along the Hopper's western defile as you turn gradually northeast to summit Greylock. At 3,491 feet, Mount Greylock is the highest point in

---

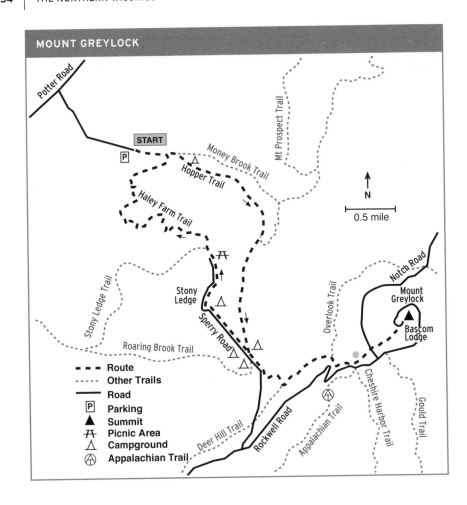

MOUNT GREYLOCK

Massachusetts. Beginning at 3,000 feet, its summit zone is forested with the postglacial remnants of subalpine vegetation. Colder temperatures and increased precipitation create favorable conditions for red spruce, balsam fir, paper birch, and mountain ash—the upper-elevation companions that hikers tend to equate with wilderness. And, while the scenic auto byway to its summit minimally imposes upon Mount Greylock's serenity, hikers can find isolation just a short way off the summit on any of the mountain's many trails.

Prepare for a long outing with significant climbing. From the parking area at Haley's Farm trailhead, follow the blue-blazed Hopper Trail along an old road lined with sugar maples, through fields of alfalfa. Pass the Haley Farm Trail (your return route) on the right, and the Hopper Brook Loop Trail (a.k.a. Money Brook Trail) on your left. Your route, the Hopper Trail, goes right, off

The long Greylock massif is seen from the Hoosic Valley.

the woods road. (If you were to continue straight ahead another 300 feet, you'd reach the dispersed group camping area.)

The Hopper Trail ascends through hardwoods, sidehilling above Money Brook, growing steeper as it turns southeast, and you have sparse and intriguing glimpses of Greylock up to the left (east). Within an hour of hiking, you'll be happy to find that the trail relents, finally becoming level in a forest where red spruce appears in isolated stands. Now the trail bears left as it reaches a road, where you will walk for about 10 minutes through the heavily wooded Sperry Road camping area. (Many people park or camp in the campground for a substantially easier ascent of Greylock. Still others backpack to this point, make camp, and day-hike to the summit. Reservations for camping are advised.)

Hike a few hundred feet past the campsite check-in cabin where the Hopper Trail goes left (northeast) back into the woods. The steepest ascent lies behind you now, but there's more vertical rise ahead. Rising to a T with the Deer Hill Trail, the Hopper Trail bears left on level ground. Follow it, bearing right at a Y, where the Overlook Trail departs to the left (north). As you ascend easily, you'll draw near to Rockwell Road (the summit road) on your right. At a

Y, bear left at the Cheshire Harbor/AT connection, joining in with the Hopper Trail from the right. Walk carefully over a long string of half-log-and-plank puncheons through a wet alpine zone of balsam fir, witch hobble, and paper birch. You'll skirt the natural-looking, manufactured pond and disused pump house that originally provided Bascom Lodge with water (the lodge uses a well now). Just ahead, the trail crosses Rockwell Road, and climbs again. Signs for Bascom Lodge appear. One last rocky ascent remains. Soon you pass the communications tower and service garages and cross the access road, where you'll come upon a large, circular, steel relief map of the Greylock Range just below the summit. Carry on until you reach the expansive overlooks at the base of the memorial tower, where the viewshed is inscribed in stone. To the right is Bascom Lodge, where from May to October you can relax, find rest rooms and buy refreshments, AT souvenirs, books, and sundries. Built by the CCC in the 1930s, this rustic stone-and-wood lodge accommodates 34 guests in both bunk rooms and private rooms. Have a look at the AT thru-hikers' journal, and enjoy a picnic on the enclosed porch with its remarkable 100-mile views and mountain house atmosphere. (Drinking water is available outside, behind the lodge.)

After climbing the tower for the 360-degree view, you can watch hang gliders and sport kites taking off from the summit and landing in the valley far below you. Also of interest is the Thunderbolt Shelter (built in 1934), located adjacent to the parking lot. This rustic emergency hikers' shelter was originally the ski lodge of the Mount Greylock Ski Club, the organization that hosted the first U.S. Eastern Amateur Ski Association downhill championship races.

Retrace your steps to Sperry Road and the campground, back to the point where the Hopper Trail joined the campsite road. Leave the Hopper Trail to your right now and remain on the campsite road as it makes its way northwest to Stony Ledge. From the scenic overlook and picnic area at Stony Ledge, where you'll be treated to a spectacular close-up of Mount Greylock, Mount Prospect, and the Hopper, follow the Stony Ledge Trail to the north (it appears on your left as you look toward Greylock). Pass the Stony Ledge Shelter, soon appearing to your right, and watch carefully on the right for the Haley Farm Trail, your route of descent. The Haley Farm Trail is not intensively used. It winds and switches its way back down the mountain through dense hardwoods, meandering west to gentler contours. Within 35 minutes of hiking from Stony Ledge, it cuts back into the north and east, following a graded old farm road through a beautiful and extensive sugar-maple forest. Soon you cross the fields of Haley's Farm and turn left onto the Hopper Trail, arriving in short order at the trailhead parking area.

DID YOU KNOW?

Mount Greylock has the only taiga (boreal, or sub-arctic forest) in the state.

MORE INFORMATION

For more information, contact the Mount Greylock Visitor Center, 30 Rockwell Rd., P.O. Box 138, Lanesborough, MA, 01237; www.mass.gov/dcr/parks/mtGreylock/; 413-499-4262.

NEARBY

A number of interesting museums, restaurants, and shops are found along Route 2 in Williamstown. The Williams College Museum of Art (open Tuesday to Sunday year-round) features more than 13,000 works spanning the history of art, with an emphasis on modern and contemporary art, American art from the late 1700s to the present, and the art of world cultures; www.wcma.org; 413-597-2429.

THE CIVILIAN CONSERVATION CORPS (CCC)

The Emergency Conservation Work Act (1933) brought great numbers of unemployed men and the environment together. Organized by the Departments of Agriculture and Interior and managed by regular and reserve officers in the Coast Guard, Navy, and Marines, this peacetime "army" of 500,000 men set about improving federal and state lands and parks. Enlistees were housed in tent camps and paid $25 a month. In 1937, the Civilian Conservation Corps (CCC, affectionately known as Roosevelt's "tree army") was formed, and education and training elements were added. Eventually, every state had a CCC camp, as did Hawaii, Alaska, Puerto Rico, and the Virgin Islands.

In addition to the CCC's primary duties of planting trees and fighting fires, it built 3,470 fire towers and 97,000 miles of truck and fire roads. The corps also acted as an emergency service organization, assisting with flood and disaster control in the Ohio and Mississippi valleys, and with drainage and irrigation of croplands in the Midwest. Nearly 300 CCC veterans were reported as missing or dead during the Labor Day hurricane of 1935 in the Florida Keys after a train derailed on its way to rescue them. Although a close congressional vote in 1942 ended the CCC, its spirit lives on in the state trails and plantation forests you'll enjoy on many of these hikes.

TRIP 28
PINE COBBLE

Location: Williamstown, MA
Rating: Moderate
Distance: 3.2 miles
Elevation Gain: 1,000 feet
Estimated Time: 2.5 hours
Maps: USGS North Adams L; Williams Outing Club, North Berkshire Trails; AMC, Mount Greylock Reservation

This popular short hike leads to a quartzite limestone summit over-looking the Hoosic Valley and the Greylock Range.

DIRECTIONS
From Williamstown at the corner of Cole Avenue and MA 2 (at the only light in town), turn north onto Cole Avenue. Cross the Hoosic River at 0.7 mile. Turn right on North Hoosac Road (note that the variance in the spelling of "Hoosic" is accepted) and go another 0.4 mile to Pine Cobble Road. Turn left and park on the left at 0.1 mile in the designated trailhead parking area. *GPS coordinates:* 42° 43.100′ N, 73° 11.117′ W.

TRAIL DESCRIPTION
The scenic hike to Pine Cobble (1,893 feet) is Williamstown's most popular short outing. Lying north of the Hoosic River on the southernmost slopes of the Green Mountains less than 2 miles from the Vermont border, it represents the northeastern-most hike in this book. What makes Pine Cobble such an interesting landmark is its position between the Greylock massif, the Green Mountains, the Hoosac Range, and the eastern slopes of the rambling Northern Taconics, where the Green River valley and the fertile farm flats of the Hoosic floodplain sprawl out before you.

Although relatively short, this hike has a few steep sections and a substantial vertical rise, so be prepared for a moderately strenuous outing. (A longer, less-popular approach is along the Appalachian Trail [AT] from Blackinton. See the *North Berkshire Outdoor Guide* for details.)

From the trailhead parking area, locate the blue-blazed trail and signboard across the road and climb adjacent to it for a short distance. The trail soon heads east and away from North Hoosac Road, climbing past the unexpected

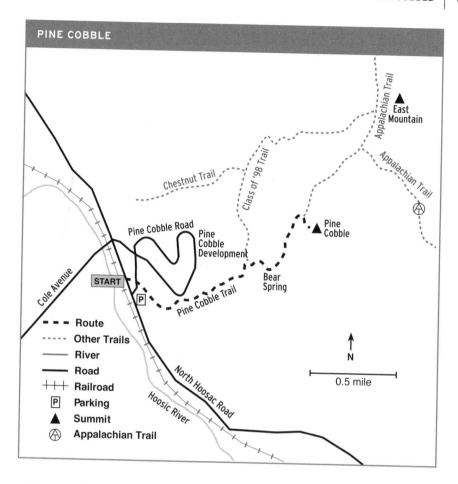

PINE COBBLE

East Mountain

Appalachian Trail

Chestnut Trail

Class of '98 Trail

Appalachian Trail

Pine Cobble Road

Pine Cobble Development

Pine Cobble

START

Cole Avenue

P

Bear Spring

Pine Cobble Trail

- - - Route
····· Other Trails
—— River
—— Road
+++ Railroad
P Parking
▲ Summit
Ⓐ Appalachian Trail

N

0.5 mile

North Hoosac Road

Hoosic River

sight of the Pine Cobble development area, where you'll see a handsome residence or two. Pay attention to the blazes, as there are several unmarked side trails and skid roads. After this initial pitch, the trail departs for the deep woods and relaxes for a while, climbing gently. Soon the trail levels and passes another blue-blazed trail on the left (the Class of '98 Trail). Bear right, avoiding it (it loops around to the north, connects with the Chestnut Trail, and ascends East Mountain to a point south of Eph's Lookout on the AT). This marks the halfway point at 0.8 mile. Now the trail ascends and within a few minutes brings you into the Pine Cobble Summit Natural Area, owned and stewarded by the Williamstown Rural Lands Foundation (WRLF).

The trail climbs steeply now, joining an unidentified old tote road and climbing to a marked T with a trail sign. To the left the trail joins the AT; to the right it leads 0.1 mile to Pine Cobble summit. Bear right, and note that the trail splits, the right fork leading to the ledges above Williamstown and the left to

The limestone outcroppings of Pine Cobble provide a great setting for far-reaching views of Williamstown and the Hoosic Valley.

those facing North Adams. Both forks have the character of herd trails at this point, and faint trails appear here and there on the "summit," a collection of isolated south-facing outcroppings with extensive east-to-west views.

The more pronounced of the two trails—the left fork—will lead you to an easterly lookout, where a series of open rock ledges face the long ridge of the Hoosac Range stretching north and south above North Adams. The predominantly hardwood summit area yields a few pitch pines and white pines and a sparse blueberry heath. The summit rock is a curious-looking quartzite limestone, resembling unpolished marble. Most prominent of the peaks on the Hoosac ridge are Spruce Hill and, north of it, West Summit, both lying across the Hoosic River's north branch. More arresting by far is the view looking across Blackinton, where the AT comes down from Greylock to cross the Hoosic Valley. Then you gaze up the long ridgeline south of Braytonville to the summit of Mount Williams, companion to Mount Greylock, rising unmistakably in the south in company with westerly Mount Prospect. Look to the southwest now. With a little searching, locate a faint trail that leads to the views over Williamstown. An attractive village, Williamstown looks even better from above, with its college halls, spires, playing fields, farms, and woodlands; beyond, the eastern slopes of the Northern Taconics flatten into the valley where prominent Mount Brodie juts into the floodplain. Easily identified across the Hoosic's west branch are the Petersburgh and Berlin passes, which split the long Taconic ridge where the Taconic Crest Trail roughly defines the border between New York and Massachusetts. White Rock, Mount Raimer, Berlin Mountain, Bald Mountain, and Misery Mountain extend the ridge to the south. The centerpiece of this rural dominion is the Greylock massif itself, lying squarely across the southern viewshed, a wrinkled jumble of hills created, remarkably enough, by the smashing of South America into North America. Imagine that you are looking at the floor of a 1,000-foot-deep glacial lake (Lake Bascom), easily re-created in your mind if you envision pouring water to the tops of the surrounding ridges.

The "pocket" wilderness represented by the unexpectedly wild landscape of the Hoosic River valley is in the heart of a natural wonderland that lies at the gateway of yet another. To the north, the Green Mountains present a route into the Northeast Kingdom, defined by the 265-mile Long Trail that begins just north of Pine Cobble on the Vermont–Massachusetts border. You may be tempted to extend your hike by continuing to its trailhead north of Eph's Lookout (named for Ephraim Williams, founder of Williams College), or by visiting the closer summit of East Mountain, where you can set foot on the AT—just to say you did.

Return by the route you came.

MORE INFORMATION

The Pine Cobble Trail runs on land owned by Williams College, Williamstown Rural Lands Foundation (WRLF), the Massachusetts Department of Conservation and Recreation, and private owners, and is maintained by the Williams Outing Club and the WRLF.

NEARBY

The Clark Art Institute in Williamstown is one of the most beloved and respected art museums in the world. The main gallery is open year-round; the Stone Hill Center, with galleries and walking paths, is open June to October; www.clarkart.edu; 413-458-2303.

TRIP 29
WHITE ROCK

Location: Petersburg, NY
Rating: Moderate
Distance: 5.5 miles
Elevation Gain: 300 feet
Estimated Time: 3.5 hours
Maps: USGS North Pownal; USGS Berlin; Williams College Outing Club, Northern Berkshire Trails; Williams College, Center for Environmental Studies, Hopkins Memorial Forest

An easy, east-facing, scenic ridge hike along the Taconic Crest leads to the Snow Hole, a deep, icebound crevice.

DIRECTIONS

This section of the Taconic Crest Trail (TCT) begins at the Petersburg Pass Scenic Area on NY 2, at the height-of-land equidistant from Williamstown, Massachusetts, and Petersburg, New York. Find the trail on the north side of NY 2. *GPS coordinates: 42° 43.405′ N, 73° 16.642′ W.*

TRAIL DESCRIPTION

This fairly relaxed hike will take you along the skyline trail that roughly defines New York's border with Vermont, Massachusetts, and Connecticut—the TCT. On the TCT you will walk briefly through Vermont and come within a few feet of the Massachusetts border. But, because most of the TCT in this section travels through the forested crest of the ridge or on the Taconics' western slopes just below, your views will be west-facing only.

Some confusion surrounds the place-name and location of the area defined as White Rocks. White Rocks is a topographical feature identified on maps close to the Petersburg Pass trailhead of the TCT, while a scenic lookout on this hike, White Rock, lies farther to the north. Because of the appearance of white quartz in this area, the first mile or so of this trail is locally referred to as White Rocks. The landmark (and your destination) White Rock, at 2,400 feet in elevation, is just less than 2 miles north of the trailhead. Your turn-around point is the unmistakable Snow Hole, a deep fissure at 2.75 miles from the start.

From the trailhead parking area, head north and climb a short distance, passing the prettiest trail kiosk you'll ever see as you enter Hopkins Memorial Forest. There's a map posted here, along with a box of trail maps.

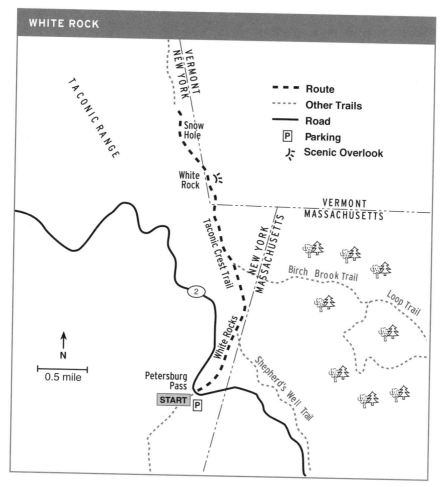

The TCT is marked with white diamonds against a blue background. Marking is often scarce but the trail is well defined. To the left (west) above this initial steep rise, a short herd trail leads to an overlook. Continue as the trail flattens out, passing a spring on the right. At the 0.5-mile point, you will pass the Shepherd's Well Trail on your right (signed). The trail remains mostly level now, making its way through thick mats of hay-scented fern and an over-story of hardwoods. A few apple trees come into view, escapees from the early subsistence farms that covered the eastern slopes in the town of Williamstown. (The upper-elevation western slopes are too steep to farm.)

At 1.1 miles, the Birch Brook Trail (also signed) appears on the right, and descends to the upper Loop Trail in Hopkins Memorial Forest.

Climb the TCT on a long, easy ascent to a point where the trail divides in a patch of ferns, where you may notice an unmarked logging trail leading to the right, to private lands. Continue left on the TCT, where the forest cover

The Taconic Crest Trail provides interesting views to the east.

diminishes to the west, revealing views to the south and west of Berlin Mountain (2,828 feet). Five minutes ahead, there's another viewpoint with a fire ring or two, and finally, after walking through Vermont for a while, a third (and best) lookout at White Rock. Views to the west across the Hudson Valley are far reaching, including the northern Catskills and the Helderbergs. You're about an hour and a half into the hike at this point.

Continuing, the TCT begins to descend. In 10 minutes, look for red trail markers to the right. Avoid this trail; it is the south end of the nameless loop trail around the Snow Hole, now faint and unmaintained. Instead continue on the TCT to a point where the better-marked north part of the red trail appears on the right. There is an informal hand-painted sign indicating the Snow Hole. Follow the red trail to the right for a few hundred feet to the Snow Hole, an unlikely looking deep fissure that emits cool air. This crack is said to hold snow through the summer, or well into it, and has been a curiosity over time. Etchings scrawled by early visitors are inscribed among newer ones. The Hole is sometimes "spelunked" by caving enthusiasts, who warn against doing so without proper guidance and equipment. It seems odd to think that such an isolated spot in the woods would ever have been discovered, until you realize that this was all open pastureland—70 percent or more of it cleared for graze by the 1700s.

Turn around here, retracing your footsteps to your point of origin in Petersburg Pass, passing along the way lumps of white rock contrasting against the green ferns.

MORE INFORMATION

Hopkins Memorial Forest is managed by the Williams College Center for Environmental Studies; www.williams.edu/ces/hopkins.htm; 413-597-4353.

NEARBY

The Massachusetts Museum of Contemporary Art in North Adams is one of the world's premier centers for making and showing contemporary visual and performing arts. The museum is open year-round; www.massmoca.org; 413-662-2111. Combination tickets are available with the Clark Institute of Art in Wiiliamstown and the Norman Rockwell Museum in Stockbridge.

TRIP 30
HOPKINS MEMORIAL FOREST

Location: Williamstown, MA
Rating: Moderate
Distance: 4.3 miles
Elevation Gain: 450 feet
Estimated Time: 2 hours
Maps: USGS Berlin R; Williams College Center for Environmental Studies, Hopkins Memorial Forest; Williams Outing Club, North Berkshire Trails

This quiet, easy hike winds through an old settlement area now managed as a research forest and as a cross-country ski trail.

DIRECTIONS
From the rotary intersection of US 7 and MA 2 at the site of Field Park in Williamstown, follow US 7 north past the information booth 0.3 mile to Bulkley Street (go slowly—it comes up quickly). Turn left and go 1.2 miles to Northwest Hill Road. Bear right, then left into the Hopkins Memorial Forest. Park on the left in the designated lot and walk up to the trailhead. *GPS coordinates: 42° 43.419′ N, 73° 16.642′ W.*

TRAIL DESCRIPTION
The 2,500-acre Hopkins Memorial Forest lies in the extreme northwest corner of Massachusetts. Belonging to Williams College's Center for Environmental Studies (CES), its trails are well marked and open to the public.

Consisting of two loops that form a figure-eight, this hike offers two options for hikers, snowshoers, and cross-country skiers. The Lower Loop, is an easy 1.5-miler; the Upper Loop is steeper and longer at 2.8 miles. The trail follows an old settlement road over rolling terrain, through the dense forests and reclaimed fields of the Northern Taconics' eastern slopes.

Begin your outing from Rosenberg Visitor Center, the college's research base, housed in the 1906 carriage house and stables of the original Buxton Farm. Walk between Buxton Garden and the Moon Barn (the Moons were the original subsistence farmers who lived along the north branch of Birch Brook), following the dirt road to the northwest. (If you're on skis, go left of Moon Barn onto the Lower Loop to climb the steepest ascent first.) Pass the Outing Club cabin on your right and the sugarhouse on your left. Soon you

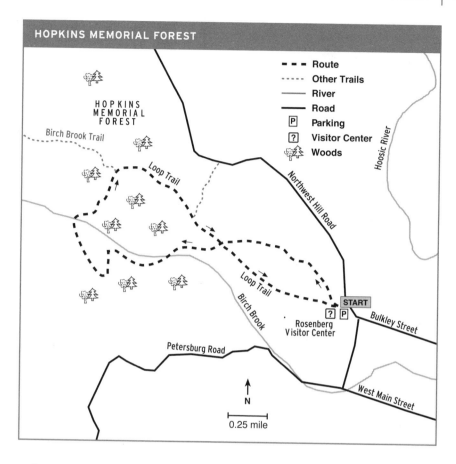

will see an open field to your left, where a weather station appears. As you re-enter the woods, see if you can spot the forest canopy platform and walkway 75 feet above you. Interpretive signs describe many of the CES' research projects.

As you ascend, a red-pine plantation appears to your left. The trail flattens out at the intersection of the figure-eight, where a ski-trail map is located. Continue diagonally across the intersection, onto the Upper Loop. The wide, dirt road descends slightly, crosses a plank bridge over the north branch of Birch Brook, and follows the south branch, passing a tiny hemlock glen. As the trail turns away from the forest's blazed southern boundary, it ascends into a sparse red-spruce wood, then into beech and oak woods. At the top of the loop, the trail becomes narrower and bumpier; skiers will want to have a good base and some new snow to negotiate this section safely.

The apex of the trail is at its crossing of the Birch Brook's middle branch. Thereafter the trail descends, crossing a bridge on the north branch where the Birch Brook Trail appears on the left. (The Birch Brook Trail climbs the eastern ridge to join the Taconic Crest Trail north of White Rocks and Jim Smith

Hill. See Trip 29.) Soon you will walk through an open, airy woods along a flat section of the trail where you can see the Taconic Ridge up to your right. Avoid the Carriage Road Trail that appears to your left and continue straight ahead to the intersection of the loops. Go straight through the intersection (skiers should turn left here). This is a flat and sometimes wet section of trail that passes first through a monospecific glade of hay-scented fern. See the interpretive sign describing the ongoing research. Farther on, you will pass a Norway spruce stand and many large specimens of field-grown oak. Soon, the relocated, reconstructed Moon Barn comes into view again amid the old reclaimed fields and stone walls of Buxton Farm, at one time considered the "agricultural showplace" of Williamstown.

DID YOU KNOW?

Hopkins Memorial Forest inspired William Cullen Bryant to write his best-known poem, "Thanatopsis," in 1811. Bryant, the budding writer and Berkshires native, was then a student at Williams College.

MORE INFORMATION

Hopkins Memorial Forest is managed by the Williams College Center for Environmental Studies; www.williams.edu/ces/hopkins.htm; 413-597-4353. Rest rooms, maps, and information can be found at the Rosenberg Visitor Center.

NEARBY

While in Williamstown, take the time to visit its many points of historical interest. Founded in 1750 as West Hoosuck, its first settlers were soldiers who served at the northern front of the French and Indian wars. Their leader, Colonel Ephraim Williams, provided the means by which Williams College was established in 1791 (with the requirement that the town be renamed Williamstown). The small house in Field Park (a remnant of the original town green) was built in 1953 for the Williamstown Bicentennial. It is a handmade reproduction of a 1753 "regulation" house—in order to gain title to a lot, a settler's house had to measure 15 by 18 feet.

6

THE CATSKILLS

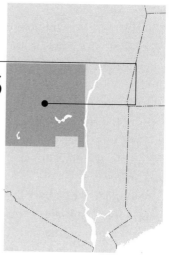

THE CATSKILLS OCCUPY 1,102 SQUARE MILES (705,500 acres, 287,514 of them publicly owned) and, along with the Adirondacks (6 million acres), are the highest and most rugged peaks in New York State. In spite of their appearance and character, the Catskills are not mountains in strict geological terms because they are not the result of tectonic collision. They are a dissected plateau, formed by the erosive action of rivers and streams when vast sheets of thick glacial ice melted and retreated along a north–south axis.

What is perhaps most interesting about the geology of the Catskills is the soil and hence the vegetation that flourishes there. The region represents the southernmost occurrence in North America of boreal coniferous forests on glaciated uplands. In contrast with this summit forest of spruce–fir and paper birch is the valley forest type, known as the Carolinian Zone Forest, which consists of oaks, hickories, occasional black birch, tulip trees, and, until recently, chestnut.

After the Contact Period (in the 1600s) and its destructive consequences for the indigenous peoples of the valley, these same people sold for pittances large blocks of lands that were then "granted" to small groups of patentees. The largest of these land grants was the Hardenburgh Patent, a grant by Queen Anne of England of more than 2 million acres to Johannes Hardenburgh in 1708. For the next hundred years or so, the Catskills remained agricultural.

But with the 1781 capitulation of the British, and with the remainder of General Washington's troops still in New Windsor, the Catskills began to grow commercially. Farm products were shipped to New York City on sloops. Dairy products and fruit followed wheat. In 1825, the Erie Canal opened, creating a widening market and turning a good deal of commerce away from Canada. Gristmills turned to steam power by the middle of the eighteenth century, and by 1840, more than 100 steamships plied the Hudson River. Still, by the mid-eighteenth century, permanent settlement of the original Hardenburgh Patent was limited.

Alongside the tanbark industry (the stripping of hemlock bark for the tanning process) and, later, commercial bluestone quarrying, the great era of hotel tourism began on the high Catskill ledges. Hotel owners were uneasy about the destruction these industries wrought upon their saleable assets—namely the scenic beauty and, less and less it seemed, the peace and serenity of the wilderness. The Catskill Mountain House set the standard for leisure tourism as early as 1823 when it opened on the Escarpment in Haines Falls.

The biggest dividend the Hardenburgh Patent would yield was not wealth for its patentees, but the unintended preservation of open space, which led directly to the creation of the Catskill Forest Preserve. In 1885, by an act of Congress, the forest preserve was created in the Adirondacks and the Catskills, leading to the famous "forever wild" clause in the state's constitution: "All lands now owned or which may hereafter be acquired by the State of New York . . . shall be forever kept as wild forest lands."

By 1887, there was a log observatory on Balsam Lake Mountain. In 1892, the state financed the first trail up Slide Mountain. The Catskill Park was created in 1904, and the first fire tower appeared in 1905, replacing the original log structure on Balsam Lake Mountain. Between 1926 and 1931, four public campsites were created. President Roosevelt formed the Civilian Conservation Corps (CCC) in 1933, which led to a vast reforestation and trail building era. In the ensuing years, the park grew.

Today, in the four forest-preserve counties of Delaware, Greene, Sullivan, and Ulster, there are 143,000 acres of wilderness, 130,000 acres of wild forest, and 5,200 acres of intensive-use lands. There are 7 campgrounds, 303 miles of hiking trails, 76 miles of snowmobile trails, 30 miles of horse trails, 33 lean-tos, and 187 primitive campsites. Based on recent trail register sign-ins, a half-million people use the forest preserve annually.

There are three trunk trails contained within the forest preserve itself: the Escarpment, the Devil's Path, and the Delaware Ridge trails, each roughly 25 miles long. Two longer regional trunk trails, the Long Path and the Finger Lakes Trail, pass through it. (See "The Long Path" on page 270.)

The Finger Lakes Trail is incomplete at this time, with the exception of the main trunk section in the Catskills. Planned to connect the Allegheny Mountains with the Catskills using a route through the most remote sections of New York State's Southern Tier, the trail will provide hikers with the opportunity to traverse nearly the entire length of New York State.

JOHN BURROUGHS

Naturalist, poet, and essayist John Burroughs (1837–1921) is considered the guardian spirit of the Catskills, the John Muir of the East. From his boyhood on a farm in Roxbury, New York, to his later years at Riverby in West Park on the Hudson, he rose to international prominence as a spokesman for America's wilderness. Most of his writing was done at his handmade cabin, Slabsides, built in 1895 and now a National Historic Landmark. Among his visitors were Theodore Roosevelt, John Muir, Thomas Edison, and Henry Ford.

During his lifetime, Burroughs became the most popular author in the field of nature writing. He bridged the gap between his day and the early Romantic artists and writers, alerting his readers to the more concrete, physical wonders of nature. He wrote *Wake-Robin* (1873) while a bank examiner and clerk in the Treasury Department, and followed with another 24 books, among them the first biographical volume on Walt Whitman (*Notes on Walt Whitman*). There are 2 miles of hiking trails in the Burroughs Sanctuary, which is open year-round free of charge. Slabsides is open for tours on the third Saturday in May and the first Saturday in October. The sanctuary is located 10 miles south of Kingston, 0.5 mile off US 9W on Floyd Ackert Road in West Park, New York.

TRIP 31
SLIDE MOUNTAIN

Location: Shandaken, NY
Rating: Strenuous
Distance: 7.0 miles
Elevation Gain: 1,700 feet
Estimated Time: 5.5 hours
Maps: USGS Phoenicia; USGS Shandaken; AMC Catskill Mountains; NY–NJTC Southern Catskills

A scenic, day-long hike climbs the Catskills' highest peak, in the Slide Mountain Wilderness area.

DIRECTIONS

From Exit 19 of the NYS Thruway (I-87) in Kingston, take NY 28 west 31 miles to CR 47 (Slide Mountain Road) in Big Indian. Set your odometer to zero. Turn left (south) onto CR 47, passing the Giant Ledge trailhead at 7.3 miles and Winnisook Lake at 8.4 miles. At 9.0 miles, park at the trailhead lot on the left side of the road. *GPS coordinates: 42° 0.529′ N, 74° 25.653′ W.*

TRAIL DESCRIPTION

Slide Mountain (4,180 feet) defied naturalist John Burroughs's climbing efforts in the early 1880s. In Burroughs's time, Slide was, as he suggested, "probably the most inaccessible; certainly the hardest to get a view of, it is hedged about so completely by other peaks, the greatest mountain of them all and apparently the least willing to be seen; only at a distance of 30 or 40 miles is it seen to stand up above all other peaks." Yet within a few years of Burroughs's first ascent in 1885, Jim Dutcher, a bark peeler living at the foot of the mountain, introduced the peak to hikers. Some of Dutcher's trail (constructed in 1886, with many stone steps) remains, but it leads onto the private lands.

There are several popular approaches to Slide, but the easiest (and fastest) route is from the northwesterly Slide Mountain trailhead parking area, using a combination of the Phoenicia–East Branch Trail (PE, yellow markers), the Wittenberg–Cornell–Slide Trail (WS, red markers), and the Curtis–Ormsbee Trail (CO, blue markers). For the final ascent, you again join the WS Trail.

Orient yourself at the map kiosk in the parking lot, and locate the yellow-marked PE Trail. Once under way, you immediately cross the upper reaches of

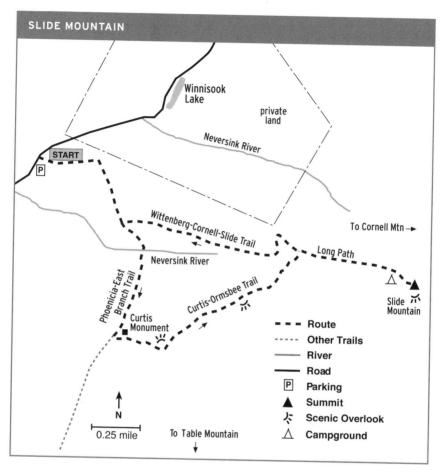

SLIDE MOUNTAIN

Winnisook Lake

private land

Neversink River

START

P

Wittenberg-Cornell-Slide Trail

To Cornell Mtn →

Long Path

Neversink River

Phoenicia-East Branch Trail

Curtis-Ormsbee Trail

Slide Mountain

Curtis Monument

- - - Route
······ Other Trails
——— River
——— Road
P Parking
▲ Summit
Scenic Overlook
△ Campground

N

0.25 mile

To Table Mountain ↓

---

the Neversink's west branch (it is often dry here, but can present a problem at very high water), which flows into the Delaware River. Originating on Slide's northwest watershed is the Esopus Creek, running down through Big Indian Hollow into Phoenicia and the Ashokan Reservoir water supply, its "wastewater" continuing to the Hudson.

Ascend through a stand of maples over rocks and roots, go up a flight of stone steps, and within 15 minutes bear right at the T, following a level Jeep trail (a.k.a. the Truck Trail, the Bridle Path, or the Firetower Trail). After 5 minutes on this section, pass a spring on the left side. Soon you'll arrive at a junction with the red-marked WS Trail that goes off to the left. (The WS Trail follows the old truck trail up Slide Mountain. It is the shortest way up, but it's rocky and without views. Instead, this road will be used for the descent.) Continue straight ahead on the yellow-marked PE Trail. Cross a wooden bridge over an unnamed tributary of the Neversink's west branch. From here, the trail

Slide Mountain is seen from the westerly slope of Cornell Mountain.

climbs slightly. In another 15 minutes, you'll reach the Curtis–Ormsbee Trail (this is the Long Path). Bear left, following blue markers.

Note the vandalized stone monument near the junction. William "Father Bill" Curtis and Allen Ormsbee, for whom the trail was named, both died of hypothermia caused by a sudden snowstorm on Mount Washington, New Hampshire, in the summer of 1900. They were on their way up the mountain to attend a meeting of the Appalachian Mountain Club. This trail was laid out to commemorate them. (These men were among the most experienced hikers of their time, and still they were caught unprepared.)

The trail ascends. Soon you will arrive at a small ledge with westerly views, including of Doubletop, Graham, Wildcat, and various peaks in the Big Indian Wilderness Area. In another 15 minutes, after a steep but short climb, you'll encounter a beautiful viewpoint to the north. The trail levels off, soon passing the 3,500-foot sign, and within 5 minutes a short, marked spur trail to the right leads 200 feet to an outstanding overlook at 3,550 feet. Below and ahead of you is the valley of the east branch of the Neversink River. Table Mountain, distinguished by its long, flat summit, is directly ahead, and Lone Mountain is to its left. You also see Rocky and Balsam Cap. With binoculars, you can see High Point Monument on the Kittatinny Ridge in New Jersey. You'll probably want to rest here for a few minutes and savor the spectacular view.

After leaving the viewpoint, the trail remains relatively level for a while and then resumes its ascent of Slide's southwestern slopes in a thick spruce–fir forest. Within 40 minutes of the previous lookout, following a fairly steep climb, you'll arrive at the junction of the WS Trail.

Bear right (east). This section of trail is relatively flat, and you have only about another 200 feet of elevation gain and an additional 20 minutes of hiking before you reach Slide's summit. Extensive views appear from a northeast-facing outcropping on the left of the trail. Continue ahead to the summit, passing the site of the former fire tower to arrive at a flat rock with good views to the east. (In Burroughs' time, the encroaching spruce–fir forest had been cut down.) Ahead of you and just to the left are Cornell and Wittenberg mountains, and the Ashokan Reservoir is visible beyond. Directly below the ledge, affixed to the rock face is a plaque commemorating John Burroughs that reads in part: "Here the works of man dwindle in the heart of the southern Catskills."

Slide's views include nearly 70 named Catskill peaks as well as a wide view of the Hudson Valley, Green Mountains, Berkshires, Taconics, Hudson Highlands, and Shawangunks. This is the same view that Forest Commissioner Townsend Cox, climbing Slide in 1886 (to recognize the Catskills as members of the New York State Forest Preserve), pronounced "every bit as fine as anything to be seen in the Adirondacks."

Highly recommended is a short descent (off route) to a year-round spring; it's ahead on the WS Trail, 200 feet lower in elevation, and about a 20-minute hike beyond Slide's summit along the trail (as if you were continuing to Cornell Mountain). The trail switches back across Slide's eastern face before descending two flights of log stairs, after which the spring appears at the end of an unmarked spur on the left.

To return to your car, retrace your steps on the red-marked WS Trail, leaving the CO Trail to your left and continuing on the red markers. The presence of white quartz here gives the trail the appearance of a "garden path."

Descend for 40 minutes or so over the rocky footpath. Soon after passing a designated campsite on the left, you arrive at the junction with the yellow-marked PE Trail, which you'll recognize. Turn right and follow the yellow markers to the next T (the trail continues to Winnisook lands and is usually barricaded with sticks), where you bear left and descend to the parking lot.

DID YOU KNOW?

Slide was not recognized as the Catskills' highest peak until Arnold Guyot, a Princeton professor of geology, published his map of 1879. Previously, Kaaterskill High Peak and later Hunter Mountain competed for the title.

MORE INFORMATION
For more information on the Catskill Forest Preserve, visit www.dec.ny.gov/lands/5265.html. For the DEC Region 3 office in New Paltz, call 845-256-3000.

NEARBY
The Belleayre Beach at Pine Hill Lake, off NY 28 in Pine Hill, has swimming, picnicking, horseshoes, volleyball, and fishing, as well as rowboat, pedal boat, and kayak rentals; www.belleayre.com/summer/lake.htm; 845-254-5202.

BICKNELL'S THRUSH

A regular visitor to Slide Mountain in the later years of the nineteenth century, naturalist John Burroughs noted that "Slide Mountain enjoys a distinction which no other mountain in the state, so far as is known, does—it has a thrush peculiar to itself." Burroughs would later learn of the work of amateur ornithologist Eugene Bicknell, who collected a species of thrush on Slide in 1881. Bicknell shot for collection what he thought was a gray-cheeked thrush, but on further examination, and to the ornithological community's surprise, it seems Bicknell had discovered a new species. The taxonomic status of the thrush remained in question for a long time, however, until recent DNA examinations confirmed that the Bicknell's and gray-cheeked thrush share no common ancestor in the last million years. Not until 1995 did the American Ornithological Union's Committee on Classification and Nomenclature grant full species status to Bicknell's thrush.

The thrush is a very shy and reclusive species. Bicknell's thrush, said to be the shiest of them all, is found only in high boreal "fog forests" like Slide Mountain's. It is seldom seen in the open, and is small—the size of a sparrow. The bird is olive-brown, gray and white underneath, and yellow at the base of the lower bill. It can be distinguished by its song, a higher, throatier sound than that of the gray-cheeked thrush; both Bicknell and Burroughs noted the Bicknell's song as peculiar to the species. Burroughs reserved his finest prose to describe it: "It is . . . a musical whisper of great sweetness and power. It seemed as if the bird was blowing in a delicate, slender golden tube, so fine and yet so flutelike and resonant the song appeared . . . a strain as fine as if blown on a fairy flute . . . it was of the purest harmony. It was but the soft hum of the balsams, interpreted and embodied in a bird's voice."

TRIP 32
WITTENBERG AND CORNELL MOUNTAINS

Location: Ulster, NY
Rating: Strenuous
Distance: 9.4 miles
Elevation Gain: 2,480 feet
Estimated Time: 7 hours
Maps: USGS Phoenicia; USGS Shandaken; AMC Catskill Mountains; NY–NJTC Southern Catskills

A steep climb from the rustic Woodland Valley leads to a scenic area that is a favorite of many Catskill hikers.

DIRECTIONS

From the junction of NY 28 and NY 214 in Phoenicia, drive 0.6 mile west on NY 28 to Woodland Valley Road. Follow Woodland Valley Road to its terminus at the Woodland Valley Campsite (4.8 miles). The trailhead parking area is located opposite the campsite, 0.1 mile east of the campground entrance. *GPS coordinates: 42° 2.178′ N, 74° 21.487′ W.*

TRAIL DESCRIPTION

Wittenberg Mountain (a.k.a. The Wittenberg; 3,780 feet) is a favorite among hikers, who regard its scenery as among the Catskills' finest. A key figure in the skyline peaks of the Burroughs Range (Slide, Wittenberg, and Cornell), Wittenberg's popularity, based on hiker registrations, lags only slightly behind that of Slide, the Catskills' highest peak, and nearby Giant Ledge, the shortest scenic hike in the Slide/Panther Wilderness Area. An interesting side trip with open views to the northeast and an area for camping is reached from the Terrace Mountain Trail (TM), a short hike from its junction with the Wittenberg–Cornell–Slide Trail (WS).

Park in the hikers' parking area on the north side of Woodland Valley Road. Note that the WS Trail does not leave directly from this parking lot, but from the south side of Woodland Valley Road within the campsite itself. From the parking area and map kiosk, walk across the road and bear left, keeping the campsite to your right. Within 300 feet, you'll find the red-marked WS Trail on the right. Follow the red markers into the campsite area, bearing left along the edge of Site 46, and cross Woodland Creek on the wooden bridge. The

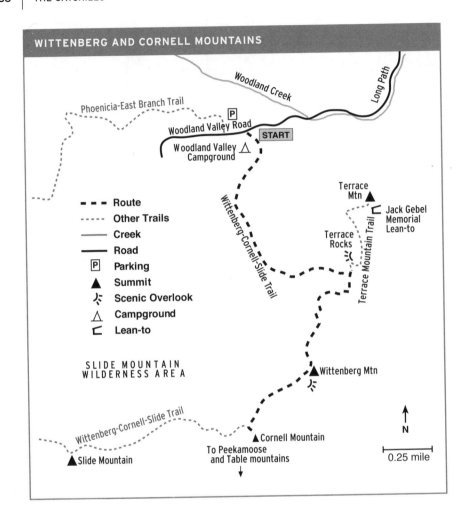

WITTENBERG AND CORNELL MOUNTAINS

trail ascends at once, soon passing the trail register and climbing thereafter through a heavily forested, boulder-strewn hardwood forest. The trail is well marked here, but because of the many boulders, it is not always self-guiding. Keep an eye on the red foot-trail disks.

After 20 minutes of hiking, you'll note the dramatic change in forest type to a nearly pure hemlock stand on a flat ledge at 1,950 feet, with spare, seasonal views to the east. Late-coming backpackers will find many suitable places to camp in the hardwood flats to the right (west) of the trail as they continue past the hemlock stand. After this welcome break, the ascent resumes and the trail crosses a seasonal brook before switching back hard to the left at an obscure arrow (south southeast). The ascent continues, not as steeply now, through attractive hemlock ledges and soon relaxes, becoming nearly level as

Easy ledge climbing during Cornell's ascent is part of the excitement of this trip.

the trail turns east–southeast along Wittenberg's northern flanks at 2,700 feet. Often lively, nameless seasonal brooks increase in volume as you travel east. Beyond the last of these, you'll enter the transition zone from mixed northern hardwoods to stunted paper birch and spruce–fir, and suddenly the trail junction appears in the low saddle between Wittenberg and Terrace. At this point, you are one and a half hours or more into the hike. Wittenberg is 1.3 miles to the right (south and 1,100 feet higher), and the Jack Gebel Memorial Lean-to is 0.9 mile to the left (north, 200 feet lower) on the yellow-marked Terrace Mountain Trail (TE).

The ascent to Wittenberg from the WS/TE trail junction is characterized by attractive (albeit steep), terraced ascents, sedimentary rock ledges, and penetrating vertical crevices. The forest cover will have changed notably into spruce and fir at 3,000 feet. Within 45 minutes to 1 hour of fairly strenuous hiking from the junction, you will arrive at the summit, an east-facing, exposed ledge. Although not panoramic, Wittenberg's view encompasses a 180-degree hemisphere of mountain and valley extending north over the Devil's Path range and the Escarpment, east over the Hudson and Taconics, and south over an expanse of hills and valleys, where the Gunks taper off into endless flatlands. To the southwest, hikers are enticed by intimate observations of the nearby peaks of Peekamoose and Table, along with the trailless Lone, Rocky, Balsam Cap, and Friday, each of the latter being popular bushwhacking summits above

3,500 feet. In the eastern lowlands, you will see the Ashokan Reservoir (part of New York City's water supply), the impoundment created by the damming of the Esopus Creek. Wittenberg's summit impressed John Burroughs, who reached it after a "long and desperate" attempt at Slide: "The view from The Wittenberg is in many respects more striking, as you are perched immediately above a broader and more distant sweep of country . . . and the earth falls away at your feet and curves through an immense stretch of forest until it joins the plain of Shokan, and thence sweeps away to the Hudson and beyond."

After experiencing Wittenberg, you may feel up to the short hike to Cornell (add 30 minutes each way) via "Bruin's Causeway," an interesting, boreal section of the WS Trail. As you gain Cornell's uppermost elevations (requiring the ascent of one low but nearly vertical ledge that can be hazardous in icy conditions), a short, unmarked spur trail to the left will take you to the summit. This is Cloud Cliff, the site of an illegal, impacted campsite with limited views. Only Cornell's nearby westerly shoulder provides a good view to the west, including the slide on Slide's north side that occurred around 1820. To see this memorable view, proceed west 0.1 mile on the trail as if you were hiking to Slide.

John Burroughs traveled the range in 1880, relating anecdotes of the porcupines in Volume 6 of his complete nature writings, *Riverby*. If you've dropped your pack off on Cornell's summit to find the westerly view of Slide, don't be surprised to discover the omnivorous quill pig sorting through its contents.

Return by the route you came.

DID YOU KNOW?

Many bears have been sighted along a narrow section of trail between Cornell and Slide mountains, giving rise to the name Bruin's Causeway. In the unlikely event that you do sight a bear in close quarters, back away slowly.

MORE INFORMATION

There is an in-season parking fee at the campsite office, 0.2 mile farther along Woodland Valley Road from the parking lot. For more information on the Catskill Forest Preserve, visit www.dec.ny.gov/lands/5265.html. For the DEC Region 3 office in New Paltz, call 845-256-3000.

NEARBY

There are shops and restaurants in Phoenicia, plus tubing and trout fishing on the Esopus Creek. Tube rentals are available from Town Tinker Tube Rental (www.towntinker.com; 845-688-5553) or FS Tube Rental (www.fstuberental.com; 845-688-7633).

TRIP 33
GIANT LEDGE

Location: Shandaken, NY
Rating: Moderate
Distance: 3.0 miles
Elevation Gain: 1,000 feet
Estimated Time: 2.5 hours
Maps: UGS Phoenicia; AMC Catskill Mountains; NY–NJTC Southern Catskills

This is a short and rewarding hike to the scenic cliffs of a glacial cirque in the epicenter of an ancient meteorite impact zone.

DIRECTIONS

At the intersection of NY 28 and CR 47 (Slide Mountain Road) in Big Indian, set your odometer to zero, turn left, and drive south on CR 47 to the Giant Ledge trailhead at 7.3 miles. *GPS coordinates: 42° 1.598′ N, 74° 24.238′ W.*

TRAIL DESCRIPTION

This fairly short, rewarding hike will take you to the vertical lip of a glacial cirque in the heart of the Catskill High Peaks area. The Giant Ledge–Panther–Fox Hollow Trail (GP) to Giant Ledge has become extremely popular with day-hikers and backpackers, so expect company, especially on weekends. Giant Ledge (3,200 feet), so named for its vertical cliffs, forms the lower, southerly ridge of Panther Mountain (3,720 feet). On the east it is flanked by the extensive wilds of Woodland Valley and the Slide Mountain Wilderness Area, and to the west by the Big Indian Wilderness Area. It is here that the Esopus Creek (an important source of New York City's drinking water) gains momentum, nurtured within Panther's long ridge and the west-lying Big Indian Valley, with its Bavarian-style homesteads and rustic mountain hotels.

The trail to Giant Ledge begins across the road from the parking lot, where it is well identified. Enter the woods and follow the yellow markers of the Phoenicia–East Branch Trail. Within 300 feet of the road you'll see the trail register and information kiosk. The initial section of trail climbs steeply at times, goes over a rough and rocky footway, crosses a (seasonal) streambed on a wooden bridge, and again ascends through a hardwood forest. The rest of the hike is easier, except for the last short pitch to the ledges.

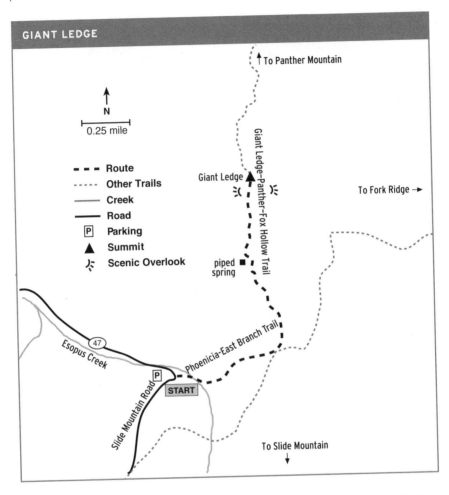

GIANT LEDGE

To Panther Mountain

N
|—————|
0.25 mile

- - - Route
..... Other Trails
——— Creek
——— Road
P Parking
▲ Summit
)(: Scenic Overlook

Giant Ledge ▲

Giant Ledge-Panther-Fox Hollow Trail

To Fork Ridge →

piped spring

Esopus Creek
47

Phoenicia-East Branch Trail

Slide Mountain Road

P
START

To Slide Mountain

Within 20 minutes or so of rigorous ascent, the trail flattens out at 2,700 feet in the col between Slide and Panther mountains. Avoid the faint, unmarked trail to your right, which heads southwest across the lands of the Winnisook Club (this is a legal and significant shortcut to the Slide Mountain trailhead for hikers doing the "loop" from Woodland Valley across the Burroughs Range). Bear left here, and within a stone's throw you will be at the trail junction where the PE Trail heads for Woodland Valley, passing the blue-marked GP Trail to Giant Ledge. Bear left again (north) on the GP Trail, following blue markers now. The trail is flat for a while, and hops across a series of stones where the footway is often muddy. These conditions vanish as the trail rises again, ascending a long set of stone steps to arrive at a Y. At this point, a spur trail marked Spring goes left (west) 600 feet to a piped spring. (Pass the first small pool of water appearing next to a boulder and continue to the pipe. This is the

**A hiker relaxes on
Giant Ledge.**

only reliable water source on the GP between here and Fox Hollow.) Bear right over level ground for a while and then ascend steeply as the trail rises to ridge elevation, where the first of several herd trails leads to a ledge on your right (east). Explore more lookouts to the north along the trail, each very exposed and dangerous, most poised on fractured sandstone ledges above high, vertical drops. The views are spectacular.

From these easterly points, you look toward Fork Ridge and into Woodland Valley, with Terrace, Cornell, and Wittenberg to your right (southwest). To the northeast, you can identify the lower peaks of Garfield and Sheridan, with Romer to the east and Tremper beyond it, including various peaks of the Devil's Path Range from northeast to east. With binoculars, you can see three of the Catskills' five fire towers from here: Overlook (easy to spot), Hunter (around the middle of the long ridge top to your left, or northeast), and Mount Tremper (the cab can be seen sticking up between you and the col of Twin Mountain).

From a point roughly in the middle of Giant Ledge, a trail leads to the west into the designated camping area, marked with yellow disks. Continue through the campsites—there are two crude fire rings—where you will discover a west-facing rock with a view revealing Hemlock, Spruce, Fir, Big Indian, Eagle, Haynes, Balsam, and Belleayre mountains in the Big Indian Wilderness Area. The appeal of Giant Ledge is that it's a short, fairly easy, and ruggedly scenic hike. You're likely to find many friendly people wandering around or camping here on a nice weekend. To have the place to yourself, plan to come on an off-season weekday.

Giant Ledge is predominantly forested with maple, beech, cherry, and birch, but at its north end there is a virgin spruce grove extending to the ledge's base. A few remaining drought-killed red spruce can still be seen below the eastern cliffs. More recently, forest tent caterpillars and gypsy moths have defoliated much of the mid-elevation forest here, the long-term results of which remain to be seen.

Many hikers elect to continue to Panther's summit for a longer outing. Panther is another 1.75 miles beyond Giant Ledge and an additional 750 feet in elevation. If you'd like to extend your hike from Giant Ledge to Panther's summit, you have another 40 minutes of hiking (each way), dropping slightly downhill at first and then climbing vigorously through large boulders and thick hardwood forest. On the ascent, you will have several views of Slide, Wittenberg, and Cornell as you cross open rock terraces, most of them similar if not inferior to Giant Ledge's. Panther's "summit" is a very small scenic outcropping beneath the true, viewless, fir-clad summit. The trail (completed in 1936) continues to the north and descends to the Fox Hollow trailhead. Most thru-hikers on the GP Trail spot a car at both ends. (Consult AMC's *Catskill Mountain Guide* for details.)

From Giant Ledge, return by the route you came.

DID YOU KNOW?

This area was hit by a meteor 375 million years ago, which left behind a crater and spherules—tiny iron droplets of condensed gas. Satellite images clearly show the circular crater, defined by the circuitous route of the Esopus Creek.

MORE INFORMATION

Aside from its tremendous appeal as a scenic destination hike, Giant Ledge is an ideal overnight trip for those new to backpacking or wishing to prepare for longer outings. For more information on the Catskill Forest Preserve, visit www.dec.ny.gov/lands/5265.html. For the DEC Region 3 office in New Paltz, call 845-256-3000.

NEARBY

Belleayre Mountain off NY 28 in Pine Hill offers mountain biking and eco-adventure programs in summer and skiing in winter; www.belleayre.com; 845-254-5600 or 800-942-6904. Performances at the Belleayre Music Festival (www.belleayremusic.org; 845-254-5600 ext. 1344) include folk, rock, opera, classical, Broadway, dance, and jazz.

TRIP 34
PEEKAMOOSE AND TABLE MOUNTAINS

Location: Denning, NY
Rating: Strenuous
Distance: 10 miles
Elevation Gain: 2,200 feet
Estimated Time: 5 hours
Maps: USGS Peekamoose Mountain; AMC Catskill Mountains; NY–NJTC Southern Catskills

This remote wilderness hike leads to a pair of quiet boreal summits with southwesterly views.

DIRECTIONS

From NY 28 in Big Indian, go south on CR 47 through Oliverea, Winnisook, and Frost Valley, then turn left in Claryville onto CR 19 (Denning Road) and follow it to the trailhead parking area, about 30 miles from Big Indian.

Alternately, from NY 28 in Boiceville, turn south onto NY 28A and go 3 miles to West Shokan, then turn right onto CR 42 (Peekamoose Road), passing the Peekamoose–Table trailhead 10 miles from West Shokan. Bear right into Grahamsville, Unionville, and Curry on NY 55, turning right at Curry to Claryville, and again right into Denning and to the trailhead, also a total of 30 miles.

From NY 17 (the shortest approach to this area from the south), take NY 55 east from Liberty, turning north onto CR19 at Curry. Bear right (staying on CR19) at Claryville, and follow Denning Road to the trailhead. *GPS coordinates: 41° 57.933′ N, 74° 27.144′ W.*

TRAIL DESCRIPTION

What will impress you most about Peekamoose and its environs are its storybook forests and the remarkable clarity of the Rondout Creek and Neversink River. The Rondout is conceived on the south- and east-facing slopes of Rocky, Lone, and Peekamoose mountains and is joined by the malachite waters of Peekamoose Lake as it swells through Bull Run and joins its east branch at Sundown. Naturalist John Burroughs loved this flashy, pellucid brook, vowing, "If I were a trout I should ascend every stream till I found the Rondout." If you're coming from the west, you follow the Neversink's east branch from Claryville. It too is famous trout water.

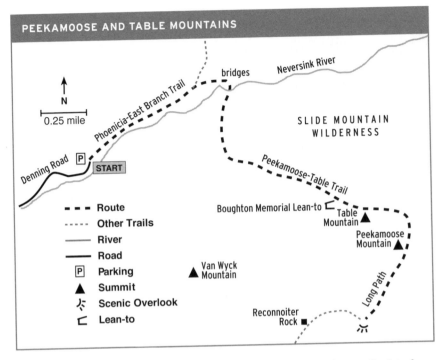

PEEKAMOOSE AND TABLE MOUNTAINS

SLIDE MOUNTAIN WILDERNESS

Neversink River

Phoenicia–East Branch Trail

bridges

Denning Road

START

Peekamoose-Table Trail

Boughton Memorial Lean-to

Table Mountain

Peekamoose Mountain

Van Wyck Mountain

Long Path

Reconnoiter Rock

N
0.25 mile

- - - Route
..... Other Trails
——— River
——— Road
P Parking
▲ Summit
Scenic Overlook
Lean-to

The most popular approach to Peekamoose Mountain (3,843 feet) is from the southern trailhead in Sundown Wild Forest along Peekamoose Road, and involves a 2,643-foot elevation gain within 3.5 miles. The recommended (and more interesting) Denning Trail, or Phoenicia–East Branch (PE) Trail, with its crossing at Deer Shanty Brook, is the gentler and more scenic option, and it will save you a few hundred feet of (cumulative) elevation. If you wish only to climb Peekamoose (these days it has a better view than Table's), the trail from Peekamoose Road provides the shortest route. The distances and logistics of spotting a car at each trailhead make this an impractical hike to shuttle.

Park at the end of Denning Road where trail signs to Slide Mountain are posted. The setting is a high farming–valley plain with frequent plots of old-growth forest. You may see deer feeding close to the road here, where old apple trees provide them with seasonal treats.

Follow the PE Trail through a hemlock woods on an old woods road, crossing a small plank bridge and a seasonal brook. Within 25 minutes you will reach a trail junction, where you turn right onto the blue-marked Peekamoose–Table Trail. Go downhill into a wet area (seasonal), keeping an eye on the blue markers and continuing downhill to cross two log stringer bridges, one of which spans a dry bed at various times of year. This is the confluence of Deer

Peekamoose and Table Mountains are seen from the boreal Bruin's Causeway.

Shanty Brook and the Neversink. The bridges are kept simple because these two creeks rise considerably during runoff, and they must be replaced frequently. Be careful crossing the stringers. The lean-to that existed mid-stream here has been removed as a non-conforming structure, due to its proximity to the creeks and the difficulty of siting a privy so close to a water source, but there are a few legal, designated campsites in the area. Most of the heavily impacted, old, now-illegal sites along the banks of both Deer Shanty Brook and the Neversink have been closed for recovery.

Continue uphill through a lush forest of fern, oxalis, club moss, and huge birch. Within a half-hour, the trail will level somewhat, skirting a ridge exposing Woodhull and Van Wyck mountains to the southwest. The trail varies in pitch, generally gaining elevation as you go through thin stands of hardwood, climbing through broken rock ledges. Within 45 minutes of leaving the confluence, you will reach a ledge among the cherry trees with a view of Peekamoose to the south. Several more spur trails lead to the right 20 or 30 feet off the trail, some with worthwhile views. Beware—these are dangerous ledges. Through the trees to the left (north) as you continue, you may see Slide and its neighboring peaks, and, as you gain in elevation, you'll identify Panther, parts of Giant Ledge, Lone, Rocky, Balsam Cap, and Friday. Just below the 3,500-foot mark (and a short way beyond a spur to a piped spring), a spur trail to the right leads to the Boughton Memorial Lean-to.

Within 2 hours of the Neversink, you'll reach Table's summit (3,847 feet). There is no view here. At one time, a herd trail led to an extraordinary north-facing viewpoint, but this location has been lost over time, obscured by heavy spruce–fir growth. Several herd trails appear in the summit area, heading no-where in particular and creating an undesirable pattern of sustained overuse.

Continue on the main trail to Peekamoose; you can see it ahead as you de-scend. Some faraway views are available along this downhill section of trail—extending beyond the Shawangunks and into the Highlands. Even Anthony's Nose and the deep gulch spanned by the Bear Mountain Bridge can be seen with binoculars, or good eyes.

As you drop into the fragrant, balsam saddle between Table and Peeka-moose, the trail becomes wet, and within 10 minutes you begin climbing again. You may see a vague Y in the trail as you approach the summit of Peekamoose. Go right to reach the summit, where a large boulder sits in a small clearing surrounded by scrub evergreens. This boulder can be climbed for more views, but they are inferior to those ahead.

Continue south another 0.6 mile, going steeply downhill through a series of ledges and overlooks, following the backbone of a long ridge extending south–southwest. Within half an hour of leaving the summit, following frequent blue trail markers, you will cross several open areas with interesting ledges and flats to reach an outstanding viewpoint at 3,500 feet. This spot exposes the Rondout, Neversink, and Mongaup valleys; Samson Mountain, Bangle Hill, Breath Hill, and Little Rocky; and some interesting ridges and peaks to the west, among them Big Indian, Doubletop, and Balsam Lake Mountain, with its fire tower (319 degrees). Any additional descent to see the limited (seasonal) views from Reconnoiter Rock would be counterproductive—the views are better here on the high southern flanks of Peekamoose.

Return by the route you came.

DID YOU KNOW?

The 350-mile-long Long Path crosses the summits of both Table and Peeka-moose mountains. The romantic place-name of the latter is a shortened ver-sion of "Peak of the Moose."

MORE INFORMATION

For more information on the Catskill Forest Preserve, visit www.dec.ny.gov/lands/5265.html. For the DEC Region 3 office in New Paltz, call 845-256-3000.

NEARBY

You can visit the New York State Catskill Fish Hatchery near Livingston Manor, on the road into the state campground at Mongaup Pond. The hatchery is open daily for visitors; www.dec.ny.gov/outdoor/7742.html; 845-439-4328.

TRIP 35
ASHOKAN RESERVOIR

Location: Shokan, NY
Rating: Easy
Distance: 4.5 miles
Elevation Gain: 150 feet
Estimated Time: 2 hours
Maps: AMC Catskill Mountains; USGS Ashokan

**This flat hike along a popular section of the Ashokan Reservoir—
the scenic middle dike—affords the most intimate views of the
Catskills from the Hudson Valley lowlands.**

DIRECTIONS

From Exit 19 of the NYS Thruway in Kingston, set your odometer to zero and
travel west on NY 28 toward Phoenicia. At 12 miles, turn left at Winchell's
Corners in Ashokan, a small, easily missed intersection. Soon you will recognize the managed forests of the Ashokan's buffer zone. As you cross the dividing weir separating the upper and lower basins, you'll see the Slide Mountain
Wilderness Area on your right (west), across the upper basin. At 13.8 miles,
(cumulative from Exit 19), turn left onto Monument Road. Go down the hill
and bear left onto NY 28A. At 15.3 miles, turn left into the area known locally
as the Frying Pan. The "pan" is formed by Leonard Hill Circle, where you will
park. *GPS coordinates: 41° 56.870′ N, 74° 10.925′ W.*

TRAIL DESCRIPTION

Although the Ashokan Reservoir's middle dike has been a well-known hiking
and cycling destination for decades, the western section of Reservoir Road
(which extends this hike and crosses the dam) was open to vehicular traffic
until September 11, 2001, after which it was closed indefinitely. Today, hikers can travel these joined sections of the dike and dam (paved), which on
clear days are popular not only with pedestrians and cyclists, but also with
landscape artists, who set up their easels before the sweeping panorama of the
Catskill high peaks. The scenic value of this unusual viewshed cannot be over-
stated. Many of the peaks you will see on this hike have been the subject matter of the Hudson River School of landscape painters. It was landscapes such
as these that spawned a new concept of a picturesque and sublime American

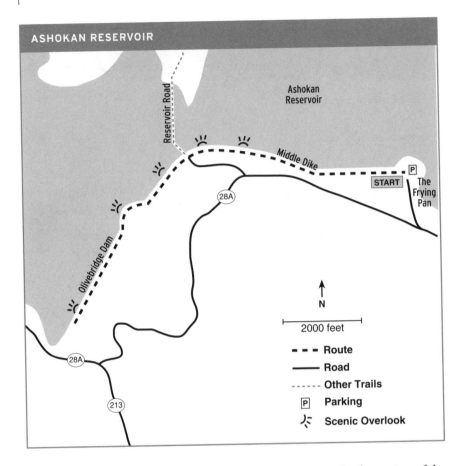

wilderness, and the values derived from that vision led to the formation of the National Park Service.

From the parking lot, walk west through the barrier gate and onto the paved middle dike. Immediately you are greeted with the extraordinary array of the major Catskill peaks running from Overlook Mountain in the east to the Sundown Wild Forest in the southwest. Between these two mountainous regions lies the bulk of the Catskill Forest Preserve, where many of the region's finest hiking trails are located. A 26-mile-long trunk trail known as the Devil's Path traces the skyline to the north, and the Slide Mountain Wilderness Area features the rugged trails of the Burroughs Range. However, many of the peaks you see before you are trailless.

Many birds, such as loons, cormorants, diving ducks, ospreys, eagles, and turkeys, make their homes here. Small herds of deer feed off the mowed grass of the dike's steep, grass-covered embankments. As you approach the dividing weir, look for Ashokan High Point in the Sundown Wild Forest in the southwest.

The Catskill High Peaks dominate the western skyline over the Ashokan Reservoir.

Continue along the dike. At 1.3 miles, you will arrive at the intersection of Monument and Reservoir roads. Carefully cross the intersection onto Reservoir Road, continuing west. Down the hill on the left, you will see the aerator, which is no longer used for the aeration of drinking water but remains as a monument that is open to the public. At the intersection, a Department of Environmental Protection kiosk stands beside the roadblocks preventing vehicular access to the main dam. Walk through the blockade and continue west along the dike. This section of the route is popular with photographers and birders—it has in recent years been the domicile of several families of eagles, which maintain nests in the large white pines along the water's edge. Interpretive signs are in place to inform the public of the ongoing preservation efforts in the Ashokan buffer zone. It is not unlikely that you will see several eagles hunting and nesting in the dense tract of woods ahead. Carrying a camera with a long lens or a small pair of binoculars will add to your enjoyment here, since the eagles have become fairly comfortable with the human presence and can at times be closely observed.

Now the road passes through a beautiful section of maturing mixed woods, where planted pines of several varieties and large oaks appear. As the road straightens, you will see Ashokan Dam ahead, where the road narrows. Continue to its center span, your turn-around point (the road does continue a bit farther but there is nothing more of interest to hikers). The dam is fairly inconspicuous as far as dams go. It is not a contemporary poured-concrete and steel-gated dam, but rather an earthen dam, one of the very last to be "hand built" by steam and manual labor. The volume of earthwork comprising the dam and its surrounding dikes is astonishing, as is the story of the impoundment's creation.

The Ashokan Reservoir's construction began in 1909, as one of six that were built to supply New York City with drinking water. The city's water system had begun to leak cesspool seepage, and cholera and dysentery were repeatedly breaking out. The wealthy were able to afford kegged water, which at the time was shipped from Staten Island. The city's nearest option for a large water supply was the Ramapo Mountains, but a group of private investors who controlled the water there had anticipated the city's needs and held out at an unreasonably high price. The city instead turned to the Catskills, going around the Ramapo extortion plan, and established rights of eminent domain. This resulted in the inundation or relocation of seven towns, the relocation of 2,000 inhabitants, the disinterment of 2,600 graves from 32 cemeteries, and the building of 11 miles of railroad and 64 miles of roads. In 1913, water filled the large excavation that had once been a thriving collection of hamlets. At the time of its construction, the Ashokan Reservoir was the largest impoundment in the world.

As you emerge from the woods you will see the dam ahead, where the road narrows. The original channel of the Esopus Creek can be seen below. The creek originally flowed through a natural flat valley that the local Seepu (of the Delaware Indians) called the Plain of Ashokan, or the "place of fish." The dam and dikes that were placed around the Esopsus's original course rerouted the creek to the wastewater spillway in Hurley. The impoundment now resembles what the post-glacial lake looked like about 17,000 years ago. Looking across the upper basin, you see the edge of a high glacial cirque formed by Panther Mountain, Giant Ledge, and the Burroughs Range (Slide, Wittenberg, and Cornell mountains). Much earlier in time, as recent research has demonstrated, the Panther Mountain area was the epicenter of a meteor impact that defined the topography of the upper Esopus Valley.

From the dam, retrace your steps back to the Frying Pan and your car.

DID YOU KNOW?

When the Ashokan Reservoir was being built in the early 1900s, kegged water in New York City cost more than gin.

MORE INFORMATION

There is an information kiosk with maps and interpretive matter in the trail-head parking lot. Though this hike is relatively short and seemingly tame, carry the appropriate outerwear to protect you from possible high, cold winds blowing across the 12-mile-long, 8,300-acre reservoir. In the interest of maintaining the highest-quality water, no dogs are permitted here. Unfortunately, there is no way to form a loop out of this attractive hike without walking busy roads, and access to the reservoir property itself is restricted to fishers with permits. Hikers interested in finding out where they can hike on New York City reservoir lands can inquire through the DEP police headquarters office on Beaverkill Road, just west of the aerator and Ben Nevis laboratory on NY 28A, or call 212-639-9675.

NEARBY

If you are returning to the NYS Thruway (I-87) from here, detour past the West Hurley Dike and the spillway, which are scenic locations similar to the middle dike, though they are not walking destinations. To see these areas, bear left out of the circle and set to zero at NY 28A. At 0.6 mile, you'll pass over the spillway. This is a spectacular sight in early spring, when, at times, a large volume of wastewater is channeling its way into the gorge below. At 6.1 miles, leave NY 28A and bear left onto Basin Road. Within 0.2 mile, you will cross the West Hurley Dike and be treated with another fine view of the Indian Head Wilderness Area, only you'll be closer this time. At 7.3 miles, turn left in front of the Reservoir Inn restaurant, and at 8.0 miles, turn right onto NY 28, back toward I-87.

TRIP 36
ASHOKAN HIGH POINT

Location: West Shokan, NY
Rating: Moderate
Distance: 7.5 miles
Elevation Gain: 1,980 feet
Estimated Time: 5.5 hours
Maps: USGS West Shokan; AMC Catskill Mountains; NY–NJTC
Southern Catskills

A gradual climb to a scenic and extensive blueberry heath affords intimate views of the high peaks.

DIRECTIONS

Turn south onto NY 28A from NY 28 in Boiceville, west of Kingston. (At this time, automobiles cannot use the Ashokan Reservoir route on Monument Road.) Follow NY 28A for 3.0 miles to West Shokan, then follow Peekamoose Road (NY 42) west and reset to zero. At 4.0 miles, turn right into the Kanape Brook parking area. Cross the road to the footbridge and the trailhead. *GPS coordinates:* 41° 56.140′ N, 74° 19.685′ W.

TRAIL DESCRIPTION

The trail to Ashokan High Point (3,080 feet) follows an old but very well-built (dirt) settlement road along hemlock-fringed Kanape Brook. Bluestone walls and ditches constructed by the Civilian Conservation Corps in the 1930s have protected the trail from erosion, and trail maintenance is carried out by a local Boy Scout troop from the Rip Van Winkle Council.

Follow the trail uphill through a slope forest of beech, birch, and maple, gently climbing up and away from Kanape Brook, to your right. Within 10 minutes you'll cross one of several stone culverts running under the trail, draining the northwest watershed of the mountain. These are structures you ordinarily won't see on Catskill trails. Several are entirely handmade; the ditch itself is lined and capped with large, flat stones. You will see some very attractive bluestone walls along this part of the trail, as well as stone bridges spanning seasonal creeks. You'll cross two such bridges and climb gradually but steadily into an area where mountain laurel appears.

Within 30 minutes or so, at 1.4 miles and at 1,600 feet in elevation, the trail crosses Kanape Brook at a clearing with a designated campsite. This is a pretty

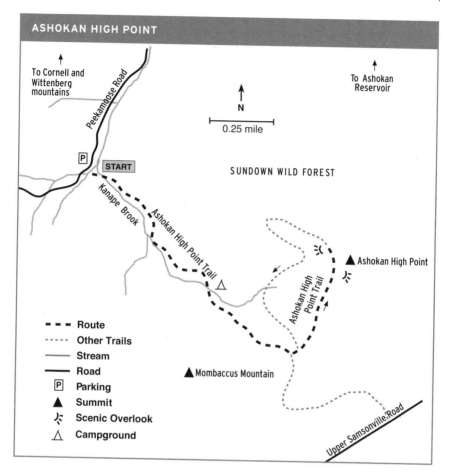

ASHOKAN HIGH POINT

To Cornell and
Wittenberg
mountains

Peekamoose Road

N

0.25 mile

To Ashokan
Reservoir

P

START

SUNDOWN WILD FOREST

Kanape Brook

Ashokan High Point Trail

Ashokan High Point Trail

Ashokan High Point

- - - Route
- - - - Other Trails
——— Stream
——— Road
P Parking
▲ Summit
⅄ Scenic Overlook
△ Campground

▲ Mombaccus Mountain

Upper Samsonville Road

spot—the brook forms a large pool as it flows from the shady Norway spruce forest upstream. Keep going uphill, never strenuously, for another 20 minutes through a second-growth forest. Curving gradually toward the east, the trail soon reaches higher open forest, becoming level and grassy amid the oak and laurel. Within 5 minutes you'll arrive at a T in the airy, forested saddle between High Point and Mombaccus Mountain (trailless) at 2.5 miles and 2,060 feet. This is the border of state land. The adjoining property, south to Freeman Avery Road, is private.

Turn left (north) at the trail junction for the 1.0-mile, 1,000-foot ascent to Ashokan's summit. Slightly beyond the trail intersection, take note of another red trail marker (this is where you'll come back to the main trail if you choose to complete the loop), but continue straight ahead, climbing gradually over broken rock. Views appear as you climb through this hardwood forest over steeper, terraced terrain. The vague side trails you may notice lead to older, treed-in views. From saddle to summit takes nearly 1 hour.

Ashokan High Point is seen from the middle dike of the Ashokan Reservoir.

At 3.5 miles from the trailhead, Ashokan's summit is a rock ledge with an east-to-southwest aspect, revealing the edge of the Ashokan Reservoir, the Kingston–Rhinecliff Bridge, the Shawangunks from Mohonk to Minnewaska (Sky Top Tower and the Mohonk Mountain House are visible at 165 degrees), down to Sam's Point, and deep into the Hudson Highlands. Weathered carvings from 1878 show in the summit stones, along with several anchor bolts from an early observation tower and a few benchmarks. There is a shallow overhang just beneath the summit ledge. The best is yet to come.

From the summit, the trail continues to the north, crossing open balds with exciting, close-up views of Slide, Friday, Balsam Cap, Rocky, Lone, Table, and Peekamoose. Most hikers will stray from the trail here to explore the bald and the broken views of the Ashokan Reservoir to the east through the trees. The popularity of camping (legal) is obvious on the bald, where there are a few large, informal fire rings. Very few places in the Catskills provide such an intimate look at the interior high peaks area. But what may astonish you the most are the lowbush blueberries, ranking easily as the best in the Catskills. The thick heaths cover the entire unshaded summit.

Many hikers take the short bushwhack to Little High Point (2,800 feet), where herd trails have developed. From Little High Point, you can see almost the entire Ashokan Reservoir, appearing as a long, flat strip of indigo. Spun into the scene are the somber, drab outcrops of rock that pockmark the summits and ranges beyond, and short stilts of wind-battered, nut-brown tree trunks, festooned with the scarlet berry clusters of mountain ash. Looking left (north) from east to west, you observe the Devil's Path Range. To the north are Wittenberg and Cornell. To the east and beyond the reservoir are the Taconics and the Berkshires. Moving westward is the long Shawangunk ridge and the plain of the Neversink, Rondout, and Mongaup. Suddenly Mombaccus again fills your eye, and you've covered about 270 degrees for what promises to be one of the best overlooks in the Catskill Mountains. Return to Ashokan High Point summit and descend by the route you came.

You can also complete the loop discussed earlier, time allowing. To do so from Ashokan High Point's summit (where the benchmarks are), follow the trail as it skirts the balds on the mountain's northwest side, soon descending through a thick and viewless forest. This is a longer option (add about 2 miles) than returning the way you came; the only advantage is that it's a little easier on the knees. The descent back to the main trail will take more than an hour. The loop is completed near the saddle between Ashokan High Point and Mombaccus, where you turned north for the final ascent. (It is much easier to return the way you came, and safer if your time is running short. It's not a good idea to be caught in low light on the less established, sometimes vague loop connection—it's not as well marked or as self-guiding as the main trail. If you plan to spend the day and do both Little Ashokan Point and the loop, it's a good idea to carry a headlamp and extra provisions.)

DID YOU KNOW?

Through the early 1900s, Ashokan High Point's summit yielded a commercial blueberry harvest.

MORE INFORMATION

For more information on the Catskill Forest Preserve, visit www.dec.ny.gov/lands/5265.html. For the DEC Region 3 office in New Paltz, call 845-256-3000.

NEARBY

An interesting attraction in the city of Kingston to the east is the Hudson River Maritime Museum, located at Rondout Landing on Rondout Creek. This museum preserves the maritime history of the Hudson with a collection of paintings, photographs, blueprints, artifacts, ship models, and small craft. It is open May 1 to October 31; www.hrmm.org; 845-338-0071.

Also in Kingston is the Trolley Museum of New York; www.tmny.org; 845-331-3399.

TRIP 37
MOUNT TREMPER

Location: Mount Tremper, NY
Rating: Strenuous
Distance: 5.6 miles
Elevation Gain: 1,960 feet
Estimated Time: 4 hours
Maps: USGS Phoenicia; AMC Catskill Mountains; NY–NJTC
Northeastern Catskills

An interesting hike leads past a quarry and two lean-tos to the summit fire tower.

DIRECTIONS
The Phoenicia Trail begins on the east side of the Esopus Creek, 2.3 miles northwest of Mount Tremper Corners and 1.6 miles southeast of Phoenicia, off CR 40 (Old Plank Road or old NY 28). *GPS coordinates:* 42° 3.964′ N, 74° 18.190′ W.

TRAIL DESCRIPTION
The hike up Mount Tremper (2,740 feet; previously Timothy Berg) is most direct and interesting from the southwest, following the red-marked Phoenicia Trail. This trail, a longtime favorite of Catskill hikers and backpackers, has become even more popular with the reopening of its now-reconditioned fire tower.

The trailhead lies along the northeastern banks of the Esopus Creek, an important trout fishery and New York City water source. Mount Romer (2,240 feet) can be seen to the southwest across the Esopus Creek from the trailhead parking area. Follow the trail across two wooden bridges to a flight of stone steps. The trail levels, heading northwest to join an old truck trail at 0.5 mile. Turn right (northeast), passing the trail register.

Several larger feeder streams intersect the trail. Evidence of logging is visible in the abundance of second-growth hardwood. Yellow blazes running north and southwest mark the forest-preserve boundaries. This piece of trail also sports a few of the Long Path's blue blazes.

As the trail steepens to 15 or 20 degrees, you cross an energetic brook that cuts a deep gully into the mountainside as it bursts from an unevenly aged

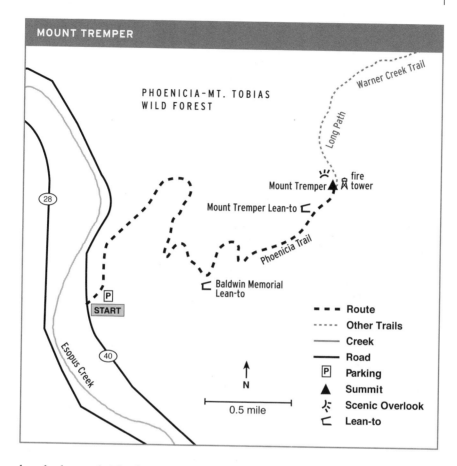

MOUNT TREMPER

PHOENICIA-MT. TOBIAS
WILD FOREST

Warner Creek Trail

Long Path

fire
Mount Tremper ▲ 𝕉 tower

Mount Tremper Lean-to ⊏

Phoenicia Trail

⊏ Baldwin Memorial
Lean-to

28

40

Esopus Creek

P
START

↑
N

⊢————————⊣
0.5 mile

- - - Route
· · · · · Other Trails
──── Creek
──── Road
P Parking
▲ Summit
𝕉 Scenic Overlook
⊏ Lean-to

hemlock stand. The large drainage area of Mount Tremper's southwestern slopes crosses the trail here, making it very wet at times.

You will have reached the first switchback when the trail suddenly turns south and uphill, where large maple and ash dominate an understory of young hemlock. To your left (east) and uphill, a long outcrop that has slid in many places begins an interesting visual transition. Water appears from a spring on your left. Fallen rock can be seen below the trail to your right, now heavily covered with moss and accumulated forest litter.

As you turn through the next switchback, you see a huge pile of quarry tailings on the left; the broken stone was shoved aside as longer slabs of bluestone were mined. The pile now forms a sort of manufactured ridge covered with thin soil and vegetation. The quarry itself is accessible from a small, overgrown roadbed on the trail's left that ascends gently into the quarry, covering an acre or two. You can follow it to a high, right-angled face, where the slabs were removed. Other than this vertical stone wall, only a small foundation and

The Mount Tremper fire tower overlooks the southern Catskills.

a few rusted iron remnants bear testimony to the once thriving industry. During your exploration, be alert to the possible presence of the quarry-dwelling rattlesnakes, which habitually bask in the warm sun of early spring. (There is a documented den here.)

Many of the nineteenth-century Catskills hotel owners disliked the imposing quarries. By the early 1880s, Major Jacob H. Tremper's Tremper House was competing for business with the Catskill Mountain House, so it could ill afford the nearby bluestone quarries robbing the hills of their peace and quiet.

The trail continues along a flatter section into an oak forest, joined by the laurel cover typical of higher elevations in the Catskills. At about 1,800 feet above sea level, you switchback about 120 degrees on a steepening grade, where paper birch and an occasional white pine appear. You'll have a few glimpses southwest toward the southern high peaks during early spring. Once through the switchback, you can look to the northwest at Sheridan Mountain.

The trail steepens, heading directly uphill, nearly due east. Within a few minutes you'll see the Baldwin Memorial Lean-to on your right. At this point, you are 2.0 miles from the trailhead, at 2,000 feet in elevation. Keep a sharp eye out for this shelter if you intend to use it, because it's off trail, positioned somewhat downhill, and facing south. It is in better condition than the summit lean-to, is more private, and has a water source nearby (uphill 0.1 mile off the trail), but has no summer views.

Finally, after one more switchback, you climb slightly and walk a long ridge. Just as you expect the summit to appear, you discover that the ridge continues for another 0.5 mile through a canopy of twisted oak, tormented and battered by exposure. After 20 minutes of hiking, you reach a stand of bright-barked beech trees on your left, and soon after that the Mount Tremper Lean-to. This hike ends here, but the trail continues to the north, joining the Warner Creek Trail to Silver Hollow (the Long Path route), and the Willow Trail into Hoyt Hollow and Willow.

The fire tower is just ahead and offers a 360-degree view. Plattekill, Indian Head, both summits of Twin, and Plateau Mountain in the Indian Head Wilderness Area are in view to the northeast. You see Blackhead and Black Dome in the far distance; the closer Hunter (looking carefully, you can find Hunter's fire tower with binoculars); Southwest Hunter; West Kill; and the seemingly endless array of peaks in the central Catskills, including Belleayre and Balsam. To the south are Ashokan High Point; bits and pieces of the Ashokan Reservoir; and several high peaks, including Wittenberg and Slide. To the right of Slide is Giant Ledge and Panther. To the east, you can see Cooper Lake (Kingston's water supply), as well as Overlook Mountain. You can see Sky Top and Eagle Cliff in the Shawangunks to the south, and the Hudson Highlands beyond.

This tower was built to replace the one on Slide, after New York State acquired the Mount Tremper tract between 1906 and 1910. The extractive resource and tourist industries followed the usual patterns here. In addition to intensive quarrying, the area gave heavily of its hemlock stands between 1836 and 1879, with one local tanner recording a total harvest of 170,000 cords of bark. The Tremper House hotel was built in 1879 near the existing railroad bed at the base of the mountain. It was the Catskills' first railroad hotel, built in an era when remoteness was more in fashion, and was visited by so many colorful personalities that it threatened even the popularity of Charles Beach's Catskill Mountain House. Oscar Wilde patronized the hotel (it was on his lecture circuit) by assuring the owners that "the top of a mountain is no place for a mountain house. . . it should be put in the valley; there the picturesque and beautiful is ever before you." The hotel was named for its manager, Major Jacob H. Tremper Jr., who renamed the mountain as well.

Return to the parking area by the route you came.

DID YOU KNOW?

The Mount Tremper fire tower has been restored and listed on the National Register of Historic Places.

MORE INFORMATION

Volunteers staff the fire tower on summer weekends, and they can supply information about the tower restoration and history. Mount Tremper is managed by the state of New York. For more information on the Catskill Forest Preserve, visit www.dec.ny.gov/lands/5265.html. For the DEC Region 3 office in New Paltz, call 845-256-3000.

NEARBY

In the village of Mount Tremper on NY 28 is the unique Kaleidostore, housed in a restored nineteenth-century dairy barn. Here is found the world's largest kaleidoscope, along with multi-media presentations (shows vary with the seasons) and a kaleidoscope shop; www.kaleidostore.com; 845-688-5800.

BLUESTONE

The period of bluestone quarrying in the eastern Catskills lasted from 1840 to 1880, in uneasy partnership with the tanbarking industry. In many cases, quarriers used the same roads that the tanners had cut years earlier, and many of the same laborers—most of them Irish—worked for both as the seasons overlapped.

Settlers and tenant farmers recognized immediately that the bluish, fine-grained sandstone was easily worked and made an ideal building material. They used it for their homes, barns, smokehouses, shops, roads, hearths, and lintels; some even ventured into the commercial end of quarrying. But soon, the big stone dealers who shipped their flagstones by sloop and, later, by three-masted schooner and railroad, put the small operators out of business.

Bluestone was prized for its ease of handling and shaping. It was used extensively for sidewalks, as it proved durable, attractive, and attainable in volume. As a result, it provided the first pavement for New York City, and quickly found its way to St. Louis, San Francisco, and even to Havana, Cuba. Whereas the tanning industry ended as the result of the near deforestation of the hills, the quarrying industry came to an end with the invention of cement in Rosendale and High Falls, New York, in 1825.

As you hike the trails that were once used by quarriers and their teams, you will see the old quarries, and note where some of the stones lying midtrail bear the century-old mark of a wedge or chisel. On closer examination, you can still find flags and perfect lintels lying neatly stacked, waiting for the teamsters that never came—testimony to a way of life that was changed nearly overnight.

TRIP 38
OVERLOOK MOUNTAIN

Location: Woodstock, NY
Rating: Strenuous
Distance: 5.0 miles
Elevation Gain: 1,440 feet
Estimated Time: 3 to 4 hours
Maps: USGS Woodstock; AMC Catskill Mountains; NY–NJTC Northeastern Catskills

This steep hike climbs to old hotel ruins, a fire tower, and Eagle Cliff from Meads Mountain, above the town of Woodstock.

DIRECTIONS
From the Woodstock village green, turn north onto Rock City Road. Continue straight through the intersection with Glasco Turnpike at 0.6 mile and climb Meads Mountain Road to the trailhead parking area at 2.6 miles. *GPS coordinates: 42° 4.215′ N, 74° 7.287′ W.*

TRAIL DESCRIPTION
Overlook Mountain (3,140 feet) is Woodstock's mecca. The trailhead begins at the height of land on Meads Mountain (the high saddle between Overlook and Mount Guardian), opposite the Tibetan Buddhist monastery Karma Triyana Dharmachakra and adjacent to the Magic Meadow of Woodstock Rainbow Tribe fame. The Rainbow Tribe, formed in the late 1960s, still exists. The Catholic Church of Christ on the Mount is here too, made famous in the 1960s by the "hippie priest," Father William Francis. This area is a sort of vortex zone, one that has attracted monks, hikers, and artists for 100 years or more. It was because of the view from Meads that artist Bolton Brown encouraged fellow artist Ralph Whitehead to build his art colony in Woodstock in 1902, based upon the utopian ideas of John Ruskin and the poetic vision of Walt Whitman. Whitehead named his art colony Byrdcliffe, after his wife Jane Byrd McCall, and situated it in the shadow of Overlook Mountain.

At the Overlook Summit trailhead, locate the map kiosk and trail register. The trail is an easy though not dull climb up a consistent grade on a dirt road—all the way to the fire tower. You begin at 1,700 feet in elevation following red markers, surrounded by dark hemlock woods that open up into

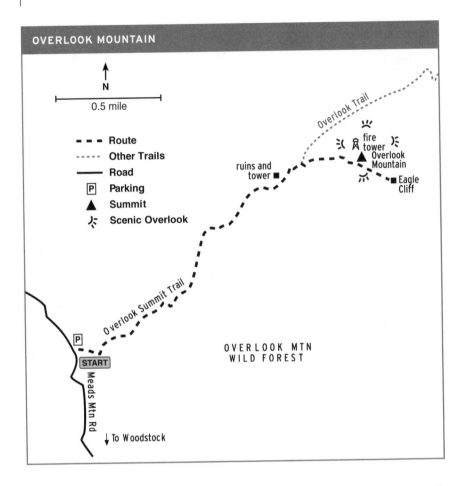

OVERLOOK MOUNTAIN

N

0.5 mile

- - - Route
····· Other Trails
——— Road
P Parking
▲ Summit
)(Scenic Overlook

Overlook Trail

fire tower

ruins and tower ■

Overlook Mountain ▲

Eagle Cliff ■

Overlook Summit Trail

P

START

OVERLOOK MTN WILD FOREST

Meads Mtn Rd

↓ To Woodstock

hardwoods and mountain laurel as the trail climbs. The forest is strewn with large sedimentary boulders, dragged off the mountaintop by retreating ice some 15,000 years ago. The ascent is consistent and at times monotonous as it follows the TV-tower maintenance road in the presence of electrical wires, having lost the character it certainly had when quarriers and tanners first built it. But soon, mountains appear everywhere, and Indian Head, a scant 3.0 miles distant, comes out of nowhere in the Devil's Path mountains.

Within 45 minutes of hiking, you will come upon the somber ruins of the Overlook Mountain House. The Mountain House opened in 1871, but despite its various distinctions (it was the highest mountain house in the Catskills), it seemed cursed. It burned completely in 1875, was reconstructed in 1878, and burned again in 1924. In 1928, under new ownership, the existing poured-concrete foundation and walls, erected near the old hotel site, were started. Walls, windows, and plumbing were about all that were completed when the

Views from the Overlook Mountain fire tower are among the best in the Catskills.

stock market crash of 1929 forced the project to be abandoned. Trees now grow in the main hall. In the 1990s, artists pasted biodegradable images and histories to the walls, most of them now faded.

Continue on the trail, rising easily, passing the TV and cell tower on your left. At 2.0 miles, pass the blue-marked Overlook Trail on your left. Continue straight, passing several herd trails that lead right (south) to limited views that aren't worth your time. At 2.5 miles, you will arrive at the summit. There's an observer's cabin, open on summer weekends and serving as a museum to the fire tower. Barry Knight, a local resident and volunteer, has climbed Overlook hundreds of times in all weather conditions. A tower enthusiast, he located, restored, and rebuilt a dismantled state fire tower on his property in Hurley. "If it weren't for the efforts of volunteers, these towers would not only be closed to the public," he says, "they'd all be dismantled!" The view would not be as spectacular without the tower. In 1997, the Overlook Mountain fire tower was recognized by the National Historical Lookout Register for its historical and cultural significance. The stewards will be happy to show you around the summit and tower.

The summit view is among the Catskills' finest and includes the Berkshires and the Taconics, the Hudson River south to the Highlands, the Shawangunks, the Ashokan Reservoir, and more Catskill peaks than you can count (remember, the Catskills have 100 peaks of more than 3,000 feet in elevation).

Compasses don't work here because of the steel tower, but a working alidade (a large, circular sight set on a compass rose) and the steward will help you identify the major peaks. Take the time to visit with the volunteer observer and have a look in the cabin. Follow the trail to the right of the cabin door to a more private view over the immediate valley (beware of the vertical drop). This is Eagle Cliff, named by the landscape painter Charles Lanman, who was inspired by the legend of an American Indian infant who was stolen by an eagle, whereupon the child's heartbroken mother threw herself over the cliff.

Just as inspiring a view is that of Overlook itself from the valley floor, a sight that merited the brushes of Frederic Church and Thomas Cole and prompted the pen of Charles Herbert Moore. The mountain continues to provide inspiration for aspiring artists from the village of Woodstock below.

Return by the route you came.

DID YOU KNOW?

From the tower, six states are seen: New York, Connecticut, Vermont, Massachusetts, New Jersey, and Pennsylvania (some will also argue for New Hampshire).

MORE INFORMATION

Parts of the Overlook Mountain House building have collapsed and the DEC has advised the public not to enter the ruin. The fire tower and the observer's cabin, open on summer weekends and serving as a museum to the fire tower, are staffed by volunteers. For more information on the Catskill Forest Preserve, visit www.dec.ny.gov/lands/5265.html. For the DEC Region 3 office in New Paltz, call 845-256-3000.

NEARBY

Take a drive through Byrdcliffe on your way home. Turn right at the Glasco Turnpike (CR 33) crossroads as you descend from Meads, then turn right again within 0.5 mile onto Upper Byrdcliffe Road. Byrdcliffe is still a thriving arts colony, with resident artists and writers, and offers many public arts programs conducted in the Byrdcliffe Theater. Attached to the barn is a box of self-guided walking tour maps for the complex. To complete your outing, visit the Woodstock Byrdcliffe Guild (gallery; www.woodstockguild.org; 845-679-2079) in town, and grab a slice at Catskill Mountain Pizza on Tinker Street.

TRIP 39
INDIAN HEAD MOUNTAIN

Location: Platte Clove, NY
Rating: Strenuous
Distance: 6.0 miles
Elevation Gain: 1,573 feet
Estimated Time: 4.5 hours
Maps: USGS Kaaterskill; AMC Catskill Mountains; NY–NJTC Northeastern Catskills

Featuring an interior forest hike to a boreal summit with exciting views, Indian Head is among the Catskills' most popular peaks.

DIRECTIONS

To reach the trailhead, turn south off NY 23A at the only light in Tannersville onto CR 16 (Spring Street). Set to zero. At 1.3 miles this road intersects Bloomer Road, where you bear left. At 1.8 miles you will reach a Y where you bear left onto Platte Clove Road. At 4.6 miles you pass Dale Lane on the right (the trail to Sugarloaf, Twin, and Pecoy Notch). Stay on Platte Clove Road, and at 5.7 miles you'll see Prediger Road on the right. Follow it 0.5 mile to the trailhead loop and park. (See Trip 44, Huckleberry Point, for alternate seasonal directions through Platte Clove.) *GPS coordinates: 42° 8.40′ N, 74° 6.260′ W.*

TRAIL DESCRIPTION

Indian Head is a beguiling triad of peaks forming a profile that appears from afar to be a face. It is best seen from the north or east, from the Taconics or from Olana, Frederic Church's Persian castle in Hudson, and from the NYS Thruway and the surrounding valleys.

At the trailhead you will see signs identifying the red-marked trail to Indian Head Mountain, Jimmy Dolan Notch Trail, and Echo Lake Trail. This is the Devil's Path trailhead. You will follow the Devil's Path a short distance to the Jimmy Dolan Notch Trail and join it again as you turn east in Jimmy Dolan Notch to summit Indian Head and complete the loop.

The foot trail leads you into the forest over a stringer bridge across one of several lively creeks that will keep you company until higher elevations are reached. Follow the well-marked (blue and red) old road uphill, reaching the trail register within 500 feet. Maps are posted here. Within 10 minutes, you'll

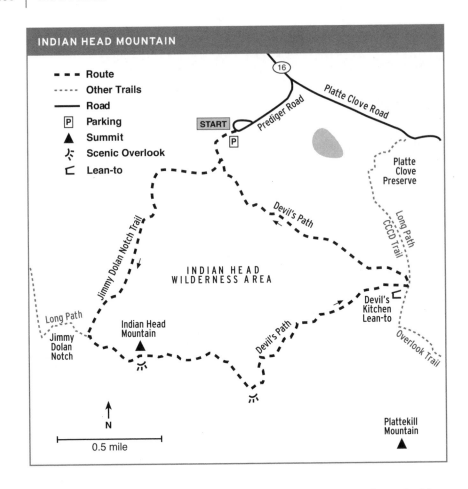

INDIAN HEAD MOUNTAIN

- - -   Route
- - - - -   Other Trails
———   Road
P   Parking
▲   Summit
⅄   Scenic Overlook
⊏   Lean-to

INDIAN HEAD
WILDERNESS AREA

Platte Clove Road

Prediger Road

START

Platte
Clove
Preserve

Devil's Path

Jimmy Dolan Notch Trail

Long Path
CCCD Trail

Devil's
Kitchen
Lean-to

Long Path

Jimmy
Dolan
Notch

Indian Head
Mountain

Devil's Path

Overlook Trail

Plattekill
Mountain

N

0.5 mile

pass a stream on your right and arrive at a trail junction. Bear right on the blue-marked Jimmy Dolan Notch Trail to Jimmy Dolan Notch and Indian Head.

The Jimmy Dolan Notch Trail rises slightly over a rocky footway with exposed tree roots into a pure beech forest. To your right, in a northerly direction, you can see Kaaterskill High Peak and Roundtop Mountain through the trees in springtime. The trail is not strenuous yet, as you slowly bend to the south, getting a view of Twin's northerly shoulder up to your right.

As you continue along a steeper, eroded section of the trail, you'll have a peek at Indian Head on your left (southeast) and will see more of Twin to the right. Climbing higher, about 45 minutes into your hike (1.5 miles), you can look back (north) at Kaaterskill High Peak, Roundtop, and the Blackhead Range. Within 10 to 15 minutes more, you will be happy to arrive in the Notch (3,100 feet) for some rest before the steep summit climb.

In Jimmy Dolan Notch the Long Path intersects with the Devil's Path, showing Indian Head at (a rugged) 0.5 mile, and Platte Clove Road at 3.9

Visitors can see Indian Head Mountain from Meads Mountain Road in Woodstock.

miles. Jimmy Dolan Notch is in every sense a classic notch, a symmetrical cut through the mountain that is scattered with large boulders and crumbling rock shelves, an ancient river canyon from which the waters have long since run away to a dried-up sea.

The trail climbs and eases alternately as you scramble uphill from the Notch, heading east. After gaining nearly 400 feet in elevation from the Notch, the trail, thick with hemlock and balsam fir, flattens suddenly. This is the only indication that you have reached the summit, which is completely surrounded by trees with no view. Within 5 minutes, you'll go downhill slightly to another flat area where climax spruce trees soar above.

Continue along through a pure evergreen forest. Some restricted views of the Sawkill Valley are available to the south if you want to push your way through the trees and explore a little, but the best views lie ahead.

You are now descending to the middle knoll, from the forehead (summit) to the eyebrow of the Indian's head. On the eastern end of the middle knoll, you'll reach a high overlook that juts out to the east with a vertical, dangerous drop at 3,200 feet above sea level. A nearly 180-degree view reveals Ashokan, the Shawangunks, Overlook, the Hudson (part of which is obstructed by the east knoll, or nose), and the Highlands, Taconics, and Berkshires. You are roughly midway through the hike, with 3.0 miles behind you.

From here, follow cautiously down a very steep section of trail into a shallow saddle separating the eyebrow and nose. Within 10 minutes, you'll encounter another thick stand of fir that would be difficult, if not impossible, to walk through without a trail. This is a prime example of "cripplebrush." Going uphill and leveling out onto the nose, in 10 minutes you'll reach a spot where views have been maintained by the DEC's cutting. (Many people disagree with maintaining vista cuts in wilderness areas and have questioned its legality.) The result is an outstanding look at the Catskill high peaks area, running from Ashokan High Point over to Slide and beyond. In this collection of peaks are also Peekamoose and Table, Lone, Rocky, Balsam Cap, Samuels, Friday, Wittenberg, Cornell, Giant Ledge, Panther, and many more. You see Overlook's fire tower, the Tibetan Monastery in Meads, the Overlook Mountain House ruin, and as far south as High Point, New Jersey (with binoculars you can see the tower at 219 degrees).

Within a few minutes of leaving this area, you'll swing toward the north, skirting the nose's easterly rim, which will give you a look at Plattekill's (trailless) western shoulder. With fair views to the east along the trail, you have the opportunity to look deep into Platte Clove, and within 5 minutes you'll reach Sherman's Lookout, which has also been cut over to provide views to the north and a previously unavailable look at the Blackhead Mountains, Kaaterskill High Peak and Roundtop, and the Hudson River. Looking beyond the deep cut of Platte Clove you can see Bash Bish Gorge in the Southern Taconics. This is the last scenic overlook before the plunge into the valley.

After approximately 20 minutes of hiking downhill with diminishing views to the east, you may find the trail wet as it terraces down, going level for a way then steep again. The footing is red shale and some broken conglomerate. The majestic stands of large virgin hemlock here, some more than 30 inches in diameter, reflect the magnificent primordial forest before the tanning period.

Within 30 to 40 minutes of leaving the nose, you'll reach a trail junction. To your right is Devil's Kitchen Lean-to (this makes for a pretty, 15-minute side trip to the bridge over the Cold Kill), and far beyond it, Echo Lake. Bear left (north), and within 500 feet or so the Devil's Path Trail dodges left (northwest). Watch closely for this turn—it's not obvious. If you go straight (north) on the Catskill Center for Conservation and Development Trail, you'll wind up a mile east of Prediger Road.

Turning left, or northwest, and back into deep hemlock woods, the trail takes you uphill slightly. In 10 to 15 minutes you'll cross a creek continuing through a fern glade, then cross another small stream, before reaching the trail junction with Jimmy Dolan Notch Trail. The 1.5-mile section of trail from Devil's Kitchen will take you about 40 minutes. Turn right, and you'll be back at the parking lot in a few minutes.

DID YOU KNOW?

Artist Thomas Cole depicted Indian Head Mountain in his 1843 painting *River in the Catskills.*

MORE INFORMATION

For more information on the Catskill Forest Preserve, visit www.dec.ny.gov/lands/5265.html. For the DEC Region 4 office in Stamford, call 607-652-7365.

NEARBY

The Mountain Top Arboretum off CR 23C in Tannersville is open year-round with free admission. There are three areas to walk through and view native trees, shrubs, and wildflowers; www.mtarboretum.org; 518-589-3903.

THE DEVIL'S PATH

Twenty-three miles long, with a cumulative elevation gain approaching 9,000 feet, the Devil's Path is one of two trunk trails in the eastern Catskills, joining Indian Head Mountain in Platte Clove to West Kill Mountain in the high Spruceton Valley. Crossing six peaks in excess of 3,500 feet (including Southwest Hunter Mountain), this rugged trail, often undertaken as a long weekend backpacking experience, begins on Prediger Road in the town of Hunter. (See Trip 39 for directions to the Devil's Path Trailhead from the east, and Trip 53 for directions from the west.) The trail can also be done as a series of day hikes from access points in the north. Hikers looking for more of a challenge can begin at the Overlook Mountain trailhead in Meads, adding 2.0 miles and 1,400 feet in elevation (where the Devil's Path ought to begin).

Few trails are so spectacular—and so difficult. Rugged, boreal peaks; deep, weather-ravaged notches; a scarcity of water; and steep, rocky terrain characterize the route. Several lean-tos are conveniently located along the way, on or near the main trunk.

The Devil's Path inspired fear in early Dutch settlers with its deep, dark cloves (ravines), where the Devil was said to dwell. In the 1940s, the DEC created Devil's Tombstone State Campground in Stony Clove Notch, putting a symbolic end to the era of superstition and legend for which the Catskills are famous. Today the trail continues beyond Stony Clove, into the west.

TRIP 40
TWIN MOUNTAIN

Location: Elka Park, NY
Rating: Strenuous
Distance: 4.4 miles
Elevation Gain: 1,740 feet
Estimated Time: 5 hours
Maps: USGS Kaaterskill; AMC Catskill Mountains; NY–NJTC Northeastern Catskills

Twin is a double-peaked mountain with superior views of the Hudson Valley and the Indian Head Wilderness Area.

DIRECTIONS

From Tannersville, turn south at the light (the intersection of CR 23C and Railroad Avenue, CR 16) to join Spring Street (CR 16), bearing right onto Elka Park Road at 1.8 miles. Go over the Schoharie Creek, pass the post office, and bear left at 2.8 miles. Go another 1.2 miles to the trailhead and park on the right. The trailhead can also be reached from Platte Clove Road (CR 16) via Dale Lane, by bearing right onto Elka Park road (a.k.a. Roaring Brook Road) at the intersection with Wase Road and going 0.7 mile to the trailhead. *GPS coordinates:* 42° 09.068′ N, 74° 07.862′ W.

TRAIL DESCRIPTION

Twin-peaked Twin Mountain is one of the Devil's Path mountains, those craggy and tempestuous summits that you see crowding the western sky as you drive on the NYS Thruway north and south between New Paltz and Catskill. Twin is best hiked from the Pecoy Notch Trail, ascending gradually along the Roaring Kill Trail from Elka Park Road (seasonal, unmaintained in winter but accessible by four-wheel-drive vehicles). From the Roaring Kill trailhead on Elka Park Road (2,150 feet elevation), take the yellow-marked Roaring Kill Trail 0.25 mile to a junction and follow the Pecoy Notch Trail to the left (southeast).

The trail ascends gradually, passing a few quarry pits where you may notice some large, hand-dressed flagstones. Enter a hemlock woods and descend to the left a bit to arrive at a large, open quarry face over an extensive talus field providing views to the north. This (Dibble's Quarry) is probably the best trailside example of a bluestone quarry in the Catskills. Several druidic bluestone "recliners" and an array of intriguing stone sculptures have been constructed

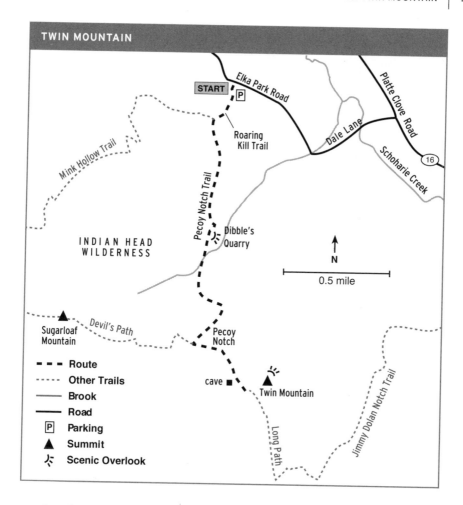

TWIN MOUNTAIN

Elka Park Road
Platte Clove Road
START [P]
Roaring
Kill Trail
Dale Lane
Schoharie Creek
Mink Hollow Trail
16
Pecoy Notch Trail
Dibble's
Quarry
INDIAN HEAD
WILDERNESS
N
0.5 mile
Sugarloaf
Mountain
Devil's Path
Pecoy
Notch
- - - Route
- - - - - Other Trails
cave ■
Twin Mountain
——— Brook
——— Road
[P] Parking
▲ Summit
Scenic Overlook
Long Path
Jimmy Dolan Notch Trail

to take advantage of the views over the Clove toward Huckleberry Point. You can get a look at Twin Mountain from here, and to the north and downhill you see the Hutterian Bruderhof. Kaaterskill High Peak and Roundtop are in the foreground. After you explore the area, continue along the trail. You'll leave the quarry and enter hardwoods, crossing a bridge and ascending.

Soon you will skirt the outlet of a beaver pond on your right. Beaver activity is spotty in this pond that feeds the high, upper Schoharie, but several dams and lodges have been evident in recent years. The pond, fed by runoff coming down the northeast slopes of Sugarloaf, attracts wildlife and has a quiet, primordial spirit about it, making a welcome stopover. As you continue, the trail heads uphill, and you begin to get views to the north of the Blackhead Range.

After about an hour's easy hiking, you'll reach Pecoy Notch, and the Devil's Path Trail. There is no trail out of Pecoy Notch to the south, only a profusion of tumbledown boulders and twisted logs. This is one of the notches, along

Twin Mountain, part of the Indian Head Wilderness, rises beyond Cooper Lake.

with its easterly neighbor Jimmy Dolan Notch, that can be seen as bright bare scrapes from points as far south as the Shawangunks.

Bear left (east) for Twin, following the Devil's Path (red) and Long Path trails. Blue and aqua are used interchangeably for the Long Path, though the official color is aqua, to distinguish it from state markings. Twin is 0.5 mile ahead, with an additional 540-foot vertical rise to its first (true) summit.

The incline is steep with a westerly aspect, soon exposing Sugarloaf and, beyond, Hunter and its fire tower. You'll pass a large rock overhang that has been heavily used by hikers and is a convenient shelter in the event of rain. The trail is very steep in places. Suddenly, through a balsam-thick shoulder of the mountain, you see views opening up to the south, the vertical ledges of stone on your path finally subsiding to a series of flat outcrops that form the northerly summit of Twin.

From this point the view is very good, extending as far south and southwest as the eye can see, but it is blocked to the north and east by mountains in the 3,500-foot class. From this southerly exposure you can survey the southern Catskills' high peaks just west of the Ashokan Reservoir. You may recognize Ashokan High Point, Samuels Point, Friday, Wittenberg, Cornell, Panther, Giant Ledge, Balsam Cap, Balsam Lake Mountain, and Graham, with many lower surrounding peaks identifiable with the aid of map and compass. You will also have a close look at the foreground mountains Tremper, Carl, and Olderbark (west to east).

During runoff, listen closely and you might hear the noisy waters of the Saw Kill or Mink Hollow Brook echoing up from below. Cooper Lake, part of Kingston's water supply, is visible 5 miles south–southwest of you, with Mount Tobias on its right. There was once a glass factory below in the Saw Kill Valley, and until recent years hikers were able to see the mirrorlike reflections of the waste glass that was cast aside, giving rise to the name the Glass Plains. The plains have since been reclaimed by nature.

The southerly summit of Twin is an additional (easy) 0.5-mile hike from here through a saddle of dense coniferous forest, bringing you to another flat-rock overlook facing south. Views to the east are of the Hudson River valley and much of the river itself. From here, nearly the entire Ashokan Reservoir is visible, as well as the Shawangunks. On a clear day, beyond them, you can see the scattered hills of the Hudson Highlands.

You'll want to visit both of Twin's summits to take in the variety of views that each cannot offer individually. If you have a lunch, plan to enjoy it at the more expansive southerly summit, where hikers feel more inclined to loaf.

Return by the route you came, and while descending the north summit, about halfway down, you can test your lungs against the echoes from Sugarloaf.

DID YOU KNOW?

Twin is the only Catskill peak with two recognized summits.

MORE INFORMATION

For more information on the Catskill Forest Preserve, visit www.dec.ny.gov/lands/5265.html. For the DEC Region 4 office in Stamford, call 607-652-7365.

NEARBY

Many hikers climb Sugarloaf as well as Twin in a one-day outing. If you choose to do so, factor in an additional 2 miles and 800 feet of ascent for a cumulative elevation gain of 2,500 feet. Twin has a far superior view, however. In fact, there's no comparison.

TRIP 41
PLATEAU MOUNTAIN FROM STONY CLOVE

Location: Hunter, NY
Rating: Strenuous
Distance: 6.0 miles
Elevation Gain: 1,840 feet
Estimated Time: 6 hours
Maps: USGS Hunter; AMC Catskill Mountains; NY–NJTC Catskill
Trails 41

**A very steep rise out of Stony Clove Notch leads to a long, level
plateau with isolated views.**

DIRECTIONS
To locate the trailhead, drive south on NY 214 from NY 23A between Hunter
and Tannersville, and go 3.0 miles to the south end of Notch Lake. Or from
the south at Phoenicia and NY 28, go north 9.0 miles on NY 214. Park at the
trailhead parking area (Devil's Tombstone State Campground day-use area) on
the west side of NY 214. *GPS coordinates:* 42° 09.564′ N, 74° 12.218′ W.

TRAIL DESCRIPTION
Stony Clove Notch is a narrow mountain pass with rugged visual appeal. It is
formed by the long ridge of Plateau meeting with that of Hunter and holds at
its apex the teardrop of Notch Lake and the Devil's Tombstone State Campground, where the Devil's Path Trail crosses NY 214. This major Catskill landmark can be seen from 50 miles away. Take a look at Plateau's western slope,
and you'll have an idea of the ascent you're about to make.

Cross the road to the east where you'll see trail signs and the red markers of the Devil's Path. Plateau Mountain Lookout (a.k.a. Orchid or Orchard
Point) is indicated at 1.2 miles, but the mountain's true summit is on the east
end of the ridge at 3,840 feet, 2.5 miles from the trailhead. What you will wit-
ness from the lookout will please you more than the boreal, viewless summit.
Plateau Mountain Lookout is an outstanding viewpoint at 3,600 feet—one that
is grossly underrated in the hierarchy of Catskill vistas.

Climb the steps and ascend over rocky terrain into a tall hardwood forest. Quickly the trail becomes very steep, with makeshift stone steps to aid
your ascent. In 10 minutes or more, as you climb over roots and rocks, you'll
encounter isolated rock slides to your left and views over your shoulder to the

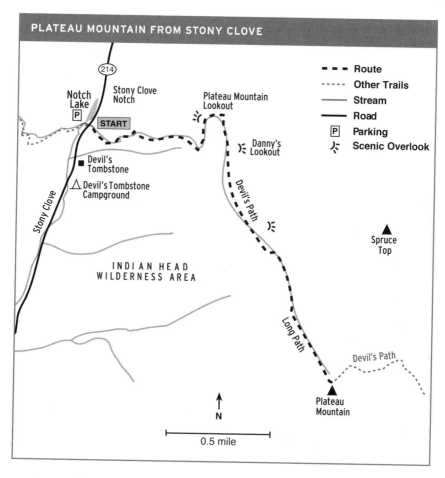

southwest of Slide and Wittenberg in the Slide–Panther Wilderness Area, as well as Cornell, Friday, Peekamoose, Table, Panther, and beyond.

These good views vanish as the trail turns north, with spring beauties and red trillium sprinkled liberally along its edge. If the trillium is in bloom during your visit, you might be surprised at its putrid scent, one that is unbecoming to such a pretty flower. All species of trillium are rare, protected, and may not be picked. In spring you also will see in bloom the very pretty viburnum, or hobblebush, with its large, heart-shaped leaves, a favorite deer food.

On this flat section of trail at 3,400 feet (the first flat stretch of trail since you set out), you can look back west for occasional views of Hunter Mountain. You'll cross the 3,500-foot mark and may see a sign indicating this point. In another 10 minutes you'll traverse some ledges that take you gradually up and onto Plateau Mountain Lookout. This is a nearly 180-degree view, reaching across the range from Colonel's Chair (and the ski trails) to Hunter Mountain's fire tower, Southwest Hunter, West Kill, the high peaks, and the Ashokan

Though challenging, the hike up Plateau Mountain provides interesting scenic lookouts.

Reservoir. You can see Belleayre Mountain, Balsam, Haynes, Eagle, Big Indian (shaped like a molar), and beyond it, Doubletop and Fir. Giant Ledge looks tiny at 246 degrees (with binoculars you can make out the cliffs). Slide Mountain is at 220 degrees. Look down into the col and then at Cornell and Wittenberg. You can plainly see the slide on Slide (snow helps to define it). Wittenberg's steep and sudden dropoff is just above Mount Tremper's fire tower (230 degrees). Peekamoose is at 228 degrees. Looking to the left of it, you see Ashokan High Point. With binoculars you can see the Lake Maratanza tower farm in Sam's Point Pitch Pine Preserve. Across Stony Clove on the east-facing slope of Hunter Mountain is Becker Hollow, the shortest route to Hunter's summit.

The summit ridge is flat now. Continue following the trail to the east until you reach an unobstructed overlook (Danny's Lookout) on the north side with a large rock upon which a crude rising sun is carved. Views include the Blackhead Range, North Point, South Mountain, Roundtop, Kaaterskill High Peak, and down into Platte Clove. Hard to your right you will see Spruce Top and then Sugarloaf, with its long ridgeline plunging into Mink Hollow to meet roaring Kill and Schoharie Creek. You can see North Lake at 86 degrees. The distant mountain groups to the northeast are the Taconics, including the Greylock Range.

Continue on the flat ridge over a soft, duff trail—dizzy with trout lilies—for another 5 minutes until you reach an overlook with the same northerly views. Use caution—this one has a dangerous drop. Many blown-down conifers lie upon this exposed ridge, like bleached whalebones against the contrasting verdant life. Continue through a forest of large spruce and fir, where the trail switches to the ridge's south side. You'll begin to go uphill slightly in a few minutes, and within another 10 minutes enter a thick understory of balsam reminiscent of Indian Head's summit, but not as enclosed. Whipped winds tear along the thin ridge as you peer through trees into Silver Hollow and Stony Clove. The forest remains coniferous on this long walk to the summit; it lends a nostalgic feel, perhaps reminding you of favorite walks in places like the White Mountains or the Maine coast.

In 20 minutes you'll reach the summit, just beyond a 90-degree left turn where the trail turns south to east. The thick spruce–fir cripplebrush will rub against your shoulders as the trail wanders along the ridge. Follow the trail for another 15 minutes to your final destination—a rock looking east. Jump across a shallow crevasse and survey Sugarloaf, Kaaterskill High Peak, Roundtop, North Point, North Mountain, Overlook, and part of Twin. The view is limited compared with the ones you had already, but it gives you an intimate feeling for the heart of the Devil's Path.

Return the way you came, listening for the *grokk, grokk* of hunting ravens.

DID YOU KNOW?

When trillium blooms in very early spring, its stench attracts pollinating insects in search of decomposing flesh. For this reason, it is called a "carrion" flower.

MORE INFORMATION

Parking for the trailhead is at the Devil's Tombstone State Campground day-use area at Notch Lake (see below). For more information on the Catskill Forest Preserve, visit www.dec.ny.gov/lands/5265.html. For the DEC Region 4 office in Stamford, call 607-652-7365.

NEARBY

Camping is available at the Devil's Tombstone State Campground for $16. Amenities include tent and trailer sites, a playground, volleyball courts, horseshoes pits, and hiking trails. It is located on NY 214 in Hunter; www.dec.ny.gov/outdoor/24462.html; 845-688-7160. Reservations can be made at new-yorkstateparks.reserveamerica.com.

TRIP 42
KAATERSKILL HIGH PEAK

Location: Platte Clove, NY
Rating: Strenuous
Distance: 10 miles
Elevation Gain: 1,855 feet
Estimated Time: 6 hours
Maps: USGS Kaaterskill; AMC Catskill Mountains; NY–NJTC Catskill
Trails 41

**A long, remote hike into the isolated Kaaterskill Wild Forest Area
offers spectacular views from Hurricane Ledge.**

DIRECTIONS

To reach the trailhead, turn south off NY 23A at the only light in Tanners-
ville onto CR 16 (Spring Street). Set to zero. At 1.3 miles, this road intersects
Bloomer Road, where you'll bear left. At 1.8 miles you'll reach a Y where you
bear left onto Platte Clove Road (still CR 16). At 4.6 miles, you'll pass Dale
Lane on the right (the trail to Sugarloaf, Twin, and Pecoy Notch). Stay on
Platte Clove Road, and at 5.7 miles you'll see Prediger Road on the right. At 6.5
miles from Tannersville, turn left onto the dirt entrance to the Kaaterskill Wild
Forest Area parking lot. (See Trip 44 for alternate seasonal directions through
Platte Clove.) *GPS coordinates: 42° 08.033′ N, 74° 04.918′ W.*

TRAIL DESCRIPTION

High Peak was far more popular 100 years ago during the hotel heyday than
it is today. Then, the mountains were defined by hotel magnates who did
everything possible to convince visitors that their establishment was indeed
positioned in the heart of the Catskills. High Peak (contending with Roundtop) was considered the highest mountain in the range until the Princeton
geologist and founder of the National Weather Bureau, Arnold Guyot, reduced
it to a lowly 23rd on the list of Catskill peaks in 1779 (actually it is 22nd). His
authority was considered absolute by many; yet his findings challenged local
belief to the point that many people claimed they were in scientific error. A
veritable empire of tourism had been built on the supposition that High Peak
was the very heart and soul of the Catskills, and to question that status was
heresy. But science often overrules even the most wishful thinking.

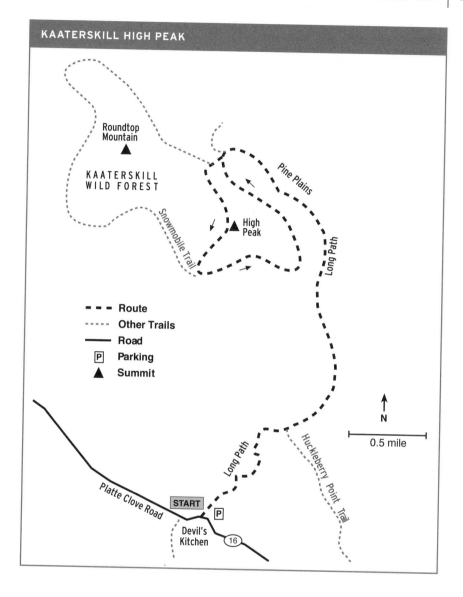

KAATERSKILL HIGH PEAK

Roundtop
Mountain ▲

KAATERSKILL
WILD FOREST

Snowmobile Trail

Pine Plains

▲ High
Peak

Long Path

- - - Route
········ Other Trails
——— Road
P Parking
▲ Summit

N

0.5 mile

Long Path

Huckleberry Point Trail

Platte Clove Road

START

P

Devil's
Kitchen 16

From low in the valley, High Peak does appear to be the highest mountain on the skyline. While it is evident from guidebooks and maps of the golden era that Kaaterskill High Peak was a very popular climbing destination, the mountain has since existed in such anonymity that only an informally marked trail crosses its summit. A snowmobile trail circles both High Peak and Roundtop, providing access to High Peak's summit trail. (Roundtop is trailless.)

At the entrance to the parking area you will see trailhead signs and orange snowmobile markers, aqua-colored Long Path disks and/or blazes, and blue

Kaaterskill High Peak and Roundtop were once thought to be the Catskills' highest mountains.

foot-trail markers. A sign denotes Junction With Loop Trail, 3.6 Miles; this is your in-transit destination. Don't be confused by the curiously useless reference to Steenberg Road, a dirt road named for an early quarryman who lived in the vicinity of Huckleberry Point. It is not identified on maps or in the field.

Follow the snowmobile trail uphill through a dense forest of hardwood and hemlock, passing old stone walls and listening to a tumbling creek on your right. The trail follows a pleasing old dirt road that has eroded well below surface grade. Within 25 minutes, you will reach a fork where arrows point to the right. Continue on the well-marked snowmobile trail, and in less than 10 minutes you'll reach another Y, where you bear right, passing the Huckleberry Point Trail (see Trip 44). Viburnum, yellow and purple violets, and trout lilies (the mottled leaf resembles a trout) form a colorful understory. The trail is relatively level for the next 20 minutes before you cross a pair of short timber bridges through a swampy area between two shallow creeks in a pretty spruce–fir swamp.

The trail then heads uphill and you begin to see beech trees and some remarkably large hemlocks and maples. Wildlife is abundant. Porcupines will scuttle away as you approach; owls will scrutinize you with haunting whispers as you rest. Here, amid the spring beauties, you can look south at Plattekill Mountain and northwest at the shoulder of High Peak. After a fairly stiff ascent, the trail levels out into a birch forest with scattered evergreens, which soon turns to a pure evergreen forest. Curiously, this pure spruce–fir forest is called the Pine Plains.

After 45 minutes of traversing this flat, swampy section of trail (wet and muddy in spring), turn sharply left, still following the snowmobile markers. The faint trail (the Long Path) to Palenville via Buttermilk Falls, Wildcat ravine, and Poet's Ledge forks to the northwest in a beech wood, becoming a narrow foot trail. This sharp left (still the snowmobile trail) heads uphill now, and within 5 minutes you'll reach a T and the start of the loop around Kaaterskill High Peak and Roundtop. Turn right (west). There is no sign indicating a trail to High Peak's summit, and marking is poor, so you must be very alert to spy it on your left. Within about 500 feet of turning, at elevation 2,933 feet, blue blazes can be seen off the trail heading in a southerly direction.

(Hint: In spring, when water is running down the mountain and when seasonal streambed scars are visible, you'll find a capillary creek at the aforementioned junction. Shortly after this creek, you cross another one, and just before crossing a third, you see the blazes on your left. Be aware, however, that conditions can change.) Look into the forest a couple of hundred feet if you don't see a blaze right away. Once you've found the marks, follow uphill, looking for blazes on rocks and trees, into an area of steep ledges and rock-strewn, moss-cloaked forest.

About an hour of strenuous hiking takes you across several ledges and through many tangled blowdowns as you gain the summit. You will get some views to the north of Kaaterskill Clove and the surrounding mountains, but mainly these are obscured by trees.

You will know you've achieved High Peak's summit when you reach a flat area among the evergreens where benchmarks can be studied in the flat stones. Pieces of a wrecked aircraft are strewn about in the woods. Herd trails leading off to the east go nowhere in particular. Continue to Hurricane Ledge and its remarkable views by following the trail for another 15 minutes. This brings you to a large expanse of grassy, open terrain with an east-to-west, south-facing aspect. The view is rare, including a variety of topography from the Hudson River valley, the Shawangunks, the Hudson Highlands, and the immediate Catskills. The ledge is a fine place to snooze, snack, photograph, or bivouac.

One of the finest representations of Kaaterskill High Peak appears in Thomas Cole's painting *Sunny Morning on the Hudson,* which depicts a highly romanticized version of High Peak from the vicinity of Roundtop.

Continue on blue markers now as you descend the mountain's southerly slopes. The trail is better marked here. There are a few steep spots, so watch your footing. Once again be on the lookout for a T, where a group of low cairns identifies the snowmobile trail loop again. Turn left (east), following the well-marked snowmobile trail for another 40 minutes. This will bring you back to the original loop intersection, where you turn right, descend, and retrace your steps to the trailhead.

DID YOU KNOW?

High Peak and Roundtop are often present in Hudson River School paintings of the nineteenth century as background or subject matter, particularly in scenes from the Catskill Mountain House area.

MORE INFORMATION

Because the trail crossing High Peak from the snowmobile trail is remote, this should be regarded as a strenuous and challenging hike that requires solid direction-finding skills, a map and compass (and your GPS), and plenty of food and water. Allow plenty of time. The Kaaterskill Wild Forest is a very quiet piece of country, even when the neighboring trails to the south and north (the Devil's Path and Escarpment Trail, respectively) are busy. For more information on the Catskill Forest Preserve, visit www.dec.ny.gov/lands/5265.html. For the DEC Region 4 office in Stamford, call 607-652-7365.

NEARBY

If staying in the area, it is worth the drive to Phoenicia for the 12-mile, round-trip ride along Esopus Creek to Boiceville on the Catskill Mountain Railroad's Esopus Scenic Train. Rides are available on weekends from Memorial Day through late October. The Empire State Railway Museum is located in the restored Phoenicia station. For details visit www.catskillmtrailroad.com or call 845-688-7400. For the museum, visit www.esrm.com or call 845-688-7501.

TANBARKING

The tanbark era in the Catskills ran roughly from 1830 to 1870, resulting in the near deforestation of the eastern or Canada hemlock (*Tsuga canadensis*) in the area. The downfall of this romantic symbol of the North Woods was its tannin-rich bark, which was ground for use in the leather tanning process, mostly for the waterproofing of boots and equipment for Civil War soldiers. After felling, trees could be peeled profitably only to the first branch, so much of the tree bark was wasted, and perhaps less than 1 percent of the lumber was used. Most of the trees were left to rot because there was no market for sawlogs. Hides were easier to transport than bark, so they were shipped to the Catskills from as far away as Argentina to be tanned.

Tanning was a wasteful process. In the estimation of the early guidebook writer H.A. Haring, "From three to ten hemlocks were felled to obtain a cord of bark [128 cubic feet] . . . probably, in the life of the industry, one hemlock was cut down for each hide tanned into leather." Colonel Zadock Pratt, for whom Prattsville is named, turned out more than 2 million hides during the lifespan of his tannery. Tannersville was previously named Edwardsville by Colonel William Edwards, one of the Catskills' most enduring "tanlords." At least 60 tanneries were running for 40 years, which gives you an idea of the vast number of trees involved.

There are a few virgin tracts of hemlock in the Catskills, most of them positioned on upper-elevation or steep slopes where oxen could not work. Chances are, some of these were in their vigorous youth as the industry waned. In addition to the tanner's hut foundations that can still be found in the hills, other evidence of the ruinous industry remains, including the old roads that many of today's marked trails follow. In a 1984 interview, the legendary forester Ed West (called "Mr. Catskill" by his Adirondack Mountain Club friends) remarked that twenty years earlier he had come across places where hemlock cut in barking days were still hard and firm, noting that "especially where it is damp it will stay like that . . . [it is] one of the most durable and long lived of woods." Hemlock is too slow-growing for plantations and was not considered a viable candidate for reforestation efforts.

TRIP 43
POET'S LEDGE

Location: Palenville, NY
Rating: Strenuous
Distance: 3.4 miles
Elevation Gain: 1,231 feet
Estimated Time: 4.5 hours
Maps: USGS Kaaterskill; AMC Catskill Mountains; NY–NJTC
Northeastern Catskills

This steep hike climbs to a quiet ledge overlooking Kaaterskill Clove, the vantage for Sanford R. Gifford's painting *October in the Catskills* (1845).

DIRECTIONS
From Exit 20 off the NYS Thruway (I-87) in Saugerties, go north on NY 32 for 6.0 miles and bear left at a light onto NY 32A. At 7.5 miles, bear left at a fork onto Malden Avenue. Proceed another 0.8 mile, crossing Woodstock Avenue, and find the Fernwood Restaurant on your left. (You must ask permission to park here.) To park in the forest-preserve access parking area, continue on NY 32A at the fork, go through Palenville, joining NY 23A at the light, bear left, and continue 0.5 mile. Park on the right and walk back through Palenville, following NY 23A to NY 32A, go right onto Woodstock Avenue, right on Mill Road, and right again onto Malden Avenue to the trailhead. *GPS coordinates:* 42° 10.406′ N, 74° 01.668′ W.

TRAIL DESCRIPTION
Poet's Ledge is identified on several very old maps, and was accessible by footpath from Haines Falls as early as 1840. It is likely that hunters and surveyors knew of it before then, for by 1820 preparations were being made just a short distance north across the Clove at Pine Orchard to build the Catskill Mountain House (1823). Hikers will revel in the magical sense of isolation of this historic destination as they peer over the precipitous cleft and its adjoining, steep ravines. Almost 20,000 years of ice and running water has conspired to create the unforgettable landscape that is Kaaterskill Clove.

This is a strenuous climb. It may look very close to the road on the map, and it is; it's the elevation you need to consider. Although this can be a hard

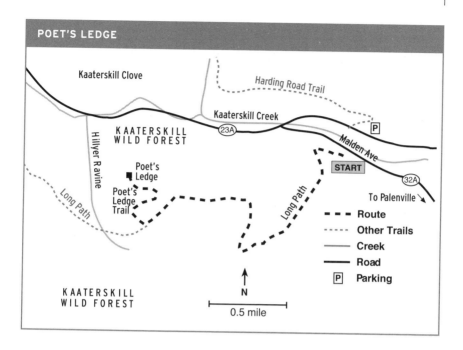

POET'S LEDGE

Kaaterskill Clove

Harding Road Trail

Kaaterskill Creek

KAATERSKILL WILD FOREST

Hillyer Ravine

23A

Malden Ave

P

START

32A

Poet's Ledge

Poet's Ledge Trail

Long Path

To Palenville

Long Path

- - - Route

· · · · Other Trails

——— Creek

——— Road

P Parking

N

0.5 mile

KAATERSKILL WILD FOREST

climb (don't use it as a season opener), finding parking near the trailhead could prove even harder. You may have to park on the street in Palenville, adding another mile to the hike. You can also park at the forest-preserve access parking area just west of Palenville on the north side of NY 23A, just before it enters the Catskill Park—but be careful, the traffic is very fast here.

Assuming you've parked at the Fernwood, walk east back the way you came on Malden Avenue and look carefully for the trailhead about 200 feet east of the Fernwood. The trail is poorly identified, but you will see the trusty aqua Long Path blazes on a telephone pole. Turn south on this little dirt road, and walk about 100 feet to a forest-preserve access gate on your right, where you will see blue state trail disks. This is Red Gravel Hill Road. Follow it uphill as it rises behind the Fernwood and switches back once or twice before maintaining a long, fairly steep southerly ascent. The road's surface improves with elevation. By the time you reach the forest-preserve boundary, identified by yellow paint blazes and wild forest signage, you'll have worked up a sweat.

Stay alert, as the trail turns off the road to the right at a trail sign and disk, heading west and uphill; Gravel Hill Road continues into the south onto private property. Now you climb on a heavily washed-out 1800s quarry road, hardly recognizable as a road anymore. As this section of trail switches north, it levels and improves. Look on the left now while the forest type changes markedly from second-growth hardwood to the typical oak and laurel cover

The hike along Red Gravel Hill Road brings hikers to the quiet and scenic Poet's Ledge.

of the mid-elevations, and you'll see the remains of a quarry tucked into the undergrowth along the uphill edge of this terrace. Hand-dressed rubble may still be found along the trail.

The trail climbs, levels, climbs again, and rises through a series of ledges and natural stone steps to a point where a fine view upriver is encountered. Across the clove, you will see Palenville Overlook and Indian Head, a pair of high ledges along the southerly flank of South Mountain. You also look out across the Hudson Valley to the vague blue-green hills of the Taconic Plateau and the Green Mountains, far beyond.

Back at it, you will soon be pleased to see the forest type changing again, this time to hemlock, promising a boreal "summitlike" experience. A frail northern hardwood forest (beech, birch, and maple) has failed to invade this almost pure stand of conifers. Once again, the trail flattens and begins to meander over a delightful and most welcome stretch of flat ground at 1,700 feet. The trail is often wet here on the northern fringes of Deer Laurel Swamp.

Suddenly you come upon the Poet's Ledge Trail, a yellow-marked spur. The sign is wrapped in hardware cloth (wire) to protect it from porcupines. The distance is marked as 0.47 mile. Descend through an area of primordial texture, past huge boulders heaped with heavy clods of thick moss and detritus. The trail is self-guiding yet needlessly overmarked. Hemlock needles and cones blanket the trail. Patches of fern and laurel, an understory of vigorous red spruce, and maturing hemlocks make up a dense transition zone. Suddenly, the trail flattens onto a bare bluestone "dance floor" hemmed in by pitch pines. Continue, bearing left and southwest and descending through ledgy terrain.

As you approach the open vista of Poet's Ledge, be alert to the existence of a substantial crevice dividing the ledge. Though narrow, this crack is deep enough to be of some consequence, especially if it is hidden by snow. It is large enough to fall into, and children should be carefully supervised.

From this small patch of rocks, you can sit and muse over the deep abysmal clove and lose your thoughts in time while gazing west at Onteora Mountain, the north-draining ravines off Kaaterskill's shoulder, and the enviable, precariously perched houses of Twilight Park at the top of the Clove.

Although not documented, it is possible that William Cullen Bryant, who together with Washington Irving created the first literary allusions to the Catskills, visited Poet's Ledge, thus engendering its name. More than likely a clever cartographer, familiar with the works of James Fenimore Cooper, Bryant, and Irving and in tune with the Romantic spirit of the times, made it up. There is little doubt, however, that the walkers and artists of the time knew about Poet's Ledge. What seems hauntingly apparent (and is a subject of recent interest by the Clark Art Institute) is that Sanford R. Gifford painted his *October in the Catskills* from the vantage of Poet's Ledge (most likely from 1845 field sketches), where the Kaaterskill rises to the south and Haines Falls is seen due west.

Return by the route you came.

DID YOU KNOW?

The trail to Poet's Ledge was lost for decades, perhaps even a hundred years. The landmark was rediscovered by the Salvador Dali scholar Albert "Cap" Field in the 1980s.

MORE INFORMATION

For more information on the Catskill Forest Preserve, visit www.dec.ny.gov/lands/5265.html. For the DEC Region 4 office in Stamford, call 607-652-7365.

NEARBY

The Mountain Top Historical Society maintains a Visitor & Art Trail Center on Route 23A in Haines Falls. Here there are interpretive panels for the Hudson River Art Trail, a restored railroad station, and walking paths. Open April to November; calling ahead is recommended. For details visit www.mths.org or call 518-589-6657.

TRIP 44
HUCKLEBERRY POINT

Location: Platte Clove, NY
Rating: Moderate
Distance: 3.5 miles
Elevation Gain: 600 feet
Estimated Time: 3.5 hours
Maps: USGS Kaaterskill; AMC Catskill Mountains; NY–NJTC
Northeastern Catskills

**A short walk through hemlock and pitch-pine woods leads to a
scenic overlook above Platte Clove and the Hudson Valley.**

DIRECTIONS

These directions bring you "the back way" over scenic Platte Clove Road, a
seasonal road that should not be attempted unless it is legally open (April
15–November 15) and clear of ice and snow. When it is closed or when the
road conditions are questionable, follow the directions to the Codfish Point
trailhead.

From Exit 20 off the NYS Thruway (I-87) in Saugerties (either northbound
or southbound), bear left a short distance to the intersection of NY 32 and NY
212. Set your odometer to zero and head west on NY 212 toward Woodstock.
At 2.0 miles, watch carefully on your right for CR 35 (Blue Mountain Road).
Follow it, bearing left at a Y, through Blue Mountain. At 5.3 miles, pass Woodstock–Saugerties Road on your left. Pass Manorville Road on your right at 5.4
miles. Now you will head straight up the mountain on Platte Clove Road. As
the road tops out, look on your right for the Kaaterskill Wild Forest parking
area at 7.8 miles. Turn right into the lot. You'll see the trail register and trail
signs here for Steenbergh Road (the trail follows this dirt road, named for an
early bluestone quarry) and the blue trail. The trail begins on the northwest
side of the lot. *GPS coordinates:* 42° 08.033′ N, 74° 04.918′ W.

TRAIL DESCRIPTION

Huckleberry Point is an ideal picnicking spot, suitable for those sunny, clear
days when an easy hike to its quiet, scenic ledges is the goal. However, especially
on nice weekends, expect to see many other hikers. And it is no wonder—this
pretty hike takes you to one of the Escarpment's most accessible and expansive
southeasterly viewsheds on an easy trail with a minimum of vertical rise.

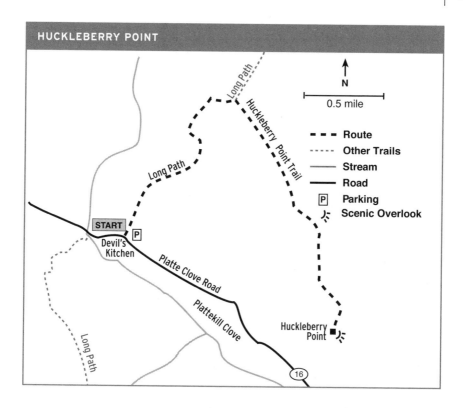

HUCKLEBERRY POINT

Long Path

Long Path

Huckleberry Point Trail

N

0.5 mile

- - - Route
.... Other Trails
——— Stream
——— Road
P Parking
)⚞ Scenic Overlook

START

P

Devil's
Kitchen

Platte Clove Road

Plattekill Clove

Huckleberry
Point

Long Path

16

The Huckleberry Point Trail is reached via the Kaaterskill High Peak snow-mobile trail, which circles Kaaterskill High Peak and Roundtop and which you follow for 1.0 mile. From the Kaaterskill Wild Forest parking area, follow the blue foot trail markers, red/orange snowmobile trail markers, and aqua Long Path blazes (sparse). The first section of trail rises through a dense hemlock forest over a deeply eroded old quarry road, within audible range of Mossy Creek, which is downhill to the east. After 20 minutes of hiking uphill, the trail reaches a Y in the hardwoods, where you bear right. Continue for 10 minutes to an arrow pointing to the right, following the blue footpath and snowmobile markers. Another 5 minutes along, you will leave the blue trail, bearing right (east) at the yellow-marked Huckleberry Point Trail (there's a sign and arrow).

Travel through a level hardwood forest with a developing hemlock under-story, where you will see obscure signs of early settlement: stone piles, walls, and an old foundation or two, the remains of an early quarrying and subsis-tence-farming community. Within a few minutes you'll drop slightly downhill into an oak woods, crossing Mossy Brook, which is several feet deep during runoff. Ford cautiously and continue directly on the other side. Don't make the mistake of following one of the old overgrown quarry roads.

The vertical ledges of Huckleberry Point offer intimate views of Platte Clove.

After the brook, you begin to climb slightly into an oak and beech transitional forest. The trail undulates easily uphill and downhill, yielding early spring views of the Devil's Path peaks, including Overlook, Indian Head, Twin, Sugarloaf, and Plateau. At this point you will enjoy the extensive "slicks" (shrub thickets) of mountain laurel (*Kalmia latifolia*), an evergreen named by biologist Carolus Linnaeus for his researcher and student, Peter Kalm (1716–1779). These bright-leaved members of the heath family are sharply contrasted against a young overstory of paper birch. Laurel blooms in late spring with large, pink flower clusters. These vigorous but fragile trailside shrubs are easily killed or damaged by overzealous (or untrained) trail maintainers.

Within a half hour of the Huckleberry Point trailhead, you'll cross the southerly slope of a pitch-pine hillock. This is the prettiest section of trail, where you begin to sense the abyss ahead. The ledgy oak–pine terrain suddenly opens up like a curtain rising onto the blueberry precipices of the Point. The views are expansive and the ledges are vertical, so be careful. You'll see the Devil's Path Mountains in the Indian Head Wilderness Area directly south, only a few miles away across the thousand-foot-deep Platte Clove (the hamlet of West Saugerties, below you, is 500 feet above sea level; you're at

2,200 feet). The north and east slopes are carved deeply by postglacial parallel drainage ravines. Overlook (with the fire tower) and the Plattekill Ridge turns into the west to Indian Head, whose profile is very apparent, lying supine with its distinct chin, nose, and eyebrow. West of it is Twin, then Sugarloaf and Plateau.

Going east from Overlook, dropping down its slopes to the small, nearly vertical outcrop of Minister's Face, you look south over the east basin of the Ashokan Reservoir to the toothy hills of the Shawangunks. The left edge of the tooth is Sky Top; you can see the Albert K. Smiley Memorial Tower (a.k.a. Sky Top Tower) with binoculars at 203 degrees. To the right is Eagle Cliff. Hidden on the flat space between them are Mohonk Lake and the Mohonk Mountain House. Moving along the descending ridge of the northern Shawangunks is Guyot Hill, and finally, the last bump is Bonticou Crag. Moving east across the rolling expanse of valley above the flatlands of the Esopus and Rondout valleys, you may see the Fishkill Ridge dipping down into the Hudson at the Highlands, and coming north, you see the city of Kingston, then Saugerties. In the middle of the Hudson's southernmost visible bay is the Esopus Meadows lighthouse at 189 degrees. Above the marshes of Tivoli Bays, just north of the Kingston–Rhinecliff Bridge, are the buildings of Bard College.

With patience, you can find Stissing Mountain at 135 degrees. The long ridge in the east is the Southern Taconic Plateau. The large birds you'll invariably see riding the thermals are not often hawks, but usually turkey vultures.

Return by the route you came.

DID YOU KNOW?

This route follows the trail of the Nature Friends, a group that originated among German expatriates who liked to wander here and, in homage to that spirit, called themselves the *Vanderverder,* or "wandering birds."

MORE INFORMATION

For more information on the Catskill Forest Preserve, visit www.dec.ny.gov/lands/5265.html. For the DEC Region 4 office in Stamford, call 607-652-7365.

NEARBY

A short distance east in Saugerties is the famous Opus 40, a sprawling rock sculpture that was crafted over 37 years with hand tools by Harvey Fite. In addition to the 6-acre sculpture area, there is a small Quarryman's Museum displaying quarrying tools and equipment. Opus 40 is open weekends, Memorial Day through Columbus Day; www.opus40.org; 845-246-3400.

TRIP 45
NORTH POINT

Location: Haines Falls, NY
Rating: Moderate
Distance: 7.0 miles
Elevation Gain: 700 feet
Estimated Time: 4.5 hours
Maps: USGS Kaaterskill; AMC Catskill Mountains; NY–NJTC Northeastern Catskills; North Lake Area

A popular outing along the Escarpment Trail's cliffs leads to the favorite haunts of the Hudson River School of landscape painters.

DIRECTIONS
From NY 23A in Haines Falls, turn north onto CR 18 (a.k.a. North Lake Road/ Mountain House Road) and travel 2.3 miles to the North–South Lake Public Campground's main gate. *GPS coordinates:* 42° 12.095′ N, 74° 03.383′ W.

TRAIL DESCRIPTION
This historic, scenic day hike begins along the legendary cliffs of Pine Orchard and reveals the best scenery of the Escarpment. This is the heart of the Catskills, the place that prompted the eloquence of James Fenimore Cooper, the fanciful pen of Washington Irving, and the Romantic vision of Thomas Cole. If you have time for only one hike in the Catskills, make it this one.

The best way to approach this hike is from the beach and picnic area parking lot of the North–South Lake Public Campground and day-use area. Pay the day-use fee and drive through the main gate, bearing left at the Y to the North Lake beach and picnic area. As you approach the bathing beach and picnic area parking lot, note the North Mountain Trails sign on the left. Park, backtrack along the road to the trailhead, and follow the yellow spur east to the blue-marked Escarpment Trail (or from the picnic area, simply walk east), toward Artist's and Sunset rocks, Newman's Ledge, and North Point. As you join the Escarpment Trail, turn left (north) and follow the edge of some vertical drops as the trail ascends easily in dense woods.

A series of historic lookouts begins as scenic vistas, opening up to the east across the Hudson Valley. The original locations of these lookouts—as they were understood by Mountain House guests—has become a hobby among

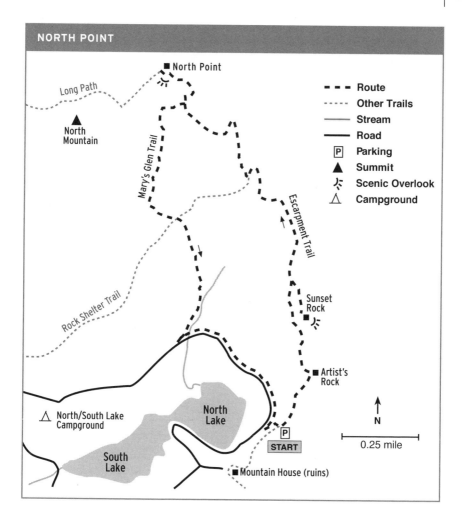

NORTH POINT

North Point

Long Path

North Mountain

Mary's Glen Trail

Escarpment Trail

Rock Shelter Trail

Sunset Rock

Artist's Rock

North/South Lake Campground

North Lake

South Lake

START

P

Mountain House (ruins)

- - - Route
··· Other Trails
—— Stream
—— Road
P Parking
▲ Summit
Scenic Overlook
△ Campground

N

0.25 mile

local toponymists. Few of today's Escarpment place-names accurately match those of the nineteenth century. I'll use the most recent ones.

Climb through broken ledges and along a rocky footway to the first signed lookout, Artist's Rock, among the well loved field studios of Thomas Cole. Cole was fond of pointing out his home in Catskill, Locust Grove, from this spot, something you can still do today with the aid of binoculars; it's easier to spot Mount Everett and the long ridge of the Taconics across the Hudson River. Continue, and soon you'll arrive at Prospect Rock (2,280 feet), a more expansive version of Artist's Rock. Continue along, passing another little dimple of rock to the right of the trail that was once known as Sunrise Rock. You'll also pass Sunset Rock and Lake View Pinnacle, recognizable by its old initial carvings and more recent graffiti.

North Lake is popular with cross-country skiers and snowshoers.

Continue along the trail, passing through pitch-pine "orchards," so named for pure stands of the pine whose crooked limbs have some resemblance to a fruit tree. (This was the result of the Romantic imagination at work, remember.) Soon, a large, monolithic rock plateau appears to the right of the trail. This is Sunset Rock, a place that was once the famous Bear's Den. As you reach the Sunset Rock Trail, bear right and follow the spur trail through the pitch pines to the rock, and you'll agree that the place-name works either way. The deep fissures and cracks make suitable bear habitat and you will want to be cautious not to slip.

From here, the westerly views are magnificent. You see Kaaterskill High Point and Roundtop above the lakes, and the long line of the southerly Escarpment heading for Overlook Mountain. Farther south, you can make out the Shawangunk Ridge, with Sky Top jutting out to the left of Overlook's easterly slopes.

Retrace your steps to the trail junction and continue north, climbing easily to Newman's Ledge, a fine open, vertical cliff looking northeast at 2,500 feet. Judging by its carvings, this was also a popular spot for Mountain House guests. Views expand to the north now, to include Albany on a good day, and the nearby valley of Rip Van Winkle Hollow (a.k.a. Sleepy Hollow). Look carefully and you might see the Old Mountain Road against the north face of the hollow. The trail continues north over a rocky surface, climbing terraces through hardwood and spruce thickets, walking the edge of a bog before meeting with the Rock Shelter Trail at the site of Badman Cave (2,650 feet). Climb to the right, remaining on the Escarpment Trail, walking the lip of a scenic, boreal ridge, and soon entering a flat hardwood forest. As you reach the junction with the Mary's Glen Trail (your return route), bear right on the Escarpment Trail to begin the only continuously steep section of the trail. After 15 minutes of strenuous and aerobic effort, you'll pass through a white-birch stand that precedes the large, flat rocks and long views from North Point's summit. Investigate views from various parts of the ledge: Windham High Peak, Burnt Knob and Acra Point, Blackhead, and Roundtop to the north; the Hudson Valley toward Albany, to the east through the Taconics and Berkshires; and south across the Highlands and into the Escarpment, where North and South lakes lie like spilled quicksilver under the shadows of Kaaterskill High Peak and Roundtop.

Descend now, retracing your steps to the previous junction, and turn right on the yellow-marked Mary's Glen Trail. You'll walk through thick spruce–fir forests as you descend to cross the Rock Shelter Trail, continuing through a wet area to cross the top of Ashley's Falls before descending into the Glen.

This spot was a favorite of Mary Scribner (the wife of Ira Scribner, who operated a sawmill on Spruce Creek above Kaaterskill Falls). Go left when you reach the bottom of Ashley's Falls (also called Mary's Glen Falls) on a spur trail to the stone rubble below the cascade. Turn around and follow the trail out to the campground road, turn left, and walk 0.5 mile back to the picnic area and bathing beach parking area.

MORE INFORMATION

You can combine this hike with a picnic or swim in spring-fed North Lake at the North–South Lake Public Campground. Or you can bring your canoe and paddle North and South lakes, reserve a campsite, and spend the night ($22 camping fee).

If you don't park at the campground, you can park outside the main gate and walk to North Lake beach (a walk-in fee applies), or take the yellow-marked Rock Shelter Trail (no walk-in fee) to connect with Mary's Glen Trail. To use the latter two options, park outside the main gate in the Scutt Road trailhead parking area. (Two miles of featureless, round-trip hiking applies to either option.) Visit www.dec.ny.gov/outdoor/24487.html or call 518-589-5058.

NEARBY

Hunter Mountain Resort in Hunter hosts several theme festivals in spring, summer, and fall and is also home to an Orvis fly-fishing school and guide service. A lift skyride is available in summer and fall, and there are three zipline and adventure courses; www.huntermtn.com; 800-486-8376.

TRIP 46
INSPIRATION POINT

Location: Haines Falls, NY
Rating: Moderate
Distance: 8.0 miles
Elevation Gain: 500 feet
Estimated Time: 4 hours
Maps: USGS Kaaterskill; AMC Catskill Mountains; NY–NJTC, North Lake Area, Northeastern Catskills

This cliff-edge hike above Kaaterskill Clove to the North–South Lake Public Campground returns along the lakes.

DIRECTIONS
From NY 23A in Haines Falls, turn north onto CR 18 (a.k.a. North Lake Road/ Mountain House Road) and travel 2.3 miles. Turn right on Scutt Road and, within 300 feet turn right again into the Escarpment trailhead parking area (a.k.a. Scutt Road Corral). *GPS coordinates:* 42° 12.039′ N, 74° 03.494′ W.

TRAIL DESCRIPTION
The scenic lookouts and labyrinthine footpaths surrounding the old mountain houses of North Lake's Pine Orchard area have been destination hikes since the early 1800s. Detailed in the many guidebooks of the day, the trail system around Pine Orchard was one of America's most popular visual attractions.

Many of the trails emanating from the grounds of the Kaaterskill Hotel and the Catskill Mountain House have since disappeared, leaving only fanciful place-names such as Fairy Spring, Druid Rocks, and the Sphinx. But the scenery remains, and today's Escarpment Trail highlights the best of it.

Walk east across Scutt Road onto the Escarpment Trail, or ET (also the Sleepy Hollow Horse Trail at this point). Descend, soon crossing two old railroad beds. Cross Spruce Creek on a footbridge and ascend slightly, passing an unmarked woods road to the left; this was once the approach to the now derelict, but still interesting, stone laundry building of the Catskill Mountain House.

Continue on the ET to the trail junction. Turn right, following signs for Layman's Monument. The trail passes a register and descends through laurels, arriving at the monument to a lost firefighter at 1.2 miles. Now the trail ascends, winding along the Escarpment's edge past steep drops. If you've

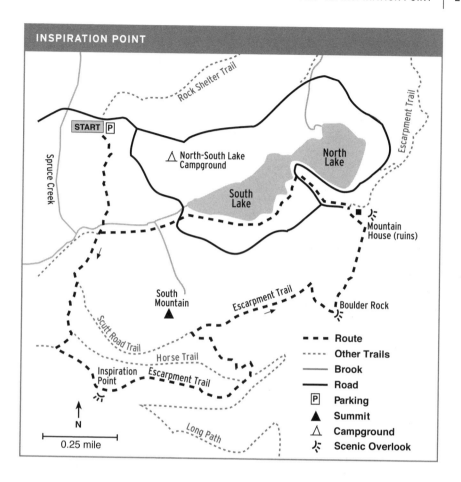

timed your visit to coincide with the appearance of the pinxter blossoms (mid-May to mid-June), you'll also see swallowtails, bronze coppers, and cabbage butterflies alighting on them and on the many-colored hawkweeds and wildflowers clinging to the weather-beaten cliffs along the way. Dodging in and out of oak and laurel woods, at 1.6 miles you'll pass the yellow-marked connector trail to Scutt Road Trail to the left. Continue straight ahead on the ET, arriving at Sunset Rock at 1.7 miles. Views improve ahead at Inspiration Point (1.9 miles).

Continue through the forest for another 20 minutes of easy walking, passing views (and precipitous, dangerous ledges) to the south and east. Note Palenville Overlook, the ragged rock outcropping jutting from the Clove's northern flank, down to your right. Here the ET joins the Horse Trail at a level intersection, where you bear right. Two hundred feet farther is Shorey Point. The Long Path joins the ET now, following the Horse Trail up from Palenville.

The high vertical ledges of Inspiration Point rise above Kaaterskill Clove.

Bear left here on the ET/Long Path toward Boulder Rock (1.3 miles) and North–South Lake Campground (2.0 miles). The trail climbs a bit now, flattening as you approach the Hotel Kaaterskill site on South Mountain. Here there is another junction, where the red Scutt Road Trail goes left (west). The hotel site is neither marked nor obvious from the junction, but lies north of it and can be explored on the herd trails that circle and penetrate it. There are few remains, only a dump and some stone foundations to which the state has contributed its own debris. Continue on the ET through a pretty oak-and-laurel forest dotted with single red spruce trees, (passing an unmarked trail that descends to the South Lake beach and picnic area road), and within 0.5 mile you'll reach a trail junction where the red-marked trail shortcuts off to the left toward the Catskill Mountain House site. Avoid this trail and continue following the blue markers, bearing right and descending slightly. In a few moments you'll reach Split Rock, a large, fractured megalith with a deep fissure lying close to the trail. Suddenly, you're at Boulder Rock, a large erratic that sits on a flat ledge with outstanding views. Old photos show an ornate gazebo perched on the rock.

Views of the Hudson Valley here are outstanding, giving an idea of what's to come over at Pine Orchard. You have fine, far-reaching views of the Shawangunks, Taconics, Berkshires, Stissing, and the Hudson River and its sprawling lowlands. Continue on the trail, leaving Boulder Rock at your back and ascending to pass the red trail on your left. Ledges—some of them dangerous—continue as you travel north along the Escarpment's edge. At Eagle Rock, where some carvings dating to 1850 are seen in the stone, bear slightly right to avoid dead-ending in a pitch-pine orchard, drop downhill slightly, and, after a switchback in the trail, arrive at the flat expanse where the Catskill Mountain House stood—the original Pine Orchard.

When you've had enough of the views across the valley (similar to Boulder Rock's), head west with the ledge at your back and watch the blue markers. Shortly, the ET departs to the right (north) and drops downhill to an open area just east of North Lake (visible nearby) and you're at the point where the Otis Elevated Railroad rose from the valley floor to the top of the Escarpment (you can see the cut in the mountain by exploring to the east a little here.).

Leave the ET now and bear left, following the road that you can see ahead (also marked as a snowmobile trail) and walk along the south shore of North Lake. You will also see yellow foot-trail markers. Follow this road around the peninsula that juts into the narrows between North and South lakes, and at a point where the snowmobile trail turns east, follow the yellow foot trail into the hemlock woods as it goes south along the lake's edge. Skirt the edge of South Lake and walk past the bathhouse, keeping it to your left. The yellow trail continues along the edge of South Lake, reentering the woods where the beach and the lake come together. (If your feet are sore, you can follow the access road back to the parking area.) Follow the yellow trail into the woods. After 20 minutes, the trail ends on the South Lake access road (paved). As you rise to the road, you'll see the lake to your right. Bear left and across the road to the yellow-marked and well-identified ski trail, a pleasant, flat trail that brings you 0.5 mile to the intersection of the ET and Scutt Road trails. From here, bear right on the ET to return to the trailhead parking area.

MORE INFORMATION

For more information on the Catskill Forest Preserve, visit www.dec.ny.gov/lands/5265.html. For the DEC Region 4 office in Stamford, call 607-652-7365.

NEARBY

After your hike, you can pay the day-use fee at the adjacent North–South Lake Public Campground and enjoy a picnic or a swim in spring-fed North Lake. Or you can bring your canoe and paddle North–South Lakes, reserve a campsite, and spend the night ($22 camping fee). For campground details visit www.dec.ny.gov/outdoor/24487.html or call 518-589-5058.

TRIP 47
KAATERSKILL FALLS

Location: Haines Falls, NY
Rating: Easy
Distance: 1.4 miles
Elevation Gain: 200 feet
Estimated Time: 1.5 hours
Maps: USGS Kaaterskill; AMC Catskill Mountains; NY–NJTC North Lake Area, Northeastern Catskills

This hike to the state's highest waterfall is the most popular short hike in the Catskills.

DIRECTIONS
From Exit 20 off the NYS Thruway (I-87) in Saugerties, take NY 32 6.0 miles to NY 32A, bearing left into Palenville. Bear left at the light in Palenville at 8.0 miles onto NY 23A, ascending through Kaaterskill Clove. The trailhead is located at 11.2 miles, at the hairpin turn on NY 23A between the towns of Haines Falls and Palenville. Park at the designated area 0.2 mile west (uphill) of the trailhead. *GPS coordinates: 42° 11.390′ N, 74° 04.443′ W.*

TRAIL DESCRIPTION
By the mid-nineteenth century Romantic period, Kaaterskill Falls had become the most popular symbol of the American wilderness, when notions of the "picturesque" and "sublime" were shifting away from European scenery. The West was still a frontier by the time the Catskill Mountain House was built on the ledges of Pine Orchard in 1823, and Niagara Falls—discovered by travelers as early as 1683—was old news by 1778. The main reason for Kaaterskill Falls' immense popularity was its proximity to the largest U.S. population center of the time—New York City—and to the fact that the rising upper and middle classes now had the time and means for destination travel.

By the late 1800s, the falls were averaging 100 visitors a day, most of them residents at the mountaintop hotels. At the time, people believed that nearby Roundtop Mountain (3,804 feet) was the highest of the Catskill peaks and therefore represented the heart of the Catskills, and they believed that the Catskills were the embodiment of a new national identity, making its definitive case in the art and literature of the times.

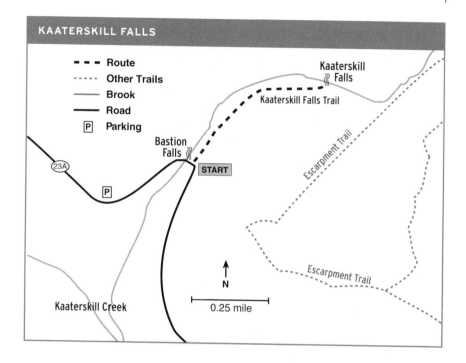

Today the hotels are gone and the falls now enjoy relative obscurity, but you won't believe it if you arrive on a sunny weekend, when the parking area is full and hikers of all ages walk single file up the trail like strings of Sherpas.

From the parking lot, descend along the road (NY 23A) cautiously, keeping to the left, where the shoulder is wider. Cross the highway bridge next to Bastion Falls, bear left, and go around the guardrail to begin the climb. There's a trail sign here, indicating the Falls at 0.5 mile on the dead-end spur trail. Follow yellow markers uphill steeply over stone and wooden steps to the trail register. Continue through a small grove of virgin hemlock (one of four such groves in the Kaaterskill Wild Forest) as the trail follows close along the shaded banks of Spruce Creek. Within 15 to 20 minutes you will arrive at the falls, hidden from view until you arrive at their base.

Try to time your visit to a period that is not too dry, and you'll be treated to the remarkable double-plumed fall; the uppermost, initial 175-foot drop is the most spectacular. The upper plume fills a huge basin (not seen from below) known as the Amphitheater, immortalized as the slumbering place of Rip Van Winkle.

Many people scramble up the slope on the south side of the creek to scale the narrow herd trail leading behind the upper falls—a practice that has created sustained impact problems and is the reason for the original Escarpment

Kaaterskill Falls' upper plume, a.k.a. the Amphitheater, illustrates why this is one of the most popular short hikes in the Catskills.

Trail's relocation to its present trailhead on Scutt Road. The DEC has long pondered the difficult management problems facing this area. Not only is the impact high, so are the dangers. Several people have died here. At least two people have (barely) survived falls from above. Several dogs are also among the deceased. The most memorable of them was Vite, a dog who, in the 1800s, had been trained to jump at his master's whistle. A thoughtless whistle caused Vite to jump over the falls. The bereaved master engaged a stone cutter to carve a lavish memorial to "Vite, the Bayard of Dogs" that can still be seen in the ledges on the steep slopes below the falls, where there was once a series of paths, ropes, and ladders leading to the Amphitheater.

The artists, poets, and other writers who focused their creative genius on Kaaterskill Falls are legion. Thomas Cole is credited with the first and most influential painting, *Falls of the Kaaterskill* (1826), which immediately created public interest in the Falls. Cole's protégés and imitators followed, among them Jasper Cropsey (a late-generation Hudson River School painter), W.H. Bartlett, Winslow Homer, Harry Fenn, Currier and Ives, and countless engravers and illustrators. The poets featured in particular William Cullen Bryant; even Thomas Cole was inspired to write poetry and essays about the Falls, as were many writers of the Knickerbocker period—Washington Irving central among them. Henry David Thoreau visited the Scribners' cabin at Kaaterskill Falls in the summer of 1844, during a brief hiatus in the construction of his cabin at Walden Pond, along with William Ellery Channing (a founder of Transcendentalism). However, for some unknown reason, Thoreau deleted references of the Catskills in the first draft of *Walden*.

John Bartram, the chief American horticulturalist of his time, and his son, the naturalist, explorer, and writer William Bartram, visited Kaaterskill Falls in 1753. The latter's book dealing with his explorations, *The Travels of William Bartram* (1791), had a clear impact on both Wordsworth and Coleridge, who would in turn influence the American Romantic imagination. Timothy Dwight, president of Yale College in 1823, contributed his *Description of Kaaterskill Falls, September 28, 1815*. Listings in gazetteers, travel guides, magazines, geographical dictionaries, histories, sketch and art books, pictorial geographies, companion guides, and parlor books further assured the immortalization of Kaaterskill Falls as a household name.

But the most memorable of all the popular literary utterances comes from the American writer James Fenimore Cooper, in a passage that historian Alf Evers has called "one of the finest pieces of promotional writing to ornament the 19th Century." The reference is from Cooper's *The Pioneers*, published in the same year that the Catskill Mountain House opened for business (1823). The protagonist, Natty Bumppo, remarks on the Falls to his young companion, Edwards: "To my judgment, lad, it's the best piece of work that I have met with in the woods; and none know how often the hand of God is seen in a wilderness but them that rove it for a man's life."

Return by the route you came.

DID YOU KNOW?

Kaaterskill Falls is higher than Niagara Falls, falling for a total of 260 feet.

MORE INFORMATION

For more information on the Catskill Forest Preserve, visit www.dec.ny.gov/lands/5265.html. For the DEC Region 4 office in Stamford, call 607-652-7365.

NEARBY

This short hike can be combined with a visit to Cedar Grove at the Thomas Cole National Historic Site in the town of Catskill, down in the Hudson Valley a few miles east of Kaaterskill Clove. Guided tours of Cole's house and studio are offered May to October, along with guided hikes to painting locations; www.thomascole.org; 518-943-7465.

TRIP 48
BLACKHEAD MOUNTAIN

Location: Maplecrest, NY
Rating: Strenuous
Distance: 4.2 miles
Elevation Gain: 1,550 feet
Estimated Time: 3 hours
Map: USGS Freehold; USGS Hensonville; AMC Catskill Mountains; NY–NJTC Northeast Catskills

This steep trail climbs into Lockwood Gap to the Escarpment Trail.

DIRECTIONS
From the corners of CR 40 and CR 56 in the village of Maplecrest, follow Big Hollow Road (CR 56) to the north and east, passing Peck Road on your left. Continue 4.5 miles to the end of CR 56, where you will see the red-marked Black Dome Range trailhead on the left. Park at the dead end just ahead. *GPS coordinates: 42° 17.355′ N, 74° 06.957′ W.*

TRAIL DESCRIPTION
The short but scenic loop trail over Blackhead Mountain (3,940 feet) rewards you with the best scenery of the Windham Blackhead Range Wilderness without the extra work of traversing the entire "big three"—Blackhead, Black Dome, and Thomas Cole mountains. The west-lying two peaks of the range, with the exception of a small group of lookouts on the south and east of Black Dome's summit (3,950 feet), have little to compare with Blackhead's enormous western viewshed. Thomas Cole Mountain—ironically—is viewless since it has become overgrown. In spite of this, one of the nicest ledges in the Black-heads is the small lookout on Black Dome, so you may want to add extra time to diverge westward when you reach Lockwood Gap, bagging Blackhead on the way out.

Begin at the rustic Batavia Kill trailhead, and follow the route of both the yellow-marked Batavia Kill and red-marked Black Dome Range trails as they make their way southeast through dense mixed hemlock and hardwoods, crossing a pair of footbridges. The trail follows the washed-out imprint of an old road for 0.5 mile to the confluence of two creeks, at a trail junction where the Black Dome Range Trail bears southwest and where your return route, the Batavia Kill Trail, continues east. Turn right on the Black Dome Range Trail,

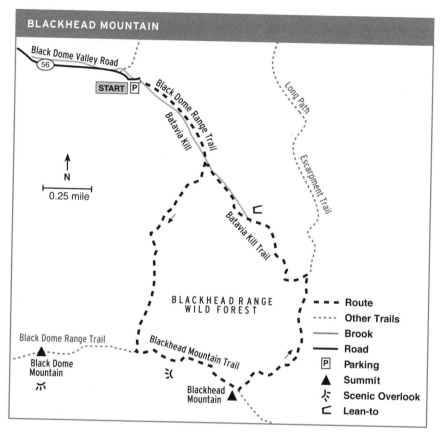

which soon climbs into the gap, becoming very steep. You will pass a reliable spring on the left, odd for this elevation in the Catskills.

The ascent continues relentlessly through Lockwood Gap and levels in the saddle between Black Dome and Blackhead. (The very worthwhile, 0.5-mile ascent of 500 feet to Black Dome's pure fir summit will add another 1.5 hours to your hike, so weigh this side trip against your time and the weather.) The route to Blackhead is to the left (east), following the yellow-marked Blackhead Mountain Trail, a short connector between the Black Dome Range Trail and the Escarpment Trail. There is a poorly sited, legal campsite in Lockwood Gap to the northeast of the junction, with very little if any flat ground.

The Blackhead Mountain Trail ascends immediately into the east, climbing the long westerly slopes of Blackhead. A succession of increasingly scenic terraces leads to a grassy outcropping with broad and penetrating views southwest. These are the hike's best views. You see West Kill over Hunter Mountain's ski slopes, Hunter's fire tower, and the Catskill high peaks area, including Slide, Table, Cornell, and Wittenberg. East of Hunter are Stony Clove, Plateau, and the Devil's Path mountains to Overlook. Kaaterskill High Peak and Roundtop

The Blackhead Range is seen from the northern Hudson Valley.

are due south. The trail climbs steeply ahead, easing up at 3,700 feet. It follows along through balsam and soon arrives at the summit, a bald but viewless dome enclosed in a fir thicket. The Escarpment Trail crosses the summit here. Follow it to the left (northeast), as it descends steeply, bending into the north and passing a scenic, east-facing overlook on the right. The trail terraces its way down through birch, beech, striped maple, and a ground cover of asters where the sun reaches through the canopy. Canada violets, trout lilies, trillium, bunchberry, and oxalis are your regular companions along the trail.

The junction of the yellow-marked Batavia Kill Trail is reached at 2,850 feet in elevation. Bear left, following it downhill and northwest, leaving only a lean-to to your right. The contours relax as you descend along the kill, and you'll find yourself back at the junction with the Black Dome Range Trail.

Continue straight ahead to arrive at the trailhead parking area.

DID YOU KNOW?

Blackhead and Black Dome get their names from their dark, virgin fir summits, which lumberers call "black growth."

MORE INFORMATION

For more information on the Catskill Forest Preserve, visit www.dec.ny.gov/lands/5265.html. For the DEC Region 4 office in Stamford, call 607-652-7365.

NEARBY

The Windham Vineyard & Winery on Route 10 in Windham is the highest-elevation vineyard in the Northeast. It is open year-round for tours and tastings. For details visit www.windhamvineyard.com or call 518-734-5214.

TRIP 49
WINDHAM HIGH PEAK

Location: Maplecrest, NY
Rating: Strenuous
Distance: 6.6 miles
Elevation Gain: 1,475 feet
Estimated Time: 5 to 7 hours
Maps: USGS Hensonville; AMC Catskill Mountains; NY–NJTC Northeastern Catskills

Windham High Peak is a charming, but strenuous, walk through mature spruce plantations to the northern Escarpment with sweeping views to the north.

DIRECTIONS

From NY 23, turn south onto CR 65 to Hensonville. From there, go 2.0 miles into Maplecrest on CR 40. Turn left onto CR 56 (Big Hollow Road) until you reach Peck Road at 1.8 miles on your left. The trail begins within a mile, at the end of Peck Road. *GPS coordinates: 42° 17.848′ N, 74° 10.149′ W.*

TRAIL DESCRIPTION

This scenic hike follows the Escarpment's northern shoulder, where the long, western-sloping ridge of Windham High Peak (3,524 feet) reaches in a high arch from Burnt Knob to Elm Ridge. Windham High Peak is the last mountain on the 23-mile Escarpment Trail that begins at Scutt Road Corral in Haines Falls. This 4,250-acre wild forest area was renamed the Windham Blackhead Range Wilderness in 2008.

Begin on the yellow-marked trail toward Elm Ridge Lean-to (1.0 mile), where you'll also see New York State snowmobile trail signs. Follow a dirt road through vestigial pasturelands, now grown into a forest of mixed hardwoods where stone walls mark the field divisions of early settlements. In 15 minutes, you should reach the trail junction. Turn right, following the blue (Escarpment Trail, Long Path) markers indicating Windham High Peak, Burnt Knob, and Acra Point. The Elm Ridge Lean-to will appear on your right as you continue.

The lean-to is nicely situated and frequently used. Nearby campsites are plentiful, however, if the lean-to is occupied and you are interested in spending the night.

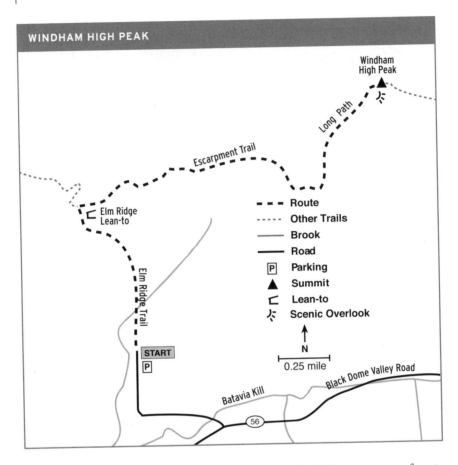

WINDHAM HIGH PEAK

Windham High Peak

Long Path

Escarpment Trail

Elm Ridge
Lean-to

Elm Ridge Trail

- - - Route
· · · · Other Trails
——— Brook
——— Road
P Parking
▲ Summit
⊏ Lean-to
⃗ Scenic Overlook

N

0.25 mile

START
P

Batavia Kill

Black Dome Valley Road

56

After a half-hour of hiking, you'll pass through dark Norway spruce forests that will spark your imagination. These trees (including the Norway pine) get their name from their nursery of origin in Norway, Maine. The trees were planted throughout the Catskills by the Civilian Conservation Corps in the 1920s and 1930s, mostly in the open fields of abandoned farmlands. Higher-elevation lands in the Catskills were never very good for farming, and when they "ran out" as pasturelands, farmers often found it more profitable to sell to the state rather than to pay taxes. This stretch used to be very wet in the early season, until an Appalachian Mountain Club trail crew improved it. The trail winds through these magnificent forests and then through hardwoods, gradually ascending. Most of the forest cover in this wild forest area falls within the northern hardwood types of beech, birch, and maple, with companion species of hemlock, basswood, red and white oak, and white ash.

Signs of early settlement are everywhere, some hidden and reclaimed by the forest, revealed by telltale, vagrant apple trees and runaway grape vines.

Windham High Peak is seen from the Hudson Valley lowlands.

An extensive, pure sugar-maple forest follows as the trail gently ascends. Thick mats of grass cover the rich soils of the western slopes, and you cross a seasonal creek. (The streams in the Windham Blackhead Range Wilderness Area are high-gradient tributaries of the Batavia Kill and Catskill Creeks and are dry most of the year.)

When you reach the southerly shoulder of the mountain at 3,000 feet in elevation, you get a look at the nearby Blackhead Range and the more westerly East Jewett Range. Blackhead and Black Dome are named for the dark balsam–fir growth you can see on their summits. At this point, you are about 3 miles into the walk; turn northeast for the 0.5-mile, 520-foot climb to the summit. During periods of scanty foliage in this birch, cherry, and maple forest, you will be able to look east at Burnt Knob and Acra Point and the long Escarpment Ridge. The last (and steepest) incline will take you about 30 minutes. Once on the long, level summit, you'll discover a benchmark and the views that have made Windham such a popular destination hike.

The most imposing of these views will be into the Blackhead Range, which feels remarkably close, only 3.0 miles south across the scenic Black Dome Valley. Down and to your right, southwest, you see the sister peaks of Round Hill and Van Loan Hill. Westerly views are available from the northwest side of the summit, on a short spur to a rocky area that you will find easily. From this point, you see a long line of lesser peaks disappearing into the Schoharie Valley; a flat stretch of open fields and farms, including Ginseng, Zoar, and Cave Mountain; and slightly to the north, Richmond and Huntersfield mountains, with Ashland Pinnacle between them.

The most popular view is from beyond the summit (east), where a graffiti-inscribed outcrop hangs above the Hudson Valley. (These inscriptions are not of the same genre as the North Lake variety, and the few decent initials have been heavily eroded and defaced.) From here you can see the Helderberg Escarpment and, on a clear day, Albany's Empire Plaza, the Egg Performing Arts Center, and the State University buildings. It is also likely that you'll see Vermont's Green Mountains, the Berkshires, and the Taconic Range, including the Greylock massif, a geological member of the Taconics. Looking down over the ridge, you see Burnt Knob (3,180 feet), the second knoll from Windham High Peak. The Escarpment Trail goes downhill at this point, to Burnt Knob, Acra Point, and points south.

Some hikers prefer to make a large loop over Windham High Peak, returning via Burnt Knob and the Black Dome Range Trail, walking west along Black Dome Valley Road and back to the trailhead on Peck Road for a total distance of more than 13 miles. Groups also can extend the hike by spotting a car at the end of Black Dome Valley Road.

DID YOU KNOW?

Gangster Jack "Legs" Diamond kept a hideout home in the town of Acra, under the shadow of Windham High Peak.

MORE INFORMATION

For more information on the Catskill Forest Preserve, visit www.dec.ny.gov/lands/5265.html. For the DEC Region 4 office in Stamford, call 607-652-7365.

NEARBY

Windham Mountain Ski Area and Adventure Park, located in the town of Windham, offers skyrides on weekends from July to October, and also has a paintball facility and skateboard park. For details visit www.windhammountain.com or call 800-754-9463 or 518-734-4300.

TRIP 50
ACRA POINT

Location: Maplecrest, NY
Rating: Moderate
Distance: 3.4 miles
Elevation Gain: 800 feet
Estimated Time: 3 hours
Maps: USGS Freehold; AMC Catskill Mountains; NY–NJTC Northeast Catskills

This short hike to an isolated lookout above the Black Dome Valley provides intimate views of the Blackhead Range.

DIRECTIONS

From the corners of CR 40 and CR 56 in the village of Maplecrest, follow Big Hollow Road (CR 56) to the north and east, passing Peck Road on your left. Continue 4.5 miles to the end of CR 56, where you will see the red-marked Black Dome Range trailhead on the left, or park at the dead end (Batavia Kill trailhead) just ahead. *GPS coordinates:* 42° 17.848′ N, 74° 10.149′ W.

TRAIL DESCRIPTION

The route to Acra Point uses the northern portion of the Black Dome Range Trail, located at the eastern end of Big Hollow Road in Maplecrest. Don't be concerned if the road is washed out along the boisterous Batavia Kill—it often is in early spring. Since this is a dead end, you can park almost anywhere. The red-marked Black Dome Range Trail begins on the left (north) side of the road. It's the first trailhead you see; the next one, a few hundred feet ahead, is the Batavia Kill trailhead (yellow markers). You can also use the Batavia Kill and Escarpment trails to reach Acra Point (or to return from it), more than doubling this hike's distance.

Acra Point is an ideal hike for days when you want a scenic outing that's not an overwhelming workout. This part of the Escarpment Trail is also less traveled than the North Lake area trails and the neighboring Windham High Peak or Blackhead Range trails, so you're likely to see fewer hikers. You may encounter thru-hikers, however. I enjoy meeting these hikers "going the distance" on the Escarpment Trail (also shared by the Long Path); in their floppy hats and rumpled bandanas, they come plodding along with their hiking

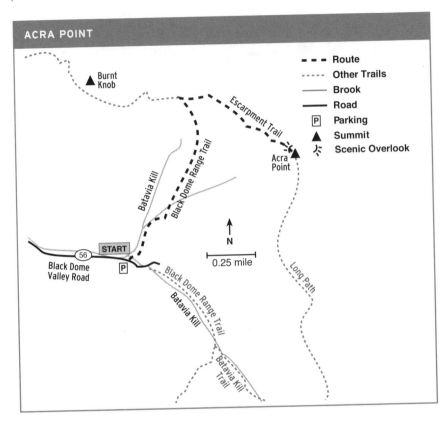

staffs, blending in with the environment. If you meet one here during summer, chances are they may try to yogi your food, especially your water, in exchange for tales of their adventures—this part of the Catskills is notoriously dry.

Note that the Black Dome Range Trail sign alongside the road at 2,200 feet indicates Acra Point at a forgiving 1.7 miles (3,100 feet). Head north into the woods following the Black Dome Range Trail across the Batavia Kill on a wooden bridge. Sign in at the trail register on the north side of the Kill and bear hard right, fording a seasonal tributary. Marking is spotty here, but soon the trail is obvious and remains self-guiding. Climb easily through an attractive stand of large red spruce trees, some snapped in two by high winds. The trail follows the Batavia Kill, passing many pretty spots where the tiny trout stream flows over low, gray ledges into shallow pools. The trail soon crosses Batavia Kill again, turning sharply northwest and north again through a northern hardwood forest. The climb is consistent but never steep. As you gain elevation, there are small pockets of hemlock and a few large, isolated cherry trees, then oaks, providing a good combination of browse for deer, wild turkey, and ruffed grouse. At 2,700 feet, the trail levels out for the last 0.25

mile of the Black Dome Range Trail, into a shallow notch on the spine of the Escarpment Trail. There are trail signs here indicating that your direction of travel is to the right (south) to Acra Point, 0.7 mile distant. This and the neighboring Dutcher Notch Trail are re-supply stations for the college outing clubs and Scout troops that regularly traverse the Escarpment Trail. Often they have drop points where you may see supplies, mostly gallon jugs of water brought in by their support staffs.

The following section of the Escarpment Trail is flat for a while then rises easily through the remaining 300 feet of ascent to Acra Point. As the trail gains the northwest-facing ridge, boreal forest takes over. Look to your right (west) for an established, unmarked spur trail, and follow it 75 feet to a flat sandstone outcropping. Although you are not on Acra Point's summit (3,100 feet), this is the best lookout. The true "summit" lies near the next spur trail to the south, where, due to sustained impact on the thin soils, No Camping signs are posted.

The intimate views of the Black Dome/Batavia Kill Valley are the attraction here, where you can lie around on the warm, flat rocks off the trail and relax. Seldom are views of such magnitude attained with so little work on the part of the hiker. The Blackhead Range—from Blackhead, Thomas Cole, and Black Dome mountains—slopes downward in a massive ellipsis over Camel's Hump (the western-most little nub) into a semicolon of Round and Van Loan hills (named for the early Catskill writer and mapmaker, Walton Van Loan). To the right (north) of these is Cave Mountain. The large, distant peak with the dorsal profile lying due west (270 degrees magnetic) is Bearpen Mountain, a trailed peak outside the Catskill Park boundary in Delaware County. It is, however, still within the forest preserve, as is Vly, just south of it, recognizable by its long, flat top.

Looking north you have Burnt Knob directly in front of you, a sort of mirror point to Acra Point (with less interesting views from a small rock ledge on the trail's west side, and better ones in the north), and to the right of it, just over 2 miles distant, is Windham High Peak. Looking south past the immense shoulder of Blackhead Mountain (194 degrees) is Arizona Mountain, a high and dry plateau seldom named on maps. Farther south, the Escarpment winds away to Stoppel Point and North Mountain. Views of the Hudson Valley are limited from the east side of the Point.

Return by the route you came.

DID YOU KNOW?

The Black Dome Range Trail has the advantage of providing the fastest and easiest approach to the top of the northern Catskill Escarpment.

MORE INFORMATION

For more information on the Catskill Forest Preserve, visit www.dec.ny.gov/lands/5265.html. For the DEC Region 4 office in Stamford, call 607-652-7365.

NEARBY

The Windham Chamber Music Festival puts on several concerts each year at the Windham Civic and Performing Arts Center. Visit www.windhammusic.com or call 518-734-3868. There are many other opportunities for enjoying the arts in the Windham area and around Greene County; visit www.greene-tourism.com/sights-and-activities/performing-fine-arts.

THE ESCARPMENT TRAIL

While the Devil's Path Trail runs east to west, the Escarpment Trail travels south to north along the edge of the Catskills' eastern ledges, the high and sudden rise to plateau elevation known as the Escarpment. This 24-mile trail begins outside the gate of the North-South Lake Public Campground at Scutt Road Corral, and is most often hiked from south to north, since many hikers stage their hike from the North Lake camping area. The elevation change and gradient is a bit more forgiving than those of the Devil's Path (6,500 cumulative feet). There are fewer lean-tos on or near the Escarpment Trail.

With the exception of the north and south extremes, the views are perhaps not as grand on the Escarpment Trail as on the Devil's Path's because there are fewer peaks above 3,500 feet (Blackhead Mountain and Windham High Peak). However, due to the relative lack of easy and convenient day hikes to this area (with the exception of the trails around North Lake), the sense of solitude is greater once you pass North Point. The Long Path uses both the Devil's Path and the Escarpment Trail as it makes its way northward through the Catskills.

TRIP 51
HUNTER MOUNTAIN

Location: Spruceton, NY
Rating: Strenuous
Distance: 7.2 miles
Elevation Gain: 1,950 feet
Estimated Time: 7 hours
Maps: USGS Hunter; USGS Lexington; AMC Catskill Mountains; NY–NJTC Northeastern Catskills

Hunter Mountain demands a long, gradual climb to the Catskills' second-highest peak, with a quiet, westerly ledge viewpoint.

DIRECTIONS

From Lexington, 8.0 miles west of Hunter on NY 23A, travel south on NY 42 for 0.8 mile and turn left (east) onto CR 6 (Spruceton Road). Drive past the West Kill Mountain trailhead, appearing on your right at 3.8 miles, and continue for another 3.0 miles to the forest-preserve access parking area on the left, where there are trail signs for Hunter Mountain. *GPS coordinates: 42° 11.050′ N, 74° 16.321′ W.*

TRAIL DESCRIPTION

The most interesting and gradual (though still challenging) climb to Hunter Mountain (4,040 feet—the Catskills' second highest) is by way of the Spruceton Trail. The considerable vertical rise of 1,950 feet is distributed evenly over this long western approach beginning at the headwaters of the beautiful West Kill Creek. (Hunter can be climbed in roughly half the time using the steeper Becker Hollow Trail from Stony Clove. See "Nearby.")

Locate the blue-marked Spruceton Trail on the north side of Spruceton Road, which indicates the direction to the John Robb Lean-to and Hunter Mountain. (There's an overflow parking area 0.2 mile farther ahead on Spruceton Road; the Devil's Path Trail is another 0.2 mile past the overflow lot at the dead end of Spruceton Road.)

Setting out along a well-defined truck trail (also an equestrian trail), you follow the old Jones Gap Turnpike (a.k.a. Old Hunter Road), built in 1880 and later improved to construct and maintain the present Hunter Mountain fire tower. After 0.5 mile, the trail turns east and steepens gradually. About 50

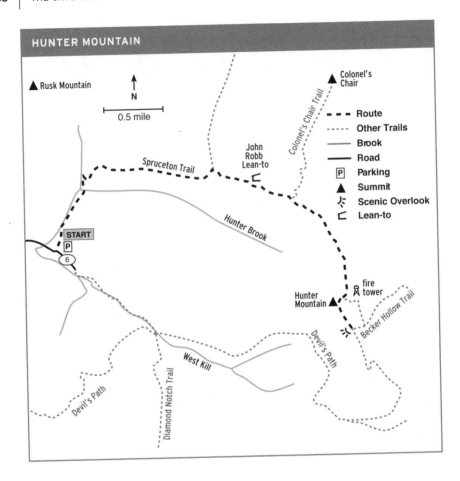

HUNTER MOUNTAIN

▲ Rusk Mountain

↑
N

0.5 mile

▲ Colonel's Chair

Colonel's Chair Trail

John Robb Lean-to

Spruceton Trail

Legend:
- - - Route
······ Other Trails
——— Brook
——— Road
P Parking
▲ Summit
Scenic Overlook
⊏ Lean-to

START
P
6

Hunter Brook

fire tower

Hunter Mountain ▲

Becker Hollow Trail

Devil's Path

West Kill

Devil's Path

Diamond Notch Trail

minutes into the hike, you'll arrive in the saddle between Rusk (trailless) and Hunter mountains, at 1.7 miles. You'll see an unmarked trail leading north and downhill onto private lands in Taylor Hollow.

The trail continues south–southeast and ascends steeply, reaching a good spring on the right within 0.5 mile. (Be careful, horses sometimes drink from the pool.) Near the spring are views to the north and southwest with Rusk and West Kill in the foreground. Within 0.1 mile, you'll see the John Robb Lean-to on your left at the 3,500-foot mark.

Continue for another 0.1 mile into a flat area of thick evergreens. Here you come upon the Colonel's Chair Trail, branching left (north, yellow markers, easily missed). This is part of the old Shanty Hollow Trail to Colonel's Chair; its last 0.5 mile has been erased by ski-trail construction. The mile-long side trip to Colonel's Chair and the ski lifts and summit lodge (open in summer) of the Hunter Mountain Ski Area is worthwhile if you've allowed the time, but

The sweeping hills of West Kill Valley are seen from below Hunter Mountain.

the views are redundant with the fire tower's, and the elevation loss (500 feet) is significant. (See the Appalachian Mountain Club's *Catskill Mountain Guide* for details.)

Continue on the Spruceton Trail. The summit is 1.0 mile ahead and 450 feet in elevation above you. The heavily rutted, often wet trail leads you through a remarkably dense forest of spruce and fir with isolated ledges to the northeast. From the John Robb Lean-to, it will take you about 45 minutes to walk to the summit. Just before the final ascent at approximately 3 miles, a yellow spur trail (marked) leads 1,500 feet to a marginal spring.

Suddenly the fire tower and observer's cabin appear. Once you have enjoyed this rocky peak and the 360-degree view from the fire tower (this is the highest fire tower in the state; it is staffed seasonally, on weekends), continue on the blue-marked trail to the true summit, where the fire tower and a lean-to were previously located. This additional distance of 0.25 mile through a level spruce–fir wood takes only 10 minutes and is well worth the effort. When you reach the small clearing of the old tower site, at the junction where the Becker Hollow Trail rises from Stony Clove, you'll see a spur trail to the right (west), leading a short distance to a west-facing ledge with excellent views from the north–northwest to the south–southwest, including West Kill, North Dome, Sherrill, Balsam, Vly, Bearpen, and many other peaks in the southern Catskills and the Shawangunks. When the tower is busy, this is the place to head for.

In his classic 1918 book, *The Catskills*, T. Morris Longstreth sums up Hunter's views: "Hunter is a climb-repaying mountain. From the steel tower on the top the entire Catskill mountainland is visible. Stony Clove…is but a gash in mother earth. The mass of the southern Catskills rises in ranged domes… dropped into gulfs made pearl gray by the mists of melting snow. Westward the chain that walls the valley toward Lexington wandered away until it grew soft with lilacs and lavendars [sic]."

Your shortest return route (from the Becker Hollow Trail junction) is the Spruceton Trail—the way you came (3.6 miles)—but consider that a loop can be completed, time allowing, by continuing ahead on the yellow-marked Hunter Mountain Trail to Devil's Path that turns west to join the blue-marked Diamond Notch Trail at West Kill Falls. It would bring you to a point about 1 mile east of the Spruceton Trail parking area (a total from Becker Hollow Trail junction of 4.6 miles, about 2 miles longer than returning the way you came).

DID YOU KNOW?

The Hunter Mountain ski trail called K2 has the steepest vertical rise of any ski trail in the eastern United States.

MORE INFORMATION

For more information on the Catskill Forest Preserve, visit www.dec.ny.gov/lands/5265.html. For the DEC Region 4 office in Stamford, call 607-652-7365.

NEARBY

Hikers wishing to make the fastest ascent to Hunter's summit (a 2.05-mile, 2,220-foot ascent) and fire tower will find the Becker Hollow trailhead and hiker's parking area 1.3 miles south on NY 214 from NY 23A, between Hunter and Tannersville. Hunter Mountain Resort is home to New York Zipline Adventure Tours, open year-round with two zipline and adventure courses and a new Skyrider tour billed as the highest and longest in North America. For details visit www.ziplinenewyork.com or call 518-263-4388.

TRIP 52
DIAMOND NOTCH TO WEST KILL FALLS

Location: Lanesville, NY
Rating: Moderate
Distance: 4.6 miles
Elevation Gain: 1,500 feet
Estimated Time: 3.5 hours
Maps: USGS Lexington; AMC Catskill Mountains; NY–NJTC
Northeastern Catskills

This classic mountain notch leads to a secluded waterfall.

DIRECTIONS

From Lanesville on NY 214, drive 5.0 miles north of Phoenicia, look for Diamond Notch Road on the left, where there are state trail signs. Go up Diamond Notch Road 1.2 miles, and into the woods another 0.3 mile to the trailhead parking area. Note that the last 0.5 mile is a rocky road that may be difficult for all but four-wheel-drive vehicles. A private landowner has posted the area, but it is legal to park on the road as long as you are not blocking traffic. Coming southeast from Hunter, take NY 214 (2.0 miles east of town), and you'll see the trailhead signs 7.0 miles into Stony Clove (or 4.0 miles beyond Devil's Tombstone State Campground) on your right. Turn right onto Diamond Notch Road and follow the above directions to the trailhead. *GPS coordinates: 42° 8.764′ N, 74° 15.829′ W.*

TRAIL DESCRIPTION

This is an easy-to-moderate hike that takes you into Diamond Notch via an old turnpike converted in 1937 to a ski and hiking trail. Forest encroachment and slides have reduced the trail's width considerably, but the footpath remains intact. From the trailhead parking area, the trail is marked with blue state trail markers and climbs next to Hollow Tree Brook. Soon you cross the brook on a flight of stone steps.

In spring you'll discover a wide variety of wildflowers: dutchman's breeches, Carolina spring beauties, yellow violets, and purple trillium. After 15 minutes of hiking, just beyond the bridge, you can make out a high ridge to your left, which is part of West Kill Mountain, the ridge that forms the west side of Diamond Notch in the Hunter West Kill Wilderness. At this point, hemlock

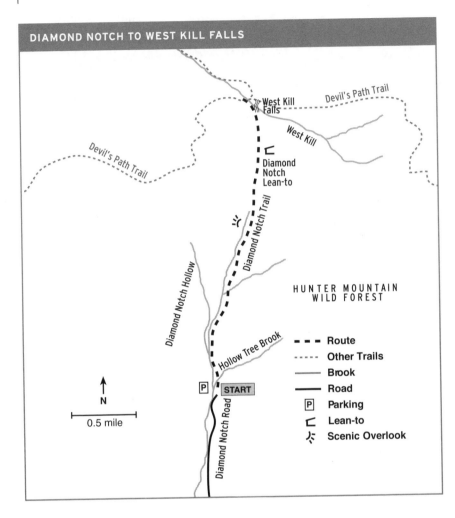

DIAMOND NOTCH TO WEST KILL FALLS

West Kill Falls

Devil's Path Trail

Devil's Path Trail

West Kill

Diamond Notch Lean-to

Diamond Notch Trail

Diamond Notch Hollow

HUNTER MOUNTAIN WILD FOREST

Hollow Tree Brook

- - - Route
- - - - Other Trails
———— Brook
━━━━ Road
P Parking
L Lean-to
Scenic Overlook

P START

N

0.5 mile

Diamond Notch Road

begins to appear, and the trail becomes heavily eroded and gullied. Soon another bridge crosses Hollow Tree Brook, and the trail begins an even ascent, continuing due north into Diamond Notch Hollow. This is most likely the spot that suggested the development of a ski trail through the notch, but you'll probably opt for the novice slopes of a sanctioned ski area after you look down from above. Look up to your left (west), and you'll see the rocky, spruce-covered shoulder of West Kill's east ridge jutting out.

About 1.5 miles into the hollow, you'll come across a miniature waterfall on your right and another small kill just beyond it, both running straight down the mountain, crossing the trail. Some outcrops of thinly stratified sandstone lie ahead, hinting that the notch is not far beyond. Within 5 minutes, there are excellent views to the southwest, highlighting (from right to left) Slide, Table, Lone, Peekamoose, Cornell, Wittenberg, and Ashokan High Point. Up to the right is a long pile of landslide talus, with birch, cherry, and maple establishing themselves in its thin soil.

An old road descends sharply into the ravine on the trail's west side. Now, 1.7 miles into the notch, you approach its highest point. After you have enjoyed the notch and its fine view, follow the trail into an evergreen forest, descending gently to reach Diamond Notch Lean-to. The shelter has a wood floor; its site is cleaner than most and it's in good shape as far as Catskill lean-tos go. Just below the lean-to is a small wetland that contributes to the upper reaches of West Kill Creek. Follow along on what can be a fairly wet trail, with a view of Rusk Mountain ahead and slightly left. To the west of Rusk Mountain is Evergreen Mountain, and to the east, Hunter Mountain, none of them visible. Within 15 minutes of the lean-to, you should reach the junction with the red-marked Devil's Path Trail and the bridge over West Kill Falls (a.k.a. Buttermilk Falls). Diamond Notch is back the way you came, about 2.3 miles away; the nearest road is ahead on the blue-marked trail, at 0.5 mile (Spruceton–Old Hunter Road).

The falls here are small but very attractive, with a succession of large pools. The Devil's Path Trail (red markers) runs east and west past the falls. To the west lies West Kill Mountain. Straight ahead, the Diamond Notch Trail continues to the Spruceton Road trailhead to Hunter Mountain (see Trip 51).

You will find the falls an ideal place to spend a hot afternoon. Hike out on the route you came in.

DID YOU KNOW?

In Diamond Notch, where the mountains of West Kill and Southwest Hunter come very close together, it's theoretically possible to stand on two mountains at the same time.

MORE INFORMATION

Because of its proximity to Spruceton Road, this area was at one time subject to intensive overuse and unregulated camping, but it has since recovered and no camping is permitted. For more information on the Catskill Forest Preserve, visit www.dec.ny.gov/lands/5265.html. For the DEC Region 4 office in Stamford, call 607-652-7365.

NEARBY

For an easy nearby outing, the Tannersville Bike Path (Huckleberry Multi-Use Trail) in Tannersville follows the bed of the old Huckleberry Railroad for 2.7 miles, from Bloomer Road to Clum Hill Road, with swimming and picnicking at Tannersville Park in the middle. For more information, call the village of Tannersville at 518-589-5850.

TRIP 53
WEST KILL MOUNTAIN TO
BUCK RIDGE LOOKOUT

Location: Spruceton, NY
Rating: Strenuous
Distance: 9.4 miles
Elevation Gain: 2,030 feet
Estimated Time: 6.5 hours
Maps: USGS Lexington; AMC Catskill Mountains; NY–NJTC Northeastern Catskills

This demanding hike crosses the elongated West Kill plateau, taking hikers to the scenic Buck Ridge Lookout.

DIRECTIONS

Turn off NY 23A onto NY 42 South in Lexington, west of Hunter. Follow NY 42 toward Shandaken into West Kill. About 3.8 miles from NY 23A , you will see signs for Spruceton on CR 6. Turn left here and go 3.8 miles to the Devil's Path on your right. *GPS coordinates: 42° 11.528′ N, 74° 19.454′ W.*

TRAIL DESCRIPTION

This is the longer but gentler approach to West Kill Mountain from Spruceton, with a slightly greater vertical rise than the approach from the eastern end of Spruceton Road (1,780-foot rise). This is the terminus of the red-marked Devil's Path Trail.

Go immediately uphill through a hardwood-and-pine forest. The trail levels out shortly, and after 10 minutes you'll find that you are walking the border of a forest transition, with hemlock on your right and hardwood on your left. To your right are Mink Hollow (not to be confused with the better-known Mink Hollow near Lake Hill) and its brook that joins the West Kill. Large, moss-clad boulders decorate the forest. Grouse may burst from dense cover as you walk along.

After 20 minutes or so, over rocky, root-covered footing, you'll meet the creek that runs into Mink Hollow. The trail then veers left, ascending into a rocky hardwood forest. In 10 minutes, you'll hear a spring bubbling beneath the trail as you look ahead into a gap, or opening, in the forest where a vernal pond sits between West Kill and North Dome. The gap runs south into the

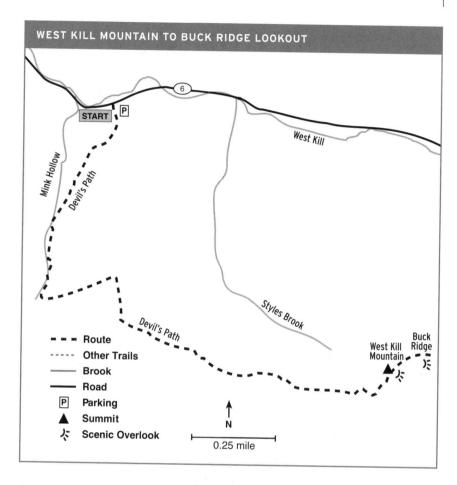

WEST KILL MOUNTAIN TO BUCK RIDGE LOOKOUT

START

6

West Kill

Mink Hollow

Devil's Path

Styles Brook

Devil's Path

Buck
West Kill Ridge
Mountain

Route

Other Trails

Brook

Road

P **Parking**

▲ **Summit**

Scenic Overlook

N

0.25 mile

head of Broadstreet Hollow and the Timber Lake Camp. There are two signs at this pond section on the trail, one indicating West Kill Mountain summit; the other shows Spruceton Road as back the way you came.

Turn sharply uphill to the north. Continue climbing for 20 minutes or more, over the steepest section of trail you will encounter. The trail eases over grassy, fern-covered flats through ledges and undulating terrain where beech and cherry appear. This pattern continues for another 20 minutes until you descend steeply. But the drop is not severe or prolonged; it flattens out and the trail climbs again. Be careful here while negotiating slanted slabs of bluestone that are slippery when wet.

As you ascend to a level walk again, it will take you 20 more minutes through winding flats to climb into alpine terrain where the trail narrows and balsam becomes prolific. A short spur to the north, just before you arrive at the summit, offers excellent views of the Blackhead Range; Huntersfield, Tower,

The upper elevations of Spruceton Valley are subject to rapid changes in weather.

and Cave mountains; and an extensive sprawl of lowlands where you have a glimpse of the Schoharie Reservoir. A sign identifying West Kill's summit (3,880 feet) appears just ahead on your right.

Continue for another 3 to 5 minutes, to the ledge of Buck Ridge (3,740 feet). This view is on many hikers' "favorites" list, and it is impressive. There is enough room for a dozen people to rest here, poised in midair looking at a 180-degree collection of peaks. From left to right you can see Windham, Thomas Cole, Black Dome, Blackhead, Hunter West with its ski trails, Hunter and its fire tower, Southwest Hunter, Plateau, Overlook and its fire tower (for hawkeyes only!), Slide, Table, Lone, Rocky, Wittenberg, Cornell, Friday, Balsam Cap, Ashokan High Point, the Mohonk Preserve's Sky Top, a piece of the Ashokan Reservoir, and down into Lanesville on NY 214. You can also see a widening in the Hudson River (Vanderberg Cove) as well as Olderbark, Little Rocky, Carl Mountain (in the foreground), and Mount Tremper to the right of the Ashokan Reservoir. See if you can find its fire tower.

On the summt, you will recognize the pungent odor of the balm of Gilead—the pitch of balsam fir, dripping from the blisters on the tree's bark. It is said to have medicinal value; it does keep bacteria and fungi to a minimum, at least in the tree's case. People once thought that it must also do that for them, recalling the prophet Jeremiah's reference to the balm that ancient Israelites found on Mount Gilead in the Holy Land. American Indians called the healing balsam salve *cho-koh-tung*, or "blisters." The resin was used commercially to create adhesives for lenses and microscope slides until synthetics were found to be superior.

Retrace your steps to your car.

DID YOU KNOW?

The West Kill Creek was the favorite trout-fishing stream of Art Flick, the grandfather of Catskill fly-fishers.

MORE INFORMATION

For more information on the Catskill Forest Preserve, visit www.dec.ny.gov/lands/5265.html. For the DEC Region 4 office in Stamford, call 607-652-7365.

NEARBY

The Catskill Mountain Foundation on Route 23A in Hunter operates a bookstore, crafts and art gallery, and organic farm market. The Foundation's Doctorow Center for the Arts presents music and film arts and is the home of the two-screen Mountain Cinema and the Pleshakov Piano Museum (by appointment only). Visit www.catskillmtn.org or call 518-263-2000.

TRIP 54
DRY BROOK RIDGE

Location: Arkville, NY
Rating: Strenuous
Distance: 10.6 miles
Elevation Gain: 2,000 feet
Estimated Time: 5 hours
Maps: USGS Margaretville; USGS Fleischmanns; USGS Seager; USGS Arena; AMC Catskill Mountains; NY–NJTC Central Catskills

Dry Brook Valley is a remote hike in the western Catskills in a first-growth forest. Off the beaten track, Dry Brook has experienced little change in thousands of years.

DIRECTIONS
From NY 28, west of Margaretville, take South Side road 2.0 miles to Hill Road. Bear left on Hill Road and go an additional 1.3 miles to the Huckleberry Loop trailhead on the road's north side. *GPS coordinates:* 42° 6.949′ N, 74° 38.740′ W.

TRAIL DESCRIPTION
This interesting loop hike across the west-facing edge of Dry Brook Ridge has become more popular with organized groups in recent years. The ridge is fairly high (3,480 feet) and remote, offering a secluded and interesting vantage above Cold Spring Hollow from Penguin Rocks. The entire length of the loop trail across the top of the ridge is covered in first-growth forest.

The suggested route begins from the north of Hill Road, using the Huckleberry Loop Trail. The trailhead lies at 1,900 feet. To save time or to maximize time spent on the ledges, some hikers choose to visit Penguin Rocks and return to this trailhead rather than completing the loop, thus saving some 500 feet in elevation and an additional 1.5 miles of hiking. But the forests and plantations of the southern end of the loop are well worth a look, so by all means plan to hike the entire route.

From the trailhead, travel uphill through several forest transitions of plantation Norway spruce and red pine, followed by native Carolinian hardwoods (you can see the plantations from the higher ridge elevations). The terrain flattens as the route turns east, soon crossing an old, disused woods road. Now the

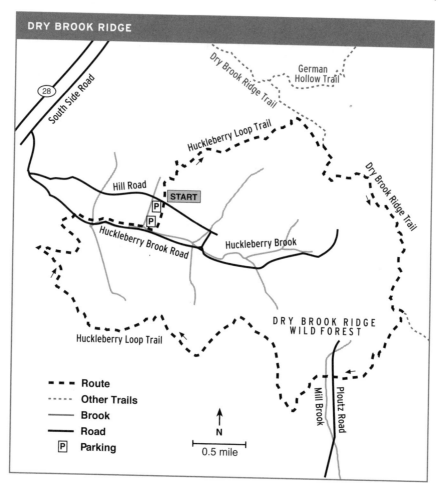

DRY BROOK RIDGE

German
Hollow Trail

Dry Brook Ridge Trail

28

South Side Road

Huckleberry Loop Trail

Dry Brook Ridge Trail

Hill Road

START

P

P

Huckleberry Brook Road

Huckleberry Brook

DRY BROOK RIDGE
WILD FOREST

Huckleberry Loop Trail

- - - Route
- - - - Other Trails
——— Brook
——— Road
P Parking

Mill Brook

Ploutz Road

N

0.5 mile

trail climbs again, until it intersects with the Dry Brook Ridge Trail at 1.7 miles. Turn right (south). You walk through a consistent distribution of beech, birch, and maple, with a corresponding appearance of moosewood, pin cherry, choke cherry, hop hornbeam, hobblebush, oxalis, wood fern, viburnum, blackberry, raspberry, and blueberry. Of course, such a profusion of fruit attracts bears, but you will be very lucky to see one in these open hardwood areas.

The trail is flat for a stretch but rises shortly and soon passes a high bog on the left at 3,100 feet. This first peat bog is about 680 years old; the next one, near the junction ahead, "the middle summit bog," is 3,450 years old. Still another on the Huckleberry Brook ridge is 6,908 years old.

After climbing another in a series of low ledges, you'll reach a boulder with limited views and, following it, weaving in and out of trees along the western ridgeline, you'll arrive at an unmarked spur to the 150-foot-long exposed

The trails of Dry Brook Ridge explore many reclaimed settlement areas.

outcrop of Penguin Rocks (3,300 feet; the place-name origin is not known). Covered in blueberry bushes, it offers some fine views to the west. As you look straight out into the valley, you see Cold Spring Hollow directly below you, with its Huckleberry Brook reaching for the Delaware. To the left, beyond Mill Brook Valley, is the long Mill Brook Ridge, running east–west from the vicinity of Woodpecker Ridge and the (unseen) Balsam Lake Mountain. You can see the Delaware's east branch as it flows from Margaretville and into the Pepacton Reservoir, a New York City water-supply reservoir that is known for producing record-setting brown trout.

Continue south along the trail, passing another view from a point above a talus field and below the ridge's otherwise viewless summit. Descend through terracing terrain another 0.5 mile, as the Dry Brook Ridge Trail bends southeast at the junction with the red-marked Huckleberry Ridge Trail. Turn right (south–southwest). The trail descends gradually through hardwoods to cross Ploutz Road at the site of an old settlement, probably that of a subsistence farmer. There's a trailhead parking area and register here, adjacent to Mill Brook. Signs of old settlements continue across Mill Brook, into an area where Norway spruce have been planted in old pasturelands. The trail rises along the grade of an old road, gradually steepening as it reenters hardwood forest and following to the southwest of a wooded knoll (2,832 feet).

The trail now works its way west, descending through ledgy hemlock woods to the edge of a large, open field where you have to keep a close watch on the trail markers. Cairns that guide the way across the open field may be obscured by high grass during summer. The trail enters the woods at the northerly edge of the field, ascends initially, and begins to switchback, downhill first into the northwest, then into the east. The extreme slope has resulted in sustained erosion here.

The trail heads downhill steeply to a woods road that can wash out and descends again from red pine to hemlock woods, finally crossing Huckleberry Brook. Turn right on Huckleberry Brook Road, following the trail markers east, crossing a small bridge, and turning right, in front of the DEC storage facility (keeping the building to your left). The trail appears next to the storage building and climbs again, arriving at Hill Road in 0.3 mile. Turn left 150 feet to the trailhead parking area and your car.

DID YOU KNOW?

The Dry Brook Ridge is among the most fascinating in the Catskills, because it is the only area that has sustained uninterrupted floral conditions since the Ice Age.

MORE INFORMATION

For more information on the Catskill Forest Preserve, visit www.dec.ny.gov/lands/5265.html. For the DEC Region 4 office in Stamford, call 607-652-7365.

NEARBY

Delaware County is a highly scenic and heavily farmed setting of low, gently sculpted hills spotted with rich, cultivated fields and long vistas. While in Arkville, take advantage of the scenery by taking a 2-hour ride on the Delaware and Ulster Raiload, running from Arkville to Roxbury and back. Railroads came to the Arkville area in 1871, fostering the great resort boom that followed. Riding the red Heifer (a combination diesel, mail, freight, and passenger car called a brill) through this scenic territory will give you appreciation for the easterly upper Delaware Valley that cannot be seen from the heights of Dry Brook Ridge; www.durr.org; 800-225-4132 or 845-586-3877.

TRIP 55
BALSAM LAKE MOUNTAIN

Location: Arkville, NY
Rating: Strenuous
Distance: 6.0 miles
Elevation Gain: 1,123 feet
Estimated Time: 4.5 hours
Maps: USGS Seager; AMC Catskill Mountains; NY–NJTC Central Catskills

This spruce–fir summit would be viewless without its fire tower, which offers 360-degree views of the western Catskills.

DIRECTIONS

From NY 28 in Arkville, go south on CR 49 (Dry Brook Road) for 6.0 miles, through Mapledale. Turn right onto Mill Brook Road and go 2.3 miles to the trailhead parking area on the right. Cross the road and locate the blue-marked Dry Brook Ridge Trail. Be sure you take this section of the Dry Brook Ridge Trail, not the one on the north (or right) side of the road that crosses northerly Dry Brook Ridge. *GPS coordinates: 42° 4.198′ N, 74° 34.446′ W.*

TRAIL DESCRIPTION

From the trailhead to Balsam Lake Mountain (3,723 feet) you enter a forest of beech, birch, maple, and cherry trees over cinnamon ferns, oxalis, and viburnum. Pass the trail register on your left.

Follow along through a flat section of the trail to an ascent that allows occasional views across Mill Brook Hollow to the west. Climb gently through a few switchbacks, where jack-in-the-pulpit, Solomon's seal, wolf's claw club moss, and haircap moss appear. The upright, branched, and densely leaved stems of wolf's claw club moss are used commercially for Christmas decorations. (Picking them here is prohibited.) The moss is widely distributed through the Catskills and northern North America. It can be confused with tree club moss, or ground pine, found in open pine woods and bogs.

In 10 minutes or so, you'll pass a spring to the right and downhill (indicated by a sign), among a series of sedimentary boulders, many of them covered with rock tripe. When soaked for several weeks in water, this lichen renders a purple dye that has some popularity among textile artisans. Rock

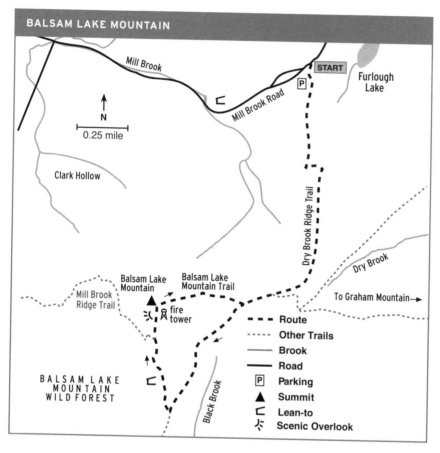

tripe is also edible, but not at all "wholesome." The dried-up, curled disks of lichen resemble moldy potato chips.

In 20 minutes, pass a grass-covered trail on your left that leads to the summit of Graham Mountain (3,868 feet). (Many hikers climb Graham along with Balsam Lake Mountain, but there is no legal public easement.)

In a few moments, you encounter several trail signs. Take the red-marked Balsam Lake Mountain Trail to your right, heading for the fire tower (0.85 mile). Continue uphill over flat rocks with visible glacial scratches. The trail includes vigorous ascents broken up by more moderate inclines, hedged in blackberry, bunchberry, and extremely dense spruce–fir thickets.

After 20 minutes, you at last see the fire tower and observer's cabin. Climb to the top of the tower where you can see in all directions (it is staffed on weekends, seasonally). Below the tower, and running north, is the Dry Brook Ridge. To the northeast on a clear day, you can see Bearpen Mountain, 15 miles away. Closer is the ridge on the east side of the Dry Brook Valley and its series of peaks. From left to right are Belleayre, Balsam, Haynes, Eagle, and Big Indian. Between the latter two is the summit of Panther. Due east of you is the range that includes Slide and Table. The two neighboring peaks are Graham and Doubletop. To the south and west are the rolling, seemingly endless lower peaks of Delaware County. You can see Red Hill and its fire tower.

Just off the summit, in an impenetrable tangle of fallen trees, is an interesting plant community.. This bog contains more sphagnum than other bogs in the Catskill region. A hurricane in 1950 caused extensive blowdown, followed by a heavy second growth of balsam fir. It has been hypothesized that this bog may never follow a bog's normal growth pattern because of the infiltration of acid rain, which acts to decompose peat. Water is retained, and the bog stage remains rather than progresses. Balsam Lake's summit has recently been the site of studies into acid rain, a phenomenon that has arisen in the Catskills despite the profusion of limestone that acts to buffer acids on the earth's surface.

The trail continues downhill past an outbuilding with signs indicating the lean-to at 0.45 mile. Follow downhill, passing the Mill Brook Ridge Trail that descends to the west and, farther on, passing a spur trail to the right (west) that leads to the Eleanor Leavitt Memorial Lean-to.

Descending, you intersect with the blue-marked Dry Brook Ridge Trail again, within 20 minutes. Go left (north) and follow this grassy road uphill for 20 minutes to the junction of the Balsam Lake Mountain Trail, which you'll recognize. Descend, retracing your steps to the parking area.

DID YOU KNOW?

Beecher Lake, to the west, once belonged to the family of American novelist Harriet Beecher Stowe, author of *Uncle Tom's Cabin* (1852).

MORE INFORMATION

For more information on the Catskill Forest Preserve, visit www.dec.ny.gov/lands/5265.html. For the DEC Region 3 office in New Paltz, call 845-256-3000.

NEARBY

The Erpf Gallery at the Catskill Center for Conservation and Development on NY 28 in Arkville presents exhibits that showcase the interconnection between humans and their landscapes. The Catskill Center supports an artist-in-residence program at Platte Clove, and maintains regional folklife and history archives; www.catskillcenter.org; 845-586-2611.

THE *CLEARWATER*–AMERICA'S ENVIRONMENTAL FLAGSHIP

Hikers peering out across the Hudson River may spot the majestic gaff-rigged sloop *Clearwater*, with her tremendous mainsail and her unmistakable topsail with the multicolored compass rose.

The *Clearwater* represents one of the most compelling and successful grass- roots environmental efforts ever undertaken. In 1966, folk singer and Hudson Valley resident Pete Seeger became disgusted with the condition of his beloved Hudson River, which was full of raw sewage and unchecked toxic waste. Indigenous fish populations were decreasing, and some had disappeared. Despairing over the Hudson's fate, Seeger brainstormed the idea of building a replica of a Hudson River sloop as a symbol and rallying point in the effort to save the river. He felt that the boat would be a cornerstone for concerned citizens, young people, school children, and educators living in the valley on which they could build their own tools and strategies for the protection of their environment.

That dream, though seemingly ambitious and idealistic, has been realized. The 106-foot *Clearwater* was built in Maine, launched in 1969, and sailed to the Hudson Valley. She is identical to the eighteenth-century, shallow, draft-freighting sloops that carried goods up- and downriver between Albany and New York City. Today her home port is in Saugerties. Each season, she sails as a floating classroom, introducing educators and children to a science-based environmental curriculum focusing on the Hudson River estuary. The *Clearwater* organization is credited with creating the first such program in the United States to be held aboard a sailing vessel–a template that has been used worldwide for similar programs. More than a half-million young people have been a part of Clearwater's onboard environmental program, and 15,000 students as well as 200 teachers are served annually.

Hudson River Sloop Clearwater, Inc., based in Beacon, New York, is a member-supported environmental advocacy group whose mission is to preserve and protect the Hudson River. But it is not simply local. Members take part in supporting the Clean Water Act, the Hudson River Park Act, and the removal of PCBs from the river.

Each year, Clearwater holds a fundraising event at Croton State Park called the Great Hudson River Revival.

In 2004, the *Clearwater* was added to the National Register of Historic Places for her part in the American environmental movement. She is often joined by her sister ship, the *Woody Guthrie*, in educational programming. Free sails are provided to the public on a scheduled basis, and anyone with interest can apply to serve as volunteer crew or as an onboard educator.

TRIP 56
PALENVILLE OVERLOOK

Location: Palenville, NY
Rating: Strenuous
Distance: 8.0 miles
Elevation Gain: 1,300 feet
Estimated Time: 5 hours
Maps: USGS Kaaterskill; AMC Catskill Mountains; NY–NJTC North Lake Area, Northeastern Catskills

This is the historic carriage road route that once led to the Catskill Mountain House and today brings hikers to a pair of peaceful lookouts over lower Kaaterskill Clove and the Hudson Valley.

DIRECTIONS
From NY 23A in Palenville, turn right onto Boggart Road, the first right after the light on NY 23A as you are driving west. Follow Boggart Road for 2.5 miles to a four-way intersection with Mountain Turnpike Road at Pelham's Four Corners (the portion to the right is dirt). There are horse trail signs here. Turn left and go 1.0 mile to the end of Mountain Turnpike Road, where you can legally park along the road. *GPS coordinates:* 42° 12.743′ N, 74° 00.451′ W.

TRAIL DESCRIPTION
To reach this quiet and isolated pair of overlooks, you hike the historic Old Mountain Road through Rip Van Winkle Hollow, which, notes the author Roland Van Zandt, became "the classic approach to the great scenic domain of the Catskill Mountain House for almost [all of] the nineteenth century." The road had its beginnings in 1823 as a tannery road and stagecoach route to the Catskill Mountain House. It remained a stage route until the railroad came in the 1880s, causing its eventual abandonment. Yet, by 1931, H.A. Haring wrote in *Our Catskill Mountains* that the road "is impassable for any sort of vehicle, but is endlessly charming for the hiker who is equal to an ascent of 2,000 feet within a walking distance of 5 miles." The road has been repaired since, and new bridges are in place for equestrians, snowmobilers, and hikers.

Begin at the western end of Mountain Turnpike Road. You will see the snowmobile trail markers as the road turns to dirt and curves uphill into Rip Van Winkle Hollow, with Stony Brook on the left. Continuing uphill, you

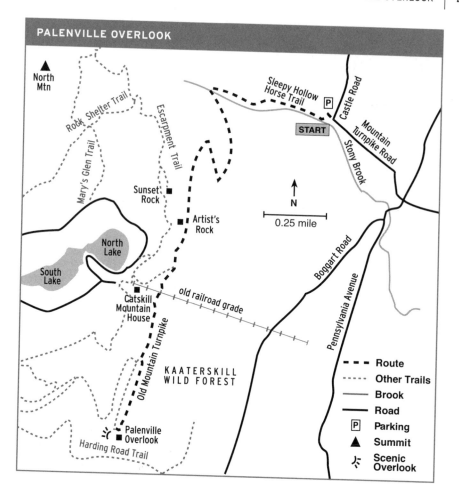

PALENVILLE OVERLOOK

▲ North Mtn

Rock Shelter Trail

Sleepy Hollow Horse Trail

P

Castle Road

START

Mountain Turnpike Road

Stony Brook

Escarpment Trail

Mary's Glen Trail

Sunset Rock ■

■ Artist's Rock

↑ N

0.25 mile

North Lake

Boggart Road

South Lake

Pennsylvania Avenue

Catskill Mountain House ■

old railroad grade

Old Mountain Turnpike

KAATERSKILL WILD FOREST

- - - Route
····· Other Trails
——— Brook
━━━ Road
P Parking
▲ Summit
⅄ Scenic Overlook

⅄ ■ Palenville Overlook

Harding Road Trail

cross Black Snake Bridge within 0.5 mile. A hardwood forest slopes steeply up to your right toward the Escarpment, while a hemlock ravine pitches steeply down to your left. At the horseshoe turn in Sleepy Hollow, you can still see the old stone foundations of the Rip Van Winkle House, a "halfway" house and early boarding house and tavern. The 1.0 mile distance to this point will take you a half-hour of uphill hiking, so you may enjoy a stop here at the traditional resting place for coach travelers to the Catskill Mountain House, who had already traveled 10 rough miles from the wharf at Catskill.

Every effort was made to assure Mountain House guests that this was the spot where Rip encountered the strange crew of Henry Hudson's *Half Moon*. Nearby was the rock upon which he took his famous slumber, and a tree could be pointed out beneath which the bones of his dog Wolf were "discovered." It's easy to imagine the Romantics of the time accepting the story as fact. Haring

The historic Palenville Overlook surveys the eastern Indian Head Wilderness.

recorded that "every summer visitors in hundreds scrambled up the perpendicular continuation of Sleepy Hollow in search of the 'flats' where Hendrick Hudson's gnomes thunderously rolled the balls in their game of ninepins." In fact, Washington Irving is not specific as to the location of the events in the legend, which appealed to the Romantic mind for its very vagueness and mystery. He did not visit the Catskills until 1832, 12 years after the publication of the story—he only observed them from the decks of a Hudson River steamboat.

Continue from here on the 0.5-mile-long Dead Ox Hill, going steadily uphill through hardwoods toward Little Pine Orchard and Cape Horn. You reach Cape Horn within 30 minutes of Sleepy Hollow at the site of a stone fireplace and rough campsite. From Cape Horn, views to the east are fair, with the Taconics and the river valley visible. Make a 180-degree right turn here onto the Short Level that takes you up a moderate grade to another horseshoe bend in 0.3 mile, or 10 minutes.

Now you turn toward the north, and then switch back south to Featherbed Hill. This path is shown on Walton Van Loan's 1876 *Map of All Points of Interest Within Four Miles of the Catskill Mountain House.* Van Loan's representation, specifically from the Saxe Farm at the end of Mountain Turnpike Road to Palenville Overlook, while not entirely reliable for navigation, accurately shows this section of the trail.

From Featherbed Hill, you walk the next 1.5 miles uphill through a hardwood forest until you reach a Y in the trail. Take a left at this Y. This point is known as the Long Level, where the grade becomes flatter.

At the Y, you follow a steep downhill grade left to the northeast that switches back almost immediately to the south. In a few minutes you cross the open gash that runs up the mountain—the abandoned Otis Elevated Railroad tracks. Opened in 1892, this incline railway saved from 3 to 4 hours' stage time for the trip to the Catskill Mountain House during the crucial period when other mountaintop resorts were challenging the supremacy of Charles L. Beach's domain. Lack of patronage and the advent of automobile travel caused the railway to be closed in 1918. Its rails and cables were sold to the government for weapons manufacturing. The bare scrape it left in the Escarpment can be seen for miles.

After crossing the railway clearing, the trail narrows through a forest of mixed hardwoods and continues along, flat and featureless (except for limited views through the trees to the east), until you reach a fork within 20 minutes. Take the right fork. One hundred feet beyond is a posted trail junction with a sign to Halfway House Lookout (0.45 mile), another name for Palenville Overlook. Follow this trail about 10 or 15 minutes on level terrain, and suddenly you stand over the abyssal depth of Kaaterskill Clove, with the village of Palenville below and remarkable views of Kaaterskill High Peak and Roundtop to the south. The open ledges of Palenville Overlook are ideal spots for picnicking, sketching, photographing, camping, or simply pondering. The vertical drops are extremely dangerous here, so be cautious.

When you have enjoyed this place to your satisfaction, you can return by the route you came. Before leaving, if you should wish to rest in the bewitching silence high above the birthplace of Rip Van Winkle, be careful lest you too sleep away a lifetime.

MORE INFORMATION

For more information on the Catskill Forest Preserve, visit www.dec.ny.gov/lands/5265.html. For the DEC Region 4 office in Stamford, call 607-652-7365.

NEARBY

The town of Catskill on the Hudson River has a self-guided walking tour along its historic Main Street, with 33 points of interest. The tour description can be found at www.catskillny.org/tour.htm. For more information contact the Heart of Catskill Association at 518-943-0989.

TRIP 57
SAUGERTIES LIGHTHOUSE

Location: Saugerties, NY
Rating: Easy
Distance: 1.1 miles
Elevation Gain: Minimal
Estimated Time: 40 minutes
Maps: Ruth Reynolds Glunt Nature Preserve, Lighthouse Trail Map

This easy, short trail provides beautiful river scenery and is an excellent starter outing for young children.

DIRECTIONS

From either the northbound or the southbound ramp of Exit 20 off the NYS Thruway (I-87), turn south on NY 32. (Northbound will turn right onto NY 32; southbound will turn left onto NY32 and left again at its intersection with NY 212. The true heading is easterly.) Head toward the village of Saugerties on Ulster Avenue. At 0.9 mile from the northbound entrance/exit to I-87, bear right at the light on Market Street and go one block. Turn left at Main Street and go one block. Stay straight to go onto US 9W/Main Street. Go 0.4 mile. Where US 9W curves to the left, turn right onto Mynderse Street. Go 0.3 mile. Take a slight left onto Lighthouse Drive and go 0.4 mile. Turn right into the lighthouse parking lot after the U.S. Coast Guard station. *GPS coordinates: 42° 4.334′ N, 73° 56.204′ W.*

TRAIL DESCRIPTION

Several lighthouses exist in the Hudson Valley, but only the Saugerties lighthouse is occupied and accessible by foot trail. And although the path to this unusual spot is short, it is fascinating and fun—especially for very young children, for whom it proves an ideal introductory hike.

The brick lighthouse itself (built in 1835, replaced in 1869) and the picnic area and walkway surrounding it are built on an artificially constructed sandbar jutting into the river, adjacent to the Esopus Creek. (The Esopus, once called Sopus, was named for the Delaware word for river, *seepu*.) The lighthouse sits upon a large granite base, 60 feet in diameter and supported by 56 wooden pilings driven into the river bottom. Views up and down the river from this point are uninterrupted for miles. To the east, across the narrow Hudson,

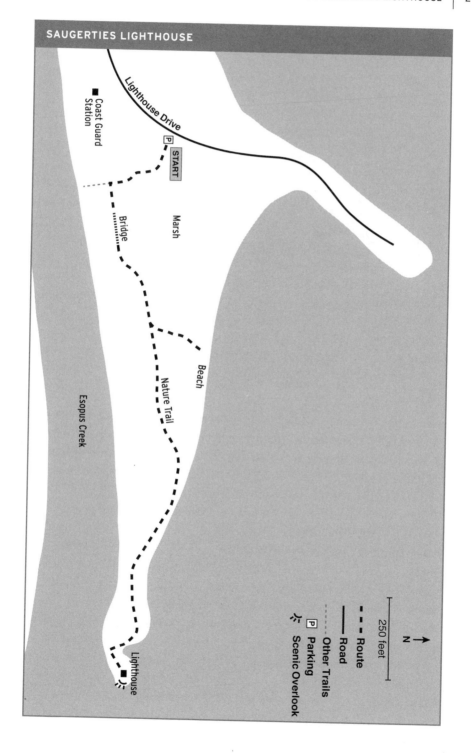

SAUGERTIES LIGHTHOUSE

Lighthouse Drive

Coast Guard
Station

P
START

Marsh

Bridge

Beach

Nature Trail

Esopus Creek

Lighthouse

N →

250 feet

- - - Route
—— Road
········ Other Trails
P Parking
Scenic Overlook

The Saugerties Lighthouse Trail follows boardwalks and sandy flats along the Hudson River.

are the estates of the rich and famous. To the west, though obstructed, are views of the Indian Head Wilderness Area peaks. The jungly tidal wetlands leading to the lighthouse are floristically rich and dense, and the footway is flat and easy to walk.

Take a trail map from the kiosk and begin at the gated trailhead that leaves from the east edge of the parking area. Immediately you will be struck by the appearance of several very large eastern cottonwood trees, members of the poplar family. These large trees with their massive trunks grow to 100 feet in height and from 3 to 4 feet in diameter—often they are larger still. They typically border streams, appearing in pure stands or mixed among willows, and are the common pioneer species on newly formed sandbars and moist, open floodplains. One of the fastest-growing native trees, they often attain 13 feet of vertical growth annually, making them a prized source of pulpwood. They are named for the cottonlike seeds that you often see blowing around the woods and across roadways.

Pass a private dock to the right and cross a short bridge over a muddy tidal channel. Ahead, a second bridge passes through swamp shrub, and a spur to the left (at the fork), where an interpretive kiosk is located, leads to a sandy beach looking north up the river. Take this spur and enjoy the scenery before returning to the fork and the main trail. Follow the main trail again, crossing a low boardwalk and passing through a swamp forest of mixed hardwood. Ahead is another low boardwalk, which is at times inundated by the tide. You'll see cables securing the walk, which has a tendency to float away with very high tides. Because there is always the chance that you and your party may arrive during such a tide, it is best to come prepared with sandals or boots, depending on the time of year. Because of the volume and nature of debris that is continually washed ashore here, it is not a good idea to go barefoot.

Soon you will reach the tall, honey-colored stalks of rushes that have taken over the eastern end of the point. These are members of an invasive species called phragmites, a common reed that grows in alkaline habitats and tolerates brackish water. These reed beds are not affected by frequent inundation from the river.

Hikers will wonder over the oddly shaped, hard-spiked seedpods of the Eurasian (European) water chestnut, another invasive species common to several eastern United States waterways. The Hudson River is among the most problematic areas for this invasive species. Mats of water chestnut severely restrict light and reduce oxygen levels in aquatic habitats. This has contributed to fish kills in some areas, and restricts recreational use. In native habitats of Europe, Asia, and Africa, the plants are kept in check by insect parasites that are not indigenous here.

Children will be enchanted by the visage of far-flung shores and the mystery of hidden, watery places as they imagine being marooned in some exotic spot and examine bits of flotsam and jetsam washed ashore with the tides, half hidden in the sands. Maybe a message in a bottle will be discovered!

Once at the lighthouse, relax on the benches and picnic tables, enjoying the view. The lighthouse beacon is still in operation and serves as an aid to navigation. It sits very close to the river's channel, which is maintained (by dredging) at a minimum of 35 feet deep. Large ships as well as pleasure craft pass very close to the lighthouse, making this an interesting and exciting spot. Freighters, tankers, and barges pushed and pulled by tugs come and go between the Port of Albany and points south. Many recreational watercraft pass through here, en route to southern climes from ports in Canada and the Great Lakes, via the Erie Canal and the St. Lawrence River. The earliest shipping in these waters was steam powered, and the first steam passenger boat to provide service from New York City to Albany was called the *Clermont,* the invention of Robert Fulton. Fulton had financial help from his father-in-law, Robert

Livingston, who resided at Clermont, which is the large white mansion seen upriver on the east shore.

The 17-acre nature preserve containing the lighthouse was named for Ruth Reynolds Glunt (1891–1979), who is credited with establishing the Saugerties lighthouse on the National Registry of Historic Places in 1978. Glunt was the author of *Lighthouses and Legends of the Hudson*. She was the widow of Chester B. Glunt, a former U.S. Coast Guard light attendant. Through her preservation efforts, Glunt became the friend of many Hudson River lighthouse keepers.

In 1986, the lighthouse and surrounding preserve was sold to the Saugerties Lighthouse Conservancy for one dollar. In 1990, the light was reactivated. With considerable community support, the SLC restored the lighthouse to its present condition.

DID YOU KNOW?

Reeds similar to the ones growing near the Saugerties lighthouse were fashioned into boats and sailed across the Atlantic Ocean from Egypt to South America.

MORE INFORMATION

The lighthouse trailhead is located at 168 Lighthouse Dr., Saugerties, NY, 12477. It is open dawn to dusk. Check the tide charts on the online tide table in order to time your hike. Avoid periods of extreme high tide. For more informatioin, visit www.saugertieslighthouse.com or call 845-247-0656. A resident keeper lives at the lighthouse year-round. The keeper not only conducts tours of the lighthouse interior (weekends Memorial Day through Labor Day, noon to 3 P.M.), but runs a bed and breakfast there as well. The B&B, established to support the Saugerties Lighthouse Conservancy's maintenance program, has proven so popular that it must be booked a year in advance.

To support the continued preservation of this historic landmark, the Saugerties Lighthouse Conservancy offers various levels of membership.

NEARBY

Visit the well-known antiques shops, eateries, and book stores of Saugerties. (See www.welcometosaugerties.com.) Horses in the Sun (HITS) presents a variety of equestrian competitions and related events in Saugerties; www.hits-shows.com; 845-246-8833. Woodstock, New York, is 10 miles west on NY 212.

TRIP 58
KENNETH L. WILSON
CAMPGROUND NATURE TRAIL

Location: Mount Tremper, NY
Rating: Easy
Distance: 1 mile
Elevation Gain: 100 feet
Estimated Time: 40 minutes
Maps: Campsite map

This easy hike is an ideal first outing for young children, featuring camping, boating, and hiking on an interpretive nature trail.

DIRECTIONS

From NYS Thruway (I-87) Exit 19 at Kingston, take the first right turn off the traffic circle onto NY 28, go 20 miles west on NY 28 to Mount Tremper, turn right onto NY 212, and continue 0.5 mile to a four-way intersection. Turn right onto Wittenberg Road (CR 40). The campsite is approximately 4 miles ahead on the right side of CR 40. From Exit 20 of I-87, take NY 212 8.5 miles to Woodstock and see the following directions from Woodstock.

Alternate route through Woodstock: From Exit 19 (Kingston) off I-87, take NY 28 heading west, go 5.5 miles, then take CR 375 for 2.7 miles into Woodstock. Turn left onto NY 212 and go through Bearsville. Turn left at the Bear Café onto CR 45, and at 2.5 miles go right onto CR 40. Continue to the campground 1 mile on the left. *GPS coordinates:* 42° 1.491′ N, 74° 13.248′ W.

TRAIL DESCRIPTION

This child-friendly hike is located within a contained and peaceful area that lends itself to the kind of multisport activities that young families typically enjoy. Although many state hiking trails begin, end, or pass through public campgrounds in the Catskills, this is one of only a few that have a marked nature trail contained within the campground itself. This feeling of security, along with the area's diverse activities, makes an ideal setting for the skills and confidence building required for more challenging outdoor adventures. The Kenneth Wilson campground is not simply an enjoyable, year-round day-use destination, but also a centrally located staging ground for attractions in the wild forests and wilderness areas of the eastern Catskills.

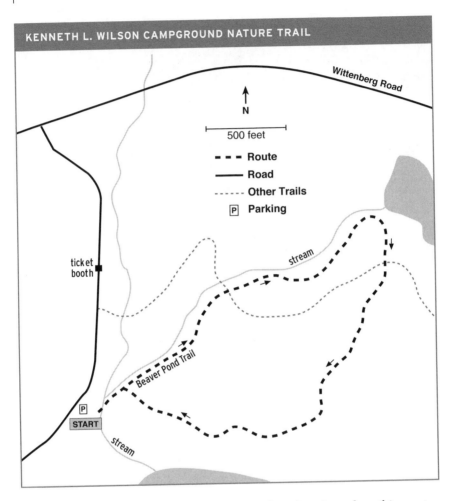

KENNETH L. WILSON CAMPGROUND NATURE TRAIL

To find the interpretive nature trail (numbered stations describing natural features), go to the northwest corner of the parking area next to the lake. There you will find a trail register. Though the trail is short and easy, it's still a good idea to sign in at any state trail register. The trail is self-guiding, and simple enough that you won't need a map, but try to get one at the entry booth so you can study the numbered interpretive stops along the way. The trail markers feature a beech leaf on a yellow background. You won't see many markers, however.

Cross a small bridge (Station 1) into a beautiful, maturing red- and white-pine forest. A small, seasonal stream flows to your left. Adjacent to Station 2 ("Two Pines"), the trail forks; bear left. (You'll be returning from the right-hand fork later.) There is no hunting allowed inside the campground, but the adjoining parcels are private, and it is not inconceivable that hunters will

A hiker enjoys the quiet hemlock woods of the Nature Trail.

position themselves in proximity to the trail—so, take the proper precautions and wear bright clothing during hunting season.

At Station 3, the forest type changes to hemlock. Through the woods to the north are some open fields. As you reach the beaver meadow at Station 4, the trail splits. The spur to the left leads to private property and is not marked. Continue through the stations, watching for wildlife in the diverse habitat of the meadows. Bear right, and climb gently into a mixed forest of large oaks with a hemlock understory. The trail levels, then descends slightly as it curves around back into the west. Some large white pines are seen, along with beech, black birch, and tulip trees (members of the poplar family). Soon you will come back into the red-pine forest you entered at the beginning of the hike. Bear left and return to the trailhead.

The final station (No. 10), is a brief explanation of the Catskills' geological history. It traces time from the Wisconsin Ice Sheet to the streamlined hill, or drumlin, represented by Ticetonyk (Dutch for "steep ladder"), which lies to the south across the Little Beaver Kill creek. The campsite's two narrow lakes were artificially created by the damming of the creek.

DID YOU KNOW?

A small but popular public campground today, this area was once the location of several farms. The land was purchased by the state in the 1960s, and the campground opened in 1979.

MORE INFORMATION

This campground has 76 tent and trailer sites, a lakeside picnic area with tables and grills, flush toilets and hot showers, and provides for mobility impaired accessibility. Bicycles are permitted on the campground roads themselves, but a formerly designated mountain-bike trail no longer exists. Kayaks and canoes are permitted, and are also available for rent at the site. Rowboats (no motors) are allowed as well. Fishing for bass, pickerel, and sunnies is permitted in the small, sheltered lake. There are baseball and soccer fields. The site is located within view of the rugged Mount Tremper Wild Forest, which you can see to the west. The campsites are large, secluded, and heavily wooded. Dogs are allowed on-leash except in the family picnic and day-use area (you must have proof of current rabies vaccination). No untreated firewood may be brought to this campsite from outside of a 50-mile radius. For more information, visit www.dec.ny.gov/outdoor/24472.html or call 845-679-7020.

NEARBY

Visit the many art galleries, restaurants, and shops in Woodstock. Hike the Comeau property trails or take the Byrdcliffe self-guided walking tour. The village of Phoenicia (6 miles west) offers tubing and trout fishing on the Esopus Creek, as well as a scenic train ride on the Catskill Mountain Railroad and a railroad museum. A good soruce of information for activities in the area is www.woodstockchamber.com.

7

THE HELDERBERGS

THE HIKES IN THE HELDERBERGS EXPLORE TWO OF THE STATE'S most striking geological formations. Here, accumulations of sand and lime mud, which
had been compressed into rock, uplifted and eroded to form the mountain
bastions bordering the plains that much later became the Sea of Albany.
These light gray ramparts derive their name from the Dutch *helder* ("bright"
or "light") and *berg* ("mountain"). The uplift of these hills in the early Ter-
tiary Period and later glacial actions expose a long segment of Earth's history.
Views from Vroman's Nose and the cliff face at Indian Ladder are phenomenal.
From Vroman's Nose, perched over the ancient Schoharie floodplain, you look
south and east from Grand Gorge to the northern Catskill Escarpment. From
Thacher Park and Indian Ladder, the viewshed extends from the southern
Adirondacks through Vermont's Green Mountains and across the Taconics.

During the time of the great patroonships (deeded tracts of land), most of
the Helderbergs were owned by the family of Kiliaen van Rensselaer, a major
shareholder in the Dutch West India Company and one of the original patentees of the royal land grants of 1629. At the time, Fort Orange (Albany) was
the center of the Dutch fur trade, which ultimately proved to be much more
profitable than the patroon system. The rich easterly bottomlands would later
be populated by the same German Palatines who arrived in the New World at
Germantown and were settled in East and West camps in a failed attempt to

produce naval stores. A hundred years later, settlers began to arrive from the west to farm the rocky Helderberg escarpment. Many settled along the rich alluvial flats of the Schoharie. Adam Vroman purchased the land in this area from the Mohawks in 1711, but did not receive the official title to it until 1714. He was among the area's earliest farmers.

Vroman's Nose and the acreage surrounding it, now protected for public use, have been in the Vroman family ever since. In 1983, the family formed the Vroman's Nose Preservation Corporation (VNPC), which manages the land as forever wild.

THE LONG PATH

Conceived by chemist and meteorologist Vincent Schaefer in 1931, the Long Path has the same purpose today as it did then: to link the outstanding scenic, geologic, prehistoric, and historic features of the area from New York City to the Adirondacks. Schaefer died in the summer of 1993. He is missed by those who continue to work on the unfinished Long Path as it forges its way north to the Adirondacks, though his memory is inextricably bound to the trail.

Beginning at the George Washington Bridge in New York City, the Long Path will eventually end in the northern Adirondacks at Whiteface Mountain. The Long Path's founders intended to construct lean-to shelters a day's hike apart along the trail, but these ambitious plans were interrupted by World War II. The Long Path still has its enthusiasts, however, and their mission it is to maintain the trail and continue it to its planned destination.

Those who walk sections of the Long Path may be frustrated by the sparingly applied blue blazes that designate the trail. Unlike present hiking trails, the Long Path was meant to be unmarked except for on topographic maps. "Thus," to quote Schaefer, "a hiker must know how to read a topographic map." Though impractical today, such a route would reduce most of the problems inherent in traditional trail systems, such as maintenance and marking, overuse, and litter.

The Long Path is managed by the New York–New Jersey Trail Conference and its affiliate clubs.

TRIP 59
VROMAN'S NOSE

Location: West Middleburgh, NY
Rating: Moderate
Distance: 2.0 miles
Elevation Gain: 480 feet
Estimated Time: 2 hours
Maps: USGS Middleburgh; Vroman's Nose Preservation Corporation handout map

This beautiful walk offers sweeping views of the Schoharie floodplain and the northern Catskills.

DIRECTIONS

From the intersection of NY 30 and NY 145 just south of Middleburgh, go south on NY 30. Vroman's Nose is obvious; its vertical cliffs rise above NY 30 in front of you. At 0.6 mile, turn right onto Mill Valley Road. Go 0.6 mile on Mill Valley Road and park on your left in the designated lot. *GPS coordinates:* 42° 35.684′ N, 74° 21.500′ W.

TRAIL DESCRIPTION

Vroman's Nose is a trip to save for a lazy afternoon when you'd rather gaze out over the countryside than take a long hike. From this geologically unique, ice-gouged cliff 600 feet above the Schoharie Valley, there are fine views of a vast alluvial farmlands floodplain, and of the long ridge of the northern Catskills.

At the kiosk, help yourself to a map. A wagon road runs south through a hay field and then through a pair of gates into a forest of large pine and hemlock, turning right as it leaves the field. This trail has been improved with water bars and grading. Follow the green diamond markers. There are no state trail signs— this is private property belonging to the Vroman's Nose Preservation Corporation (VNPC).

The path is self-guiding, and a steady climb over easy terrain (steep in places) continues through mixed hardwoods, pine, and juniper stands. At 1,100 feet or so, the trail turns from southwest to east where the Long Path joins it, then swings north as it ascends, yielding fine views of the Schoharie Valley. Twenty-five minutes from the trailhead, you will arrive at the summit, a wooded plateau of roughly 10 acres. The area of flat stone near the precipice

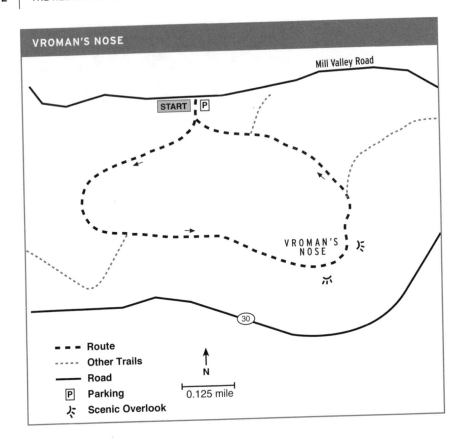

VROMAN'S NOSE

Mill Valley Road

START | P

VROMAN'S NOSE

30

- - - Route
----- Other Trails
——— Road
P Parking
Scenic Overlook

↑
N

0.125 mile

is known as the Dance Floor—dances were held here in the early 1900s during Prohibition. The eastern scarp is vertical and very high. Use caution.

The heavily scored summit of Hamilton sandstone shows evidence of its past in scratches (striae) and chatter marks of a glacier that moved from the northeast beginning about 50,000 years ago, forming the present topography of the Schoharie Valley. The cliff is defaced with engravings and graffiti, to such a point that it has had an erosive effect. Several concrete fireplaces have been built to discourage the assembling of fire rings by visitors, and impact seems to be under control.

Trees such as oak, hickory, pine, and red cedar thrive on the plateau, which is covered in bearberry (called kinikinick by the American Indians). The early spring flower fringed polygala also appears here.

Vincent J. Schaefer, founder of the Long Path, observed the presence of brachiopods, pelecypods, and trilobites that characterize the Middle Devonian Period's thin sedimentary sheets of Hamilton sandstone. Flagstones from Vroman's Nose were used for sidewalks in cities such as Troy, Albany, and

Vroman's Nose is a prominent Schoharie Valley landmark.

Schenectady. Schaefer pointed out a curious atmospheric phenomenon that generates a strong thermal updraft against the cliff, noting, "The dark-colored rocks of the cliffs of Hamilton shale and sandstone become quite warm whenever the sun is shining on them. This produces a massive upcurrent of heated air. Light objects such as grass, small twigs, and similar objects when thrown away from the cliff edge are carried upward and toward the north." You may notice birds, especially turkey vultures, taking advantage of this free ride.

The view of the Schoharie Creek is striking, and the ancient floodplain is remarkably well defined, with little farms and neatly arranged orchards fringing the creek. Beyond the valley to the east you see the Middleburgh Cliffs. Looking south you will have fine views of Windham High Peak and the Blackhead Range, beyond long esplanades of furrowed ground, a geographical contrast that is as distinctive as Vroman's Nose itself.

The long, open fields of farmland to the north, east, and south of Vroman's Nose were settled originally by American Indians, who left evidence of campfires under its thin soils. It was a Schenectady farmer, Adam Vroman, who established the first farm here, in 1713. He was followed by the German

Palatines who originally settled in the lower Hudson River valley. Crops common to the valley today are corn and carrots. The rich alluvial flats are often flooded by the Schoharie Creek, but usually this happens only in early spring and has little effect on existing crops.

If it's icy underfoot, you'll be better off returning the way you came. Otherwise, walk north now and follow the aqua Long Path blazes, passing a few more head-spinning cliffs to your right, and then descend steeply. At an intersection with an old woods road, continue on the yellow markers (don't follow right on the Long Path). The yellow trail comes out in the corner of the field where you began.

DID YOU KNOW?

Early in 1942, Vincent Schaefer visited Vroman's Nose with an employee of the General Electric Research Laboratory to photograph the testing of fog generators. The generators were used to obscure ships, personnel, and cities to prevent air attacks during World War II.

MORE INFORMATION

At the kiosk, you will find the Long Path North Hiking Club's *Hiker's Guide to the Schoharie Valley* as well as information about the Vroman's Nose Preservation Corporation. For more information, visit www.nynjtc.org/clubpages/lpn.html and www.schoharie-conservation.org.

NEARBY

In the village of Middleburgh there are specialty shops, restaurants, and historic sites. For more information visit www.middleburghnyvillage.org. Contact the Schoharie County Chamber of Commerce for other attractions in the area; www.schohariechamber.org; 518-827-3900.

Location: Voorheesville, NY
Rating: Easy
Distance: 4.0 miles
Elevation Gain: 200 feet
Estimated Time: 3 hours
Maps: USGS Altamont; John Boyd Thacher State Park Trail Map

The Indian Ladder Trail follows a narrow catwalk trail beneath the cliffs of the world's oldest exposed surface limestone, with extending trails along the Helderberg Escarpment.

DIRECTIONS

The park is 15 miles west of Albany on CR 157. From I-90, take Exit 4 and CR 85 west to CR 157. From the park's entrance sign on CR 157, continue 1.9 miles to the office and the Indian Ladder parking area. *GPS coordinates:* 42° 39.334' N, 74° 1.174' W.

TRAIL DESCRIPTION

Indian Ladder and the Thacher Park trail system offer a variety of short walks and activities, best enjoyed along with a picnic at one of the park's immaculate scenic recreation areas along the Helderberg Escarpment. By far the most interesting of these walks is along the Indian Ladder Trail and its recent extension to the north.

Verplanck Colvin, the surveyor who mapped the wilderness areas of northern New York, wrote about the Helderbergs in 1869, verifying the existence of the so-called Indian Ladder, built by American Indians to climb the steep rock wall. The 100-foot-long wooden ladder dated to about 1710, when Albany was "a frontier town, a trading post, a place where annuities were paid, and blankets exchanged with Indians for beaver pelts."

The Indian Ladder that Colvin described once leaned against this cliff, but all that exists now are the heavy steel staircases that serve a curious public. This first section of trail follows what was originally the Indian Ladder Road, which was constructed in 1828 and ran from Albany westward into the Schoharie Valley for the conveyance of farm products. At the Indian Ladder trailhead, a second trail goes off to the north and circles around the northern

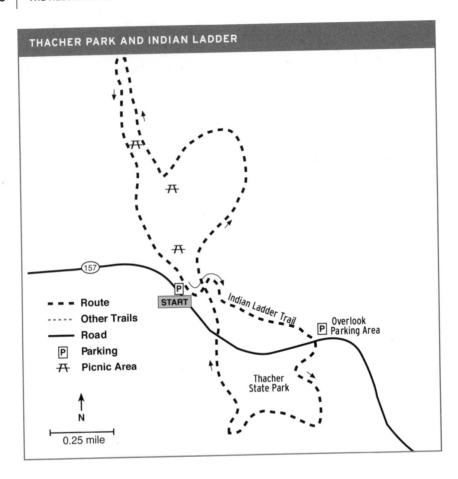

THACHER PARK AND INDIAN LADDER

Route — - -
Other Trails - - - -
Road —
Parking P
Picnic Area

N

0.25 mile

START

Indian Ladder Trail

Overlook
Parking Area

Thacher
State Park

Escarpment, which you can hike later. Descend the stairs and walk beneath the cliffs, heading south.

The upper layers of rock are the youngest, known to geologists as Coeymans limestone. That formation takes its name from the nearby town where it is well exposed. Of the two limestone formations in Thacher Park, the Coeymans is the thickest, averaging 50 feet from top to bottom. Look closely here and you may find the preserved remains of small sea creatures—crinoids, brachiopods, and tentaculites. These fossils date from the Late Silurian and Lower Devonian periods, about 415 million years ago.

Continuing down the trail, you'll notice thin layers (2 to 3 inches thick) of alternating light and dark beds of a ribbon limestone that is softer than the Coeymans and recedes beneath it as a result of erosion. This is Manlius limestone, a formation used extensively in the manufacturing of cement in Manlius, near Syracuse. Those thin limestone ribbons form a 50-foot-thick layer that also contains the preserved remains of invertebrate sea creatures and algae. Part of the formation also contains a 2-to-3-inch layer of water lime, used for making the Portland cement that will set up underwater. This forms a ledge known in the park as Upper Bear Path. At the base of the Manlius formation is limy mud-rock known as the Rondout Formation. It is a water lime that is well exposed near the Ulster County town of Rondout. It was used to produce rosendale, or natural cement—the invention that brought the Catskills' bluestone quarrying industry to a sudden end. This formation is less resistant to erosion but has eroded back to form Lower Bear Path, the ledge you are standing on.

Limestone dissolves in rainwater, causing such phenomena as disappearing streams, sinkholes, caves, and underground streams. The erosion below ground can form caves that occasionally collapse to form surface depressions, or sinkholes. The Karst topography is so-named because of its frequent appearance in the Karst region of the Dalmatian Alps. Nearby Thompson's Lake is a sinkhole that drains through a subterranean cave at its south end.

Once in the large amphitheater, or Indian Ladder Gulf, you will see Outlet and Minelot creeks. Together they have been responsible for the erosion of this impressive embayment. When the water table is high, these two creeks form spectacular falls that you walk behind on the trail. The talus slope beneath the cliff consists of rock that has broken off and fallen from the cliff face. Along the Indian Ladder Trail, watch for small, limestone-loving ferns, such as cliff brakes and spleenworts. In the moist spring woods, purple trillium (wake robin) is profuse. Among the endangered species found in the park are the Indiana bat and the spotted salamander. Neotropical magnolia warblers, having wintered in the West Indies and Panama, nest in the park's coniferous woods.

At the south end of the Indian Ladder Trail, climb the stairs and turn left. (You will see turquoise Long Path markers along the way now. When the Indian Ladder Trail is open, the Long Path follows it. When it's closed, the Long Path follows along the top, next to the fence.) Within 10 minutes, you will arrive at the (auto-accessible) Cliff Edge Overlook. Take a minute to enjoy the views of the Green Mountains and the Adirondacks, which can be identified with the aid of a large viewshed map. Continue to the south entrance of the Overlook parking area, cross CR 157, and bear right onto the paved Knowles Flat Picnic Area access road. Watch carefully to the left for the Long Path, which you'll see within 400 feet or so after crossing CR 157. Turn left and climb briefly to the Knowles Flat Picnic Area, bear left (south) again along the edge of a field, and enter the woods. Watch for the first junction, a Y, where the Long Path and the Red Trail go right (if you've reached the old rusty water tower, you've gone too far). Follow the trail through dense, extensive hemlock woods for 15 minutes.

At a T, take the Nature Trail (also marked with white disks) to your left, ascend, and turn right at a T where you'll see interpretive signpost 13 and signs that state To Red Trail. At a four-way junction, bear right at the Nature Trail sign. Follow the Red Trail downhill and cross Mine Lot Creek at the head of a tiny gorge. Bear right and descend into the beautiful Paint Mine Picnic Area. Go straight across CR 157, traverse the lawns, and turn left at the fence, following the dirt path back to the Indian Ladder trailhead.

You can finish the hike with a shorter (2.0 miles) loop on the Long Path along the recently designated northern Indian Ladder Trail that follows the Escarpment from this point. From the Indian Ladder trailhead where you originally began, bear left now, and follow the trail along the high rim of the Escarpment, passing through the Indian Ladder and Mine Lot picnic areas while threading your way through the woods on the Long Path, to the park's northern boundary. Northeasterly views are excellent. Return on the Hailes Cave Picnic Area access road, passing a red-pine plantation and arriving at the Indian Ladder trailhead and parking area in 10 or 15 minutes.

MORE INFORMATION

Thacher Park is open year-round from 8 A.M. to dusk. With some allowances made for conditions, the Indian Ladder Trail is open from May 1 through November, 15. In season, weekend fees apply. Summer swimming pool season begins June 25, and daily fees apply. There is a 1-hour free-parking limit at Cliff Edge Overlook. A comfort station is located at the top of the trailhead. Be aware that weekends here can be very crowded. Dogs are allowed on-leash with proof of rabies vaccination. For more information, call the office at 518-872-1237.

NEARBY

There are many festivals, museums, art galleries, theaters, and areas of historic and natural interest in Albany, the capital city of New York. The Albany Heritage Area Visitor Center in historic Quackenbush Square is open daily. For information on activities and attractions, visit www.albany.org, the website of the Albany County Convention & Visitors Bureau, or call 800-258-3582 or 518-434-1217.

Appendix: Helpful Information

NYS DEC DIVISION OF LANDS AND FORESTS

Central Office
625 Broadway
Albany, NY 12233
518-402-9405
www.dec.ny.gov
DEC manages the New York State Forest Preserve lands of the Catskills and detached parcels of state land outside the Catskills.

TACONIC STATE PARK AND RECREATION COMMISSION

Mills–Norrie State Parks
P.O. Box 893
Staatsburg, NY 12580
845-889-4646
The Taconic State Park and Recreation Commission manages land assigned to the Office of Parks and Recreation on the east side of the Hudson. It is responsible for state parks and historic sites there, including Hudson Highlands, South Taconic, and Fahnestock state parks.

PALISADES INTERSTATE PARK COMMISSION (PIPC)

Administration Buiding
Bear Mountain, NY 10911-0427
845-786-2701
www.nysparks.com
www.friendsofpalisades.org
The PIPC issues permits and trail information and supervises Harriman and Bear Mountain state parks and the state land of the Shawangunks.

APPALACHIAN MOUNTAIN CLUB (AMC)

5 Joy Street
Boston, MA 02108
617-523-0636
www.outdoors.org

New York–North Jersey Chapter
212-986-1430
www.amc-ny.org

Berkshire Chapter
www.amcberkshire.org

Mohawk Hudson Chapter
www.amcmohawkhudson.org

AMC helps build and maintain trails in southern New York, including some sections of the Appalachian Trail and trails in Harriman, Hudson Highlands, and Catskill state parks.

AMC publishes *Catskill Mountain Guide,* also by Peter Kick. The guide can be ordered from www.outdoors. org/amcstore, or purchased in many local outdoor shops and bookstores.

THE SIERRA CLUB

85 Washington St.
Saratoga Springs, NY 12866-4105
518-587-9166
www.sierraclub.org
Founded in 1892, the Sierra Club works to protect communities, wild places, and the planet itself. The Catskills are included in its Mid-Hudson Chapter Area. The group conducts outings and speaker socials.

THE CATSKILL 3500 CLUB

www.catskill-3500-club.org
The Catskill 3500 Club is primarily a hiking organization. A membership patch is given for completing climbs of 35 summits of more than 3,500 feet, four of which must be climbed a second time in winter.

NEW YORK–NEW JERSEY TRAIL CONFERENCE (NY–NJTC)

156 Ramapo Valley Rd.
Mahwah, NJ 07430
201-512-9348
www.nynjtc.org
The NY–NJTC coordinates the construction and maintenance of some 1,100 miles of hiking trails, including the Appalachian Trail in New York and New Jersey and Long Path. About 85 hiking clubs and conservation organizations belong to the conference, along with individual members.

ADIRONDACK MOUNTAIN CLUB (ADK)

814 Goggins Rd.
Lake George, NY 12845-4117
518-668-4447
www.adk.org
ADK has chapters in Ramapo, North Jersey, Mid-Hudson, Long Island, Knickerbocker, New York, Mohican, Albany, and Schenectady, all of which schedule regular hikes in the area described in this guide.

THE CATSKILL CENTER FOR CONSERVATION AND DEVELOPMENT, INC. (CCCD)

P.O. Box 504
Arkville, NY 12406-0504
845-586-2611
www.catskillcenter.org
CCCD is a regional advocate for land-use planning and environmental management, as well as an environmental "watchdog." CCCD owns and manages the 200-acre Platte Clove Preserve, located at the top of Platte Clove in the town of Hunter.

THE CATSKILL MOUNTAIN CLUB

P.O. Box 558
Pine Hill, NY 12465
www.catskillmountainclub.org
This club offers various hikes and outings for individuals of every ability level. It also conducts stewardship events and volunteer projects.

THE NATURE CONSERVANCY, EASTERN NEW YORK CHAPTER

195 New Karner Rd., Suite 201
Albany, NY 12205
518-690-7878
www.nature.org
The Nature Conservancy manages and protects natural areas throughout the United States.

Index

Appalachian Mountain Club

Founded in 1876, the AMC is the nation's oldest outdoor recreation and conservation organization. The AMC promotes the protection, enjoyment, and understanding of the mountains, forests, waters, and trails of the Appalachian region.

People
We are more than 100,000 members, advocates, and supporters; 16,000 volunteers; and more than 450 full-time and seasonal staff. Our 12 chapters reach from Maine to Washington, D.C.

Outdoor Adventure and Fun
We offer more than 8,000 trips each year, from local chapter activities to major excursions worldwide, for every ability level and outdoor interest—from hiking and climbing to paddling, snowshoeing, and skiing.

Great Places to Stay
We host more than 140,000 guests each year at our lodges, huts, camps, shelters, and campgrounds. Each AMC destination is a model for environmental education and stewardship.

Opportunities for Learning
We teach people the skills to be safe outdoors and to care for the natural world around us through programs for children, teens, and adults, as well as outdoor leadership training.

Caring for Trails
We maintain more than 1,500 miles of trails throughout the Northeast, including nearly 350 miles of the Appalachian Trail in five states.

Protecting Wild Places
We advocate for land and riverway conservation, monitor air quality and climate change, and work to protect alpine and forest ecosystems throughout the Northern Forest and Mid-Atlantic Highlands regions.

Engaging the Public
We seek to educate and inform our own members and an additional 2 million people annually through AMC Books, our website, our White Mountain visitor centers, and AMC destinations.

Join Us!
Members support our mission while enjoying great AMC programs, our award-winning *AMC Outdoors* magazine, and special discounts. Visit www.outdoors.org or call 800-372-1758 for more information.

APPALACHIAN MOUNTAIN CLUB
Recreation • Education • Conservation
www.outdoors.org

About the AMC in New York and the Berkshires

THE AMC HAS TWO ACTIVE CHAPTERS IN NEW YORK. The New York–North Jersey Chapter offers more than 2,000 trips per year, ranging from canoeing and kayaking, to sailing, hiking, backpacking, and social events. The chapter is also active in trail work and conservation projects and maintains a cabin at Fire Island. The AMC Mohawk Hudson Chapter serves residents of Albany, Columbia, Fulton, Greene, Montgomery, Rensselaer, Saratoga, Schenectady, Schoharie, Warren, and Washington counties. The chapter offers a variety of outdoor activities for all levels of ability. The Berkshire Chapter has nearly 3,000 members and serves western Massachusetts, maintaining almost 90 miles of the Appalachian Trail. You can learn more by visiting www.outdoors. org/chapters. To view a list of AMC activities in New York and other parts of the Northeast, visit trips.outdoors.org.

AMC Books Updates

AMC BOOKS STRIVES TO KEEP OUR GUIDEBOOKS AS UP-TO-DATE as possible to help you plan safe and enjoyable adventures. If after publishing a book we learn that trails are relocated or route or contact information has changed, we will post the updated information online. Before you hit the trail, check for updates at www.outdoors.org/publications/books/updates.

While hiking or paddling, if you notice discrepancies with the trail description or map, or if you find any other errors in the book, please let us know by submitting them to amcbookupdates@outdoors.org or in writing to Books Editor, c/o AMC, 5 Joy Street, Boston, MA 02108. We will verify all submissions and post key updates each month.

AMC Books is dedicated to being a recognized leader in outdoor publishing. Thank you for your participation.

AMC BOOKS & MAPS

EXPLORE THE POSSIBILITIES

More Books from the Outdoor Experts

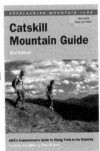
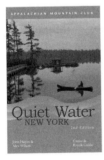
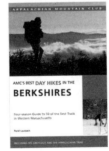